ADVANCE PRAISE FOR

betwixt
& between

"A humane, scholarly, and profoundly counter-cultural text which resists the domination of education by technical, economic, and bureaucratic considerations. For its discussions of the place of laughter in education and the role of poetry and imagination in the liberation of the human mind, this book deserves to be used in all teacher education programmes. Although written by a Catholic, it has all the power of Luther's denunciation of current corruptions in institutional culture and practice."

Gerald Grace, Professor Emeritus,
Institute of Education, University of London

"James C. Conroy is right: if we want to counter the hegemony of economic thinking in education, we need to cultivate alternative images and metaphors of what education is for and what it is about. Conroy's eloquent and erudite exploration of the idea of liminality opens up exciting theoretical possibilities. His concern for the future of liberal democracy gives his writing a clear practical edge and results in imaginative, original and highly relevant suggestions and conclusions. This is a strong book with a powerful message."

Gert Biesta, Professor of Educational Theory, University of Exeter

betwixt & between

Studies in the
Postmodern Theory of Education

Joe L. Kincheloe and Shirley R. Steinberg
General Editors

Vol. 265

PETER LANG
New York • Washington, D.C./Baltimore • Bern
Frankfurt am Main • Berlin • Brussels • Vienna • Oxford

James C. Conroy

betwixt & between

The Liminal Imagination, Education and Democracy

PETER LANG
New York • Washington, D.C./Baltimore • Bern
Frankfurt am Main • Berlin • Brussels • Vienna • Oxford

Library of Congress Cataloging-in-Publication Data

Conroy, James C.
Betwixt and between: the liminal imagination, education and democracy /
James C. Conroy.
p. cm. — (Counterpoints; vol. 265)
Includes bibliographical references and index.
1. Education—Philosophy. 2. Liminality. 3. Creative thinking—
Study and teaching. 4. Teacher-student relationships.
I. Title. II. Series: Counterpoints (New York, N.Y.); v. 265.
LB14.7.C654   370'.1—dc22   2004011044
ISBN 0-8204-6914-9
ISSN 1058-1634

Bibliographic information published by **Die Deutsche Bibliothek**.
Die Deutsche Bibliothek lists this publication in the "Deutsche
Nationalbibliografie"; detailed bibliographic data is available
on the Internet at http://dnb.ddb.de/.

Cover design by Lisa Barfield
Cover art by Anne Devine

The paper in this book meets the guidelines for permanence and durability
of the Committee on Production Guidelines for Book Longevity
of the Council of Library Resources.

Printed in the United States of America

To Jessica, Rosie and Edward whose embrace of the world is a joy to behold and to the memory of Des Kelly cfc whose love of the world was truly infectious.

Contents

Acknowledgements   IX

Introduction   1

1   The Regal Robes of Rome: Contestation and Liminality   15

2   Liminal Places and Possibilities in Education   43

3   Laughter as a Liminal Activity in Education   77

4   The Teacher as Trickster   111

5   Poetry, Liminality and the Education of the Imagination   137

6   The Liminal Possibilities of the Liminal School   167

References   197

Index   211

Acknowledgements

This work has been brewing for a few years and was completed while I was on study leave as Visiting Senior Research Fellow at the Clancy Centre for Research at the Australian Catholic University in Sydney. I am grateful to Graham Rossiter, Director of the Centre, for his kind invitation and support during my stay. But such a possibility was only made reality by the generosity of colleagues in the Department of Religious Education at the University of Glasgow, especially Gordian Marshall, O.P., who selflessly undertook the onerous administrative burdens of the department in my absence. Others in the Faculty of Education and the University have also been generous with their support, most especially Dean of Faculty, Hirek Kwiatkowski, and Vice Principal of the University, Chris Morris. My time in Sydney was made memorable by the hospitality, generosity, encouragement and support of some wonderful friends, especially Des Kelly and the Neighbourhood Watch who, although a little shaky on Aristotle, know a good Shiraz when they taste one!

I should like to thank the series editors Joe Kincheloe and Shirley Steinberg as well as Chris Myers and his team at Peter Lang, especially Sophie Appel and Justin Pelegano.

Many friends and colleagues have listened to and read parts of this essay in various guises, and their advice and comments have been invaluable. These include those who have commented on papers read at the Association for Moral Education and the Philosophy of Education Society of Great Britain. In particular I would like to thank Dwight Boyd, David Carr, David Gooderham, Jan Masschelein, Seibren Meidema, Michael Peters, Bert Roebben, Ben Speicker and Jan Steutel. Others who have in conversation helped me to move forward have included John Brick, Jude Butcher, Paul Standish, Richard Smith and Monica Taylor. Bob Davis and Doret deRuyter, two colleagues who are both my sternest critics and greatest supporters, deserve especial thanks for their unwavering kindness and support over the years. Also to Kate Adams, who has always been patient and courteous in assisting in preparing the text for publication. Finally there is my wife, friend and companion, Denise Conroy-Meagher, whose support is immeasurable.

While virtually all of this work has not been previously published, there are a few paragraphs in Chapter 4 that first appeared in an essay entitled "Poetry and Human Growth" in the *Journal of Moral Education* 28 (4), 1999. Chapter 5 also contains a small number of paragraphs first published with Bob Davis under the title "Transgression, Transformation and Enlightenment: The Trickster as Poet and Teacher" in the *Journal of Educational Philosophy and Theory* 34 (3), 2002. Much as I would like to shift blame onto any or all of these friends and colleagues, the many linguistic infelicities and conceptual inadequacies are my responsibility.

James C. Conroy
Glasgow 2004

Introduction

...I did not let the fear of death govern my life; and my reward was, I had my life. You are going to let the fear of poverty govern your life; and your reward will be that you will eat but you will not live.

George Bernard Shaw (1964, 129)

George Bernard Shaw's *Captain Shotover* offers direct access to an age-old and difficult educational controversy, one that has come to dominate public discussions of education in Britain in recent years.[1] It concerns the extent to which educational philosophies, processes and procedures should be governed by economic considerations. Given its multivalent nature, this controversy is not amenable to a straightforward answer. Its multivalence is evident in the complex network of related questions, issues and claims that arise out of considerations about the relationships between and among individuals, groups of individuals, the individual and the state, the state and the economy, the global and the local. These concerns are made even more complex by the addition of an age-old conundrum as to what constitutes both the good life and the good society. Just below this tumult bubbles the even more disconcerting thought that many of these questions are shot through with anxiety, an anxiety that issues out of the disjunction between our notions of happiness and flourishing, and our search for these in the patterns of consumption evident in late-industrial polities. This anxiety can be quickly transmuted into outright fear, which in turn can insinuate itself into the fabric of societies. Hence, the reasonable claims on liberal democracy of certain rights such as freedom of speech, opinion and association can be readily compromised by countervalent claims that a particular way of life or standard of living needs to be protected. Nowhere has this been seen in recent times more poignantly than in the aftermath of the attacks in the United States on September 11th, 2001. In the months following the attack, a range of taken-for-granted freedoms in liberal democracies have been compromised by the desire to protect a particular way of life as manifest in a particular set of economic relations (Conroy 2003).[2] These include new legal capacities to place people under surveillance, tracking and recording telephone calls and so on (see, for example, UK Government 2001). To recognise this is not to be alarmist about potential threats to civil liberties; rather it is to acknowledge that liberal democracies are prey to economic considerations that may too readily obscure their fundamental principles. This is particularly the case where such polities are witness to the demise of a sense of communal being or ethico-religious responsibility in favour of personal acquisitiveness. According to Millbank, among others, the demise of both Christianity and Communism has left what appears to be the final religion. This emerges as "something more secular than politics—a future of infinite utilitarianism, calculation by individuals, states and transnational corporations, of possible gains and losses, greater and lesser risks" (Millbank 1998, 41). What is at stake here is neither the condemnation nor the justification of some kind of neo-Hegelian belief that we have arrived at the final form of social life, but a recognition that liberal democracy is fragile, being subject to abuse from both those who effectively wield power and those who would anaesthetise themselves against the possibility of assuming personal and active responsibility in and for the world by "getting and spending," as Wordsworth[3] would have it.

The argument then, and one written into the fabric of this study, is that governance in the liberal democratic state is continuously subject to substantial pressure for political closure and a limited debate about what might count as flourishing in such a democracy; what is deemed throughout this essay to be "discursive closure." This pressure, more often than not, centres on the claim that our economic prosperity must be protected; and consequently, those things that might threaten it need to be curtailed and contained. This tendency, which is conspicuously not an exclusive feature of our own time, is manifest in an orthodoxy of the centre, wherein those who inhabit the political centre exert more control than might be desirable over the political, cultural and religious freedoms that are distinguishing features of liberal democracy. Potentially stultifying legislative steps are justified on the grounds that it is precisely these freedoms that are secured by protecting a specific version of economic functioning. Their promotion and introduction are manifestations of a ubiquitous temptation that has perennially beset governments of all kinds; that is to discursive closure.

Any particular economic account of human flourishing—the development of globalised markets, for example—may be regarded as being only contingently related to the temptations of discursive closure and the consequent need for contestation and difference in a liberal democracy. Nevertheless, it is difficult to conceive of any form of political restrictions on speech and action that do not have roots in, or are expressions of, some economic considerations. For example, while it might be argued that the political turmoil in Northern Ireland from the late 1960s had its origins in the claim to voice and the desire for political enfranchisement it is not difficult to see beyond the democratic trope to the place of economic disadvantage. Or again, on some accounts, the rise of National Socialism in 1930s Germany could be attributed to the drive to play out a reconstituted romantic conception of a people. Yet it attained its hegemonic status substantially as a result of economic insecurity. Economic insecurity and disadvantage appear to offer loose justifications for particular kinds of political doctrines about a range of social goods including education. Discussions about economic considerations are germane here because they bring in their wake deeply fissured socio-psychological anxieties about personal survival (Maslow 1968). These anxieties fuel the drive to globalisation. The globalised economy casts its shadow over this work because it casts its shadow over the entirety of education from kindergarten to university. Hence any discussion of discursive closure in and around education that ignores its energies is apt to miss the point.

Of course other forms of discursive closure that are not obviously rooted in economic fear are to be found in education. Indeed a kind of consciousness of closure has hovered around my musings on educational purposes and practices for most of my teaching career. These somewhat inchoate thoughts on closure began to take shape some ten years ago, not directly from reflections on the domains of politics and economics but from watching a student teacher work with her class teacher on a practicum. Apparently the 11-year-old children in the class, in a school serving an area of multiple deprivations, had been engaged in hostilities that had spilled over into the classroom. The teachers' response was to explore this pedagogically in the classroom where they focused on getting the children to provide an account of what they did when they lost their tempers. The children's contributions appeared to traffic between the inane and the asinine, so I took the opportunity to ask them what they *said* when they lost their temper. Their response was as revealing as it was unforthcoming. Each child that I asked either laughed embarrassedly or clammed-up, and I have yet to find out what language they were apt to use in such circumstances —though I might be able to make an educated guess! In this, as in many other cases, the classroom is seen to have been a particularly inhospitable environment for the disruptive power of the vernacular; better then to concentrate on behaviours. This has always seemed to me to be an extraordinary state of affairs but does point to the awesome power of language as well as to some of the impulses of closure. Of course, there is a significant difference between the power of the political economy and the power of the classroom. Nevertheless I began to make more and more connections.

Perhaps more important than all this is the sense of foreboding with which I enter a lecture hall or seminar knowing that what counts as appropriate teacher education has been subjected to a technicist onslaught and increasing emphasis on practical skills, with the result that the horizons of our student teachers' cultural topography is unlikely to have been expanded much after four years at university. Ironically, those who suggest that universities are failing to produce good teachers and consequently advocate an increase in schools-based training may well be right, but for entirely the wrong reasons. Their belief that learning in the classroom has more practical benefits than nurturing conceptual clarity and a certain cultural competence misses the point that teachers, at the beginning of their careers, require not more technical skills but the capacity to understand where particular roads may lead in addition to some knowledge of what obstacles might lie on a chosen path. There seems little point in having a mechanically well-tuned car and driving it into the desert with no sense as to how one might, so to speak, find the oasis and eventually move through it. Here the closure is around the existence of genuinely competing accounts of teacher education. More importantly, there is a closure around competence/benchmarks/outputs/targets—all of which find their genesis in the metaphors of the economy. Education of this kind offers too much process and rather too little promise.

A related kind of closure emerged from conversations with teachers over a number of years. Many of them harboured the desire to bring an inventiveness, creativity and excitement into the curriculum but felt themselves constrained by the increasing emphasis on a performative calculus. Indeed, many argued that the reality expressed in such a metaphor closed down their options both conceptually and pedagogically. What was, and is, absent from many of their pedagogical engagements (an absence many of them feel deeply) is a richly figurative and metaphorically powerful language. These and other pressures to contain and constrain what we mean by and do in education (for all the putative growth in pedagogical strategies and for all the growth of colourful textbooks) have surely resulted in quite significant closures.

As citizens fly into the arms of the discursive closure that binds them to their economic fears and anxieties (Fromm 1942, 24), we increasingly discover that they are incapable of exercising their singularity. This incapacity derives from a fundamental ambiguity in democracy. On the one hand the preamble of every democratic proclamation appears to give succour to the free individual in upholding rights for "all people without regard to race, sex, religion, wealth and social status." But, on the other hand, the phrase "without regard to" is, as Slavoj Žižek (1991, 163) reminds us, an abstraction from the substantial individual self. What happens in such proclamations is the dissolution of the particular individual self. One's particularity is constantly subject to erasure. This erasure of the self is heavily disguised as freedom to partake in the global economic cycle. Žižek wishes to go further than this to argue that there can be no reconciliation between the *citoyen* (the universal) and the *bourgeois* (the particularistic) ibid, 164). While possibly true in some absolute sense, this does not prevent us from proposing that the two be maintained in a relationship of tension. Indeed it might be argued that it is precisely such tension that ensures the possibilities of authentic discursive freedom.

Perhaps de Tocqueville was right, or at least partially so, in suggesting that the enemy of the citizen was the individual in the sense that the individual shares no common interest with the other; the breakdown of older community forms—be they political, social or religious—have left the individual isolated and, in that isolation, she or he searches out the mass. Like Rousseau, perhaps de Tocqueville was also wrong in thinking that the citizen embodied some surplus being not available to the individual. The worlds of neither the citizen nor the en-massed individual allow for the truly critical, because they are both constrained by and contained within the boundaries of their polity. By virtue of her very existence the citizen *qua* citizen cannot be defined without these boundaries, and by virtue of her behaviour, the en-massed individual cannot escape them.

But as for the self, that is indeed another matter. When the identity of both the citizen and the en-massed individual is exhausted there remains a surplus of being. The "I" of the self is not coterminous with the one who is a citizen because the very meaning of citizen is determined with respect to the borders where her rights are established and or guaranteed.[4] It is Rousseau's (1968) mistake that he identifies this surplus only as a particular will, to be pitted against the general will rather than as an excess of being. Equally, the identification cannot be with any other particular form of collective representation, consumer or en-massed individual since here too there is a surplus. Beyond these collective representations of the person there is a unique particularised singularity—a singularity configured for Hannah Arendt (1958) by natality and for Rosenzweig (1985) by mortality. This surplus has been variously characterised as *daimon*, soul, spirit and so on, but to render it into non-metaphysical terms it may be seen as the particular *isness* of this self that distinguishes it from all other selves. Santner (2001) well captures this in observing that when a person advertises for a partner in the personal ads of a newspaper, the stipulations are very general: "Stable professional life, loves travel, sushi, long walks on the beach and so on. All such attributes [he argues] belong to the personality: any number of people can fit the bill.... But as we all know...when one truly loves another person, one loves precisely what is not generic about them, what cannot be substituted for by someone else" (2001, 73). As he goes on to point out, this singularity is not something that stands behind the self, some ghost in the machine, but a gap in the way we identify ourselves and are represented in the social spaces

To be unique is to be distinctively oneself; it is to bring particular gifts, talents, outlooks and perceptions to the public spaces. My being unique in no way prevents my partaking in the body politic. Such a doctrine of uniqueness is a particular feature of the Judaeo-Christian tradition and is seen in various sayings attributed to Jesus (R.S.V. Matt 6: 26–34) and in the letters of St. Paul (Romans 12: 3–8). It might be argued that the shift from seeing the person as unique to seeing the person as an individual is a consequence of the construction of the masses in late-industrial society. In such societies every aspect of being, from a child's score in baseline assessments through to the calculations of pension funds, is signified numerically. The rise and rise of the arithmetic as a social imaginary signifier (Castoriadis 1997) has had a profound shaping effect on the way we construct our sense of self and our relations with each other. And so we may see that education is increasingly dedicated to the production of more goods and services; that is, for the economy. Number drives the economy, and the child's education is driven by number because her education serves the economy. So it is that the individualised person is a number in the mass. Education for the self is submerged in a discourse of number metamorphosed into the discourse of economic processes.

This powerful impetus for closure, around the numbers of the economy, gives rise to the evolution of supporting and reinforcing metaphors in fields like education. Metaphors, which depend upon numbers, tables and targets, dominate our public discussions on education. In the face of their power, workable metaphors of the surplus of being struggle to find their place and are marginalised, most particularly those that allude to the darker spaces in that surplus. This essay attempts to supply some alternative metaphors that work in an educational context, and that acknowledge and valorise the notion of the *sui generis* being. They should be sufficiently robust so as to have some impact on our thinking and be secure against the closure that comes in the wake of widespread acceptance, domestication and enumeration in and by the Centre. The first and cornerstone metaphor upon which the others are built is *liminality*; that is a metaphor which points to a space that is neither inside nor outside but lies at the threshold of our social, political, cultural and educational spaces. In so far as educators in liberal democratic polities are subject to a range of pressures to deliver on certain politically prescribed targets, *liminality* may offer the possibility of deliberately displacing our understandings, beliefs and ideals (in short, our *cogitationes*) outside the realm of others, or indeed our own, socio-psychological (and numerical) containment in order to view them afresh. Other metaphors such as laughter and play, hero myths and tricksters, poetry and ambiguity, and religion are included because they offer particular instantiations of the liminal. The metaphors which will be developed here have their roots deep in our traditions, traditions that still offer late-industrial polities fresh ways of configuring our being and our collective representations of our lives. The turn to such metaphoric roots does not entail a bout of nostalgia. Because of their complexity they are amenable to the complexity of our actual lives.

In the course of this study the metaphors of the global economy and globalisation surface and resurface against the tapestry of the liminal. Liminality has not featured much in discussions and studies of education apart from, here and there, as an anthropological tool to explore certain features of student life that stand outside the regulated spaces of the classroom. Here, it is primarily developed as a creative metaphor for approaches to both the general conceptual considerations that frame educational discussions and the practices of the classroom. But what are we to understand by the term in this context? It is most often used in anthropological descriptions of a spatio-temporal place where normal chronology and geo-political life are suspended—sometimes for a brief period, sometimes for quite long durations of days or weeks—so as to highlight particular important changes in the life of one or more members of a tribe. A classic example of this might be a right of passage entailing the removal of teenage boys from the comfort and security of the tribe so as to initiate them into adulthood. While its development in this essay retains some affinity with its traditional anthropological usage liminality is nevertheless expanded in this study to encompass a more elastic notion of the "in-between." Expressly it may be thought of as referring to those intellectual, cultural and ideological spaces that sit, or operate, at the threshold of experience. An interstitial condition, it is to be found between categories, on the margins, neither at the centre nor on the outside. In the context of education it provides a metaphor for pedagogies and practices, dispositions and attitudes and even institutions that escape the confines and constraints of the centre while fleeing neither into anarchy nor solipsism. Not being directly subject to the control of the centre, the liminal position opens up new ways of construing the myriad relationships alluded to above, and holds to account our established conceits about the worthwhile, the good and the right.

This base metaphor provides the ground for the others mentioned above, especially laughter and play, the trickster figure, poetry and religion. In other words these other metaphors are themselves particular refractions of the liminal. Let me offer some brief points of clarification here. We do not expect to open the pages of an educational journal and come across lots of stories about laughter. Indeed, each week in the *Times Higher Education Supplement*—the U.K. national weekly devoted to higher education—the educational raconteur and former sociologist, Laurie Taylor, has a witty and satirical column on the latest goings-on in higher education. But, it is not on the front page, or in the middle page spread but at the back of the newspaper running down the last column inch. Equally, in normal circumstances we do not expect the teacher to behave as a trickster figure constantly exposing her students to the vagaries of perpetual inconsistency. Or yet again, we would not expect a liberal democracy to license a religious institution to run its national educational system along purely religious lines. It may be suggested that such a list contains some things that are not, strictly speaking, metaphors at all. For example, laughter play and poetry may be regarded as activities. This is self-evidently the case. However, these activities can stand as metaphors for a particular set of approaches, dispositions and attitudes with respect to education. In any event and at this stage I wish only to make some prefatory remarks about each of these instantiations of the liminal metaphor in education.

First then let us look at laughter. Where it is seen—here and there in and around the school—laughter is generally regarded as something to be contained in the context of the classroom: that is, it is to be made safe. Where it is—or is likely to be—disruptive it is to be secured at the fringes of school life, behind the cycle sheds or in some other marginal location. Here I wish to argue for a more robust and complex notion of laughter as an educational activity that can at times be disruptive and challenging, but that discloses rather than cloaks human behaviour. Laughter can have a variety of functions but construed educationally it serves to support the development of personal critical faculties in the individual student, so that she can claim power over her own life. At different stages of her development this can involve different kinds of laughter: in early development it can be about overcoming fears from imagined dangers; in later development it can be concerned to expose hypocrisy and duplicity. In both instances it is about empowerment and empowerment is a necessary condition for engaging effectively in the public sphere.

It is in part this ambiguity that defines laughter's liminal status and it is the recognition of this ambiguity that is so important in education. The cultivation of laughter by the teacher involves working with students to explore the different ways in which laughter can be used to reinforce or to challenge the status quo. On occasion it disposes us to introduce laughter into the classroom in a manner that supports the students' perspective on the world of adults. Equally, it requires that the teacher can turn laughter on the children to assist them in discriminating behaviour from action. If it is the case, as I will argue later, that it is fear that prevents human beings from acting out of their own strength and that laughter is an enemy of fear, then it can assist students in finding their place in the world and developing their own critical faculties. Of course, the cultivation of laughter is always going to be a liminal activity in the school given that it is manifestly a structured environment where the values and aims of the dominant political centre are communicated and shored-up by its agents—funding bodies, inspectors, principals …. It is in recognition of this "brute fact" that the approach taken here is not predicated on confrontation but on the creation of alternatives that pop up here and there in the life of the classroom, the school and the system. It is virtually impossible to confront the discursive and behavioural dominance of the Centre by either trying to emulate it or by draw upon a range of conflicting stratagems since power and control are distributed asymmetrically. Moreover, it is not obvious that using the same means as the powerful to dislodge them does anything more than create mirror images. The point here is to cultivate alternative images.

The *trickster* offers such an alternative, embodying a very specific kind of laughter. He models a particular set of images and engagements through which the teacher can explore her own role in education. As education becomes increasingly seen as a *business*,[5] the arithmetic signifies the desire to maintain order and control and the teacher has been construed as the instrument of a kind of ordered morality. This formal role of the teacher as moral controller and enforcer within the civic space (as distinct from private and monastic tutors) is by and large an invention of the modern, post-Reformation era. The genealogy of the *trickster* opens up a new or different model of teacher, not as *magister* but as discloser, reflector and inverter. Where the teacher in late-industrial polities is to be imagined as one who is to ensure that students reach the sunny uplands of economic success—leader, mentor, guide, resource—the image of the teacher as trickster plays on a substantially more complex understanding of both persons and the place of education. The trickster often embodies a range of contrary and contradictory impulses; one moment a force for the good and the enlightenment of the individual or group, the next, playing tricks so as to obscure or occlude the truth.

Suppose for a moment that the arithmetic calculus, which currently dominates our public discourse in everything from student achievement to the price of housing, is misguided if not wrongheaded. Would it be possible to challenge it by quoting yet more statistics or providing a statistical analysis of the number of people who are materially or educationally damaged by so constructing or making sense of our experiences and their concomitant narratives? I suggest not, since it is unclear that putting more coal on a fire will reduce its temperature. If the arithmetic (and this includes the markets that are simply a form of calculus) does not hold the key to understanding what it is that makes people persons—or even if it does offer some, but not total, insight—then its claim to ordering our lives needs to be challenged by something quite unlike itself. Here I suggest that the trickster offers himself as customised for the task. He may be seen as offering himself as a contact zone; within but not of the polity. A liminal figure in the history of peoples certainly, but one that cultures ranging from the shamanic through the mediaeval to the modern have found it necessary to call on in order to combat hubris and recuperate that which is playful and surprising about our being. When politicians and the advocates of the non-stop technological revolution suggest that ever-new technologies will enhance our leisure time what is it that they mean? More trips to the do-it-yourself store? More sweating middle-aged men on squash courts trying to stave off the impending heart attack being induced by their arithmetically calculated working lives? If the argument is that the technology frees the individual from drudgery (probably a baseless argument in any event) then it must surely be in order that they can laugh and play, and in the course of doing so not take herself too seriously.[6] Of course, there is a serious side to the trickster as a liminal figure. He offers disruptive potential to a culture. This disruptive potential is not manifest permanently (otherwise it would be mainstream and not liminal) but comes and goes, surprisingly and unexpectedly. In education the teacher as trickster surprises children (something made pretty nigh impossible if one were to slavishly endorse current curricular guidelines and requirements in Britain). She opens up new ways of seeing old problems and she introduces such things as religion into the classroom not because of its historic power to control but because the genesis of religious movements lies in the disruptive. Neither Christ nor Buddha, Mohammed nor Guru Nanak founded great religious movements because they wished to confirm the status quo.[7] These were liminal figures precisely in that they were at the heart of their societies but not consumed by them.

Trickster stands at the apex of the mythopoeic as one of the seminal figures of myth. With the refinement of myth comes the poetic; a site not only of resistance to the apparently logical language of the forces of globalisation, but also a mode of educational engagement that enables interpretation of and immersion in aspects of a locally configured culture which has not yet been trivialised by the hegemony of the markets. Of course, the suggestion is also made here that a necessary precondition for the existence of such a hegemony is the complicity of those held under its grip; a view expounded by novelists, playwrights (Miller 1968), psychologists (Jung 1961) and philosophers (Foucault 1979). The antidote to such complicity lies precisely in the development of sites of resistance, which do not attempt to create a false sense of their being one correct voice in respect of which all others must remain subordinate. While there may be affinities with the work of Gilligan (1982), Noddings (1992) and others, especially in relation to their recognition of the actual moral complexity of life (a complexity that is ignored in the rhetoric of the market) the emphasis here is quite different.

The focus here is not so much on the interpersonal and empathetic but on the complex role that language plays in shaping identity and on exploring how literature in particular (though the arts in general may also play the same role) sits as an interstitial form of communication which enables us to escape the global while retaining our attachment to the universal. This in turn offers the student the possibility of resisting en-massing, while at the same time enabling her to expand beyond her own subjectivism. To deal with the en-massing of the self it is necessary to be in a position to make moral choices based on what can, as near as possible, approximate to an understanding of the warp and weft of living experience. Because the poetic comprises ever-changing linguistic forms and shapes it can never be entirely contained by the discourse of the market. It is true that market advertisers are constantly engaged in the attempt to harness metaphors from religious and moral life in their unending attempt to subordinate sites of dissonance. Two striking examples of this are the ways in which, during their 2001 advertising campaign, Volkswagen harnessed religious tokens of protection as a metaphor for the reliability of their cars. Thus the meta-metaphorising of such tokens appears to eat into their symbolic power and, by association, that of all such language. But the poetic offers itself as a liminal site precisely because even these assaults cannot tame it. Indeed, in the work of a number of poets it can turn the images of the market on their head reconfiguring them in the imagination.[8] It also may be regarded as liminal in the sense that it offers a contact zone in the way described above. It is not unreasonable on a "commonsense" account of such matters to regard a particular language as the means by which a given culture shapes itself and its population, enabling sense-making, communication and social engagement. Yet poetry which draws on its linguistic heartland—metaphor, aphorism, banal and sublime descriptions of the everyday—is never contained by, or reduced to, that heartland since it twists and stretches those very ordinary words so that it persistently pushes at the very edges of communicative possibility. It is worth noting that in Britain, the institution of the poet laureate is acknowledged by and given shelter in the establishment yet never contained by this same establishment; it is a contact zone at the heart of the polity, different yet connected. Seen as an educational metaphor the poetic may be reasonably construed as proffering to students a language which opens up the liminal spaces around what can be said.

The final metaphor developed in this book is religion, not as an embodiment of a given set of beliefs but as pointer to and expression of the relationship between the dominant ideology of a political centre and the range of alternatives offered by sub-groupings within it or at its edge. Religion has historically always occupied a variety of positions with respect to the centre. Sometimes, as with the mediaeval Christian church, it *is* the centre. At other times, as with the pre-Constantinian church, it is, at best, liminal.[9] It is this shifting and ambiguous character that discloses a central feature of liminality; the fluid relationship between the centre and the periphery. When a religion acquires an official (statutory) or quasi-official status within a liberal (or indeed any other kind of) state it can no longer operate as a liminal corrective, irrespective of any potentially radical doctrines it might wish to incarnate.

In the last chapter the focus switches from the practices of teaching and the teacher to look at the possible use of the liminal metaphor in the context of education as a system in liberal democracy. This is an important move since I wish to establish that particular refractions of the liminal can be applied to the whole educational enterprise as well as to its constituent parts. In exploring the relationship between a religious institution and a liberal democratic polity I am adopting a somewhat different view from the normal liberal discussion of the rights of religious groups to have their own schooling and the obligations of the state to ensure that children are not disadvantaged. Here my concern is much more on the needs of the late-industrial liberal democracy and the potential of such institutions to bring different kinds of metaphors about human being into those public spaces that embrace education. More importantly, and central to the thesis being developed in this collection of essays, I wish to distinguish the polity from the state and in doing so suggest that the polity should house the liminal and the state facilitate it. Of course, liminality in this context does carry a certain health warning. Liminal institutions such as Catholic education in Scotland cannot unequivocally exercise their right to liminality if it were to be demonstrated that it was structurally wicked or failed to have the interests of children at heart. The existence of liminal institutions may be a necessary condition of a healthy reflective and just state. That an institution is liminal, however, is not a sufficient condition for allowing its continuation within the polity. In this essay I also point out that the liminal status of an institution, and the different lens that it brings to the public spaces is constantly under threat especially where it is in receipt of state funding.

This essay has no claim to presenting an exhaustive account of the liminal metaphor in education. If anything it is but the beginning of a process of exploration merely plotting a tentative path through an under-conceptualised area of public political life. Ultimately it recognises that the public sphere has a feudatory relationship to education and must equip students who will be responsible for the maintenance of our public spaces as the best safeguard for the maintenance of the principles and practices of liberal democracy in the future. It is not enough that education prepare young people for life in a technocratic age with all the associations of ever-increasing speed and perpetual change. They must also be offered the faculties to critique and challenge it. Their capacity to engage with the world is radically tied to their sense of being an acting individual in a community of other acting individuals.

Notes

1. Many of the examples in this essay are British although they are not exclusively so and, while the British system of education and finance shares much in ideological terms with the United States, differences are more marked with respect to Europe.

2. This does not mean that other considerations are not present; these might include unspoken socio-religious attitudes, nationalist or patriotic considerations. Nor does it imply that there are not costs attached to responding to terrorists. Refracted through all of these, however, is an economic imperative.

3. As much as any late-twentieth/early-twenty-first-century philosopher, the Romantic poet Wordsworth understood the politically debilitating effects of wanton consumption. Thus one of his sonnets opens with the words, "The World is too much with us; late and soon, Getting and spending we lay waste our powers: Little we see in

nature that is ours; We have given our hearts away, a sordid boon!" ("The World is too
much with us", 1798, Lyrical Ballads, Lines 1-4)

4. Even where one holds dual or multiple citizenship, the point remains; it is just that the
borders may have changed.

5. The Department for Education and Enterprise (note the new label for what has
variously been the Department for Education, then the Department for Education and
Employment) released on September 5th, 2001, its proposals for having significant
numbers of schools managed and run on a for-profit basis by private companies.

6. Logically it might be that they have leisure so that they can sleep more but that is
hardly what is meant by the contemporary mantra that technological change will offer
us increased leisure time.

7. I think that this is true despite Durkheim's analysis of the sustaining and conserving
role of apparently disruptive religious figures within the *conscience collective*.

8. For example, see the work of Roger McGough.

9. It might be suggested that the catacombs are evidence not of liminality but beyondness
and no doubt there is some truth in this. However, it cannot be entirely true and the
Christian church at some stage had to come into a liminal relationship with the state if
its particular anthropology and ontology was to have any contact, and therefore much
more impact, on the polity. In this regard Edward Norman's model of transposition is
useful in understanding the way in which a church might come to influence the
discourse of the polity (Norman 1979, pp. 1–28).

Chapter 1

The Regal Robes of Rome:
Contestation and Liminality

Do not become a prison-officer unless you know
What you're letting someone else in for.

Roger McGough (1999, 2)

Introduction

P risons are archetypal places of closure where dissonance is neither tolerable nor (normally) officially tolerated, though admittedly it has a tendency to slip through the cracks. Closure occurs where there is no alternative. Prison warders, for a range of fairly obvious reasons, tend to see themselves as enforcing and controlling the limitations to freedom that are part and parcel of such institutions. They are there because determinations have been made elsewhere about the kinds of freedoms and limitations that are permissible here. The prison warden enacts these determinations and, while she may have some control over the enactment of the determinations, this doesn't amount to much. Similarly, from kindergarten to university, teachers are evermore required to enact the determinations about education that have been enacted elsewhere. Normally in a liberal democratic polity we would think that such determinations are made by the elected representatives of the people on behalf of the people. Equally, we might reasonably expect the liberal democratic government to make such decisions on the basis of some conception of the flourishing of both the individual and the whole social group. Increasingly this appears not to be the case. Forces other than government appear to be shaping educational policies and practices. These forces do not have a particular determined, identity but sail under the flag of convenience that we have come to refer to as globalisation. In this chapter I will sketch some features of the impact of globalisation on our reflections about what constitutes human flourishing.

Preliminary Thoughts on Globalisation

Globalisation has become one of those shibboleths that one trips over on virtually every street corner, and it is certainly not my intention to spend much time adding to the wealth of the extant literature. Nevertheless, I wish to make a couple of remarks that, it seems to me, are pertinent to the notion of discursive closure. In his analysis of a number of differing conceptions of globalisation, Beyer (1994) attempts to come to terms with the countervalent forces at work in the local/global nexus. The differing conceptions of these forces variously emphasise four domains of globalisation: the cultural, the socio-political, the economic and the linguistic. The boundaries of these four domains are not coterminous. For example, the socio-political boundaries that govern the exercise and limits of the law are not the same as those that govern the commerce in ideas—ideas can go across boundaries, where the law may be required to stop. Pressing these questions of boundaries is another set of concerns focused on the relative force each of these domains exercises in shaping and driving globalisation. Here we might see that the increasing take-up of the English language as the language of choice for international communications has a particular effect in hastening the experience of globalisation. This effect may then be greater or lesser than that of the cultural media. Whatever the relative effects of the other domains, it is hard to resist the conclusion of Beyer and others that here the economic impulse is the pre-eminent energy, and that other forms of global communication are configured in its shadow. Beyer argues that, "commodity production for a money economy has been a very powerful way of tying almost all areas of the world into a single communicative network. The political system of states both reinforces and conditions this singleness. All land areas of the globe are by now formally under the jurisdiction of one state or another, creating a continuity of political power that parallels and reinforces that of money. There is only one political system in global society and it is coextensive with the economic system" (ibid, 48). As I argue elsewhere (Conroy 1999b), the vehicle for this globalisation is the transnational corporation, which has displaced the international and that knows no limits to its consumptive appetites (see Korten 2001). There is little sign of the forces which drive consumption abating, despite the occasional collapse of some such corporations under the weight of their own avarice, and the hope of some (Habermas 2001, 58–112) that the permeability of national boundaries across a range of social goods and communications may bring about a different kind of international politics. However, we should resist the temptation to see the relationship between, say political systems and the commodity economy, as a simple equation of terms since the former may act to correct particular features of the latter. Indeed, viewed normatively, it may be that political systems are required to moderate and modify the energies and impulses of the commodity economy.

Globalisation then may be defined in terms of the expansion of the boundaries of the economy to embrace other forms of communication and, because the only apparent obstacle to this expansion is the physical limits of the earth, these boundaries are in their own turn coextensive with the territorial and resource limits of the globe itself. Nevertheless it is important to acknowledge that there is leakage across boundaries via other forms of communication. Thus, for example, the environmental movement might be construed as a global network but one that is not coextensive with either the state or the commodity economy. But even this is not simple, since it could be argued that the environmental movement has the same limits as the commodity economy. This arises because the concerns of the environmentalists track the expansion of the commodity market and are consequently their mirror image. Consequently, even those spheres of communication that might be deemed antithetical to the commodity economy are actually configured by its form and shape, if only as its negation.

Economic globalisation draws to itself other forms of communication,[1] such as the values of a polity. No longer are the values of one polity to be seen in contradistinction to another, but gradually, globalised values are processed out of economic considerations. Global fashions, global foods, global popular speech and musical forms are examples of global lifestyle aspirations that are parasitic on a globalised economy. Some may argue that there remain local conversations in those societies or strata of societies where markets have not yet penetrated and that consequently, we do not live in a globalised world. While it is true that there are, so to speak, pockets of resistance, these are small and largely in polities ill-equipped to partake of the putative benefits of globalisation (though many will be ensnared by it because they supply raw materials, cheap labour, etc.). Others may argue that religious communication provides an alternative; and this may be seen particularly with respect to Islam. However, this is not an open-and-shut case. Certain features of rising Islamic consciousness may *appear* to stand against the totalising claims of globalisation, but these have to be weighed against the inability of Islamic countries in general to avoid substantial reliance on the production of consumer goods. Additionally, the virulent Islamic reaction is not necessarily directed towards globalisation per se, but rather, imperialism. While the two may overlap, they are different. Whereas globalisation transcends the particularity of a state or states, imperialism emanates from and remains rooted in a state or states. Nevertheless, religion may offer some potential as a site of resistance to the globalising energies of the commodity economy.

Given the potential of the global commodity economy to consume other conversations, making them increasingly subject to its own force, the difficulty and the dangers for liberal democracies emerge quite starkly. As Habermas (2001) points out, nation states are ill-equipped to control the flows of capital that emerge in a globalised world, so they need to band together in order to have sufficient muscle. In banding together, however, the relationship between the individual and the state is changed irrevocably. It matters little whether this change is perceived to be good or bad, there being devotees on both sides of the argument. What does matter is the extent to which the individual and groups of citizens are equipped and empowered to dissent and resist the claims of globalisation, and the extent to which the polity, to which they belong, facilitates the exercise of their freedoms in these regards. In line with philosophers and political theorists from Hegel to the present, Habermas assumes a kind of historical inevitability about the forces of globalisation; they are but a further dialectical step in our evolution. Like Kierkegaard (1945) however, I do not accept the thesis of historic inevitability but wish to maintain that human beings are endowed with the power of choice, and that choices they make can, at least formally, be substituted for other choices, albeit with some difficulty. It should not be forgotten that it is individuals and groups who decide whether or not exchange controls are to be dropped, whether or not to fix border tariffs, or whether or not to develop free trade agreements. Admittedly, the capacity to effect such change requires that those polities in which people are governed nurture and cultivate the ability to act freely, and do so in the light of a substantial conception of personal and communal flourishing. The kind of polities with which I am primarily concerned in this study are liberal democracies, because they have their roots in a complex account of human flourishing. Moreover, they have *de jure* and *de facto* obligations to secure something approximating such flourishing on behalf of the citizens whom they serve. Any meaningful account of flourishing or well-being in a liberal democracy must embody the visibility of its citizens in those public spaces where conversations about well-being take place. This does not mean that the discussion here has little or no relevance for developing countries that are not liberal democracies. Such polities have also certain obligations towards their people and they may have mythopoeic and other resources available that continue to offer an alternative account of human flourishing to that available in the globalised heartlands.

Let us suppose that liberal democratic polities need to remain vigilant with respect to the threat they may face from the too powerful communicative form of the commodity economy. That being the case, they have to keep themselves open to *dissensus* and its attendant discursive practices. This requires the evolution and maintenance of a robust range of voices that might include the development of protest groups, the emergence of single issue protests, and the growth of particular types of comic inversion. But all these, in their own turn depend on the existence of discerning individuals and communities who are psychologically and socially equipped to act out of their own volition, and who have the ability to discern and discriminate between the interests of different forms of global and local communication. To the extent that education is a public good intended to contribute to the flourishing of citizens in a liberal democracy, it is central to this enterprise. Consequently, and despite their significance, the focus on economic considerations in these essays is subordinate to the concern for the development of an educational project equipped to maintain and support the values and practices of liberal democracy as the most desirable form of political organisation in a complex, fissiparous and pluriform world. Now it might be argued that schools are not appropriately seen as places where politico-economic principles are to be either worked out or defended per se. But they are spaces where children are taught about the world and that world, as Arendt would have it, is always in the past despite the fact that children have to live in the future (Arendt 1977). While as an adult community we may not justifiably burden our children with our anxieties or responsibilities about how the world is we should, nonetheless, prepare them to live in the future. Such a preparation should entail teaching them about and facilitating their experience of agonal engagements, dissensus and voice in the belief that liberal democracy is the political system most likely to nurture human flourishing. It is not enough to teach children negatively that a particular conception of human flourishing is under threat or that present political circumstances are detrimental to such flourishing. Neither, strictly speaking, can we teach them for the future, since by definition we do not know what that is or entails. What we can do is help them develop positive responses to the conditions of the past and present so that they can assume responsibility for their own future. To do this is to teach them to *act*. One way of conceptualising pedagogies that would contribute to this agenda is through the cultivation of the liminal in education where liminality represents an interstitial condition which is not immediately subject to the structured and dominant mainstream of political, social or educational thought. In doing this it may be possible to offer alternatives from within the polity should the centrist discourse that envelops education appear to promote a single voice and that voice go abroad in the polity largely uncontested. Such alternatives cannot legitimately be wholly outside voices since children, in the particular instance with which I am concerned, are being educated in *this* liberal democratic polity. But neither can they simply replicate the voice of the dominant centre since plural democracy depends on contestation. Consequently this study is an exercise in discovering the balance between *monoglossia* and incommensurability in education in and for liberal democracy.

Globalisation and Education: Process without End

While the next chapter deals extensively with the development of a defensible account of liminality it is important to make some preliminary remarks here. The cultivation of the liminal poses a real challenge to education inasmuch as education (or at least schooling, with which it is often conflated) functions as a socially and politically established set of centripetal arrangements designed to hold as many individuals and groups as possible to what is deemed the middle ground or centre of public, political and economic life. In this particular respect education tends to be both utilitarian and conservative, aiming to create those conditions claimed[2] to be in the best interests of the majority of the population. The consequences of such a view is the containment of any experimentation that might be judged controversial or damaging to social and economic/market stability and the particular form of well-being that is predicated upon it. A number of educationalists, significant among whom is Hargreaves (1997), wish to demolish what they deem to be a conservative educational agenda and reconfigure it, so as to meet the needs of a globalised world. A world that he believes demands increasingly creative, inventive and proactive responses and that requires a system readily capable of adapting its forms of engagement and embracing the world of technological change. Significantly, Hargreaves view is only different from conservatism if the latter is seen to be primarily concerned with the historical question (the maintenance of conventions, habits, mores and worldviews).[3] However, it is not a question of history but is rather about containment and control. It is not clear that Hargreaves' radical agenda is anything of the sort. It is clear that this is the case on a number of grounds. First, going back to Bentham and beyond it is not difficult to see technology as a primary tool of control. Indeed recent strategies for behaviour management in Scottish schools have focused on the introduction of television in the public areas of the school during breaks and recess! Second, those who see a new education rooted in technology as a means for liberation imbue the technology with capacities it simply doesn't have. Technology may well propel teachers into new and different relationships with their students and reshape pedagogies but this is quite different from claiming (as many, such as Hargreaves, do) that the technology itself has some kind of democratic impulse simply because it increases access to all kinds of new information, knowledge[4] and interactions. It is quite possible to have increased access to something, say mobile telephony, without any concomitant increase in democracy. I may be able to make lots of telephone calls, text messages and emails to all kinds of people to find out such things as football scores, where to meet for dinner, the weather, the latest prices on the stock market, which movies are "hot," but were I to multiply these communications a hundred fold it would offer no necessary increase in the democratic impulse or democratic opportunity. It is not the quantity but the quality of information and knowledge to be communicated that is paramount. Access to information and knowledge is undoubtedly a necessary but subordinate condition for democracy. Education in and for a liberal democracy is not, as many in the "learning about learning" school would have it, simply a matter of inducting students into a set of learning processes delivered through what are claimed to be increasingly "sophisticated pedagogies and technologies" so that they have a kind of interminable open access.

Third, technology has been complicit in the evolution of such popular notions as learning about learning, perennially problematising the world and learning for transformation. Contra Hargreaves these are, I would suggest part of the problem and not the solution with respect to determining how education should be configured to support human flourishing through discursive engagement within the context of globalisation. Masschelein (1998 and 2001) rightly takes issue with the currently fashionable conceit of the learning society and its attendant high moral claims. Following Arendt, he argues that attention to the distinction between the *Zoë* and the *Bios* (see

Arendt 1958) is helpful in disclosing the manner in which the bare, elemental force of life itself has come to dominate our conception of what it is to be human. *Zoë,* conceived as that which is proper to everything that lives, encompasses the drive to labour as a means for sustaining life. Metaphorically, it is encapsulated in the Genesis account of expulsion from "The Garden." The text puts it as follows:

> Accursed be the soil because of you.
> With suffering shall you get your food from it
> Every day of your life...
> With sweat on your brow
> Shall you eat your bread
> Until you return to the soil

(Gen. 3:17–19)

Here life has no meaning per se, being merely concerned with metabolising nature in the service of survival. Thus begins the cycle of labour and consumption that turns up again at the heart of Karl Marx's thought. The sense of the raw elemental force of life, shared with animals and all living creatures, is redeemed only in the post-flood covenant with Noah, by virtue of which individual life becomes important and gradually evolves a sense of meaning beyond naked survival. In her observations on Greek attitudes to labour, Arendt opines, "To labour meant to be enslaved by necessity and this enslavement was inherent in the conditions of human life. Because men were dominated by the necessities of life, they could win their freedom only through the domination of those [i.e., slaves] who they subjected to necessity by force" (ibid, 83ff). For the Greeks, slavery was not primarily driven by a desire to exploit and dominate the other so much as it was an attempt to exclude labour and raw necessity from the conditions of life. This elemental need to sustain life was quite different from the individuated self. The *Bios,* or biography as we might say, points to a sense of a self, conditioned by natality, with a *telos,* whose being is, to a greater or lesser extent, determined by the encounter with another, different self. Meaning in one's life was not, as Aristotle (1952) would have it, determined by the labour characteristic of the life force, but by how one's whole life might be looked upon to determine whether or not it had been a happy, that is a virtuous, life. In the *Ethics,* Aristotle observes that any determination about a man's happiness (that is his virtue) may only be determined teleologically. Judgements are to be rendered on the basis of how "good and noble" one was in acting out the good life as appropriate to him. But such judgements could not reasonably be made in the course of one's life, for as he says, "we must add 'in a complete life.' For one swallow does not make a summer, nor one day; and so too one day, or a short time does not make a man blessed and happy" (ibid, §1098a, L. 18ff).

So far then I have suggested that the *Zoë* and the *Bios* are to be distinguished in so far as the former refers to the relentless processes of nature and the latter to the living out of the individual life. Further, as Masschelein (2001) suggests, meaning as such can only be ascribed to the latter. However, Arendt argues that these two terms have been conflated, especially through the evolution of labour so that "as matters stand today, it has become as senseless to describe this world of machines in terms of means and ends as it has always been senseless to ask nature if she produced the seed to produce a tree or the tree to produce the seed" (Arendt, 152). Once there is no longer a distinction to be made between the processes of bare life and living the good life (between means and ends), living the good life may itself be measured by participation or non-participation in the processes themselves. The worth of a life is thus indistinguishable from life, production is indistinguishable from labour and consumption is indistinguishable from happiness. From this it is but a small step to the realisation that economic globalisation is shot through with this notion of the ineluctable cycle of production and consumption, ever expanding so that it draws into itself all forms of life including education. Education indeed becomes ensnared as but a part of the process where learning for learning displaces say, learning for meaning, much less learning for truth. In doing so it becomes entangled in the mechanisms of globalisation. Of course, if globalisation itself is the logical outworking of this mistake about means and ends it must perforce have great difficulty in accommodating itself to the discursive contest that might be deemed a feature of liberal democracies since such contests may challenge the global in favour of the local.

Masschelein takes the analysis one stage further in arguing that the preeminence of the process means that education is not concerned with the creation of a common world, where we can come to meet one another, but with ensuring that students can constantly adapt themselves to the process itself. Just as globalisation has no teleology, so too education comes to have no ultimate meaning beyond its own continuation. The process is its own end! Thus it is not clear that either the conservative or the radical liberal who subscribes to the efficacy of globalisation and its technologies are really very different. Global technologies are as apt to bring about closure as they are to open up new possibilities and ways of making sense of the world. While they may offer a different take on the processes of living this does not mean that they necessarily sustain an openness to life. In the light of this it is particularly important that we cultivate an educational project that draws upon diverse anthropological, ontological and ethical perspectives on human purpose and flourishing. Moreover, in order to instantiate the notion that the individual life is central to the educational project, it needs to go beyond the normatively determined processes to encounter both the self and the other as beings configured, to reiterate, by their natality. Education cannot focus merely on equipping students to live within a new set of technological social conditions but must ensure that they have the capacity and opportunity to credibly subject these condition to scrutiny from a variety of perspectives.

Critique and the Illusions of Criticism

In order to ground liminality as important to both education and civic society, as well as offering appropriate sites for and understandings of what would count as liminality, it is necessary to develop an understanding of not only what kinds of practices but also what kinds of spaces and encounters conduce to a discursive openness through contestation in the public spaces. It is equally important to see these contests as being situated within a larger picture where the ideological purity of Right and Left, liberals and communitarians is constantly compromised by their philosophical and practical overlap with the other. This is not to suggest that differences do not exist or that they are not deeply felt. Rather, it is to intimate that ideological positions are occasionally freighted with some confusion and contradiction and, moreover, that they generally share crucial claims about what is and is not important for the well being of the individual and/or community with countervalent ideologies. As we have noted above, more often than not disagreement appears only at the margins, with the how rather than the why or what. The difficulty for modern societies is that the overlap may increasingly occlude the differences and so de facto banish the dissenting voice from the public space. Yet, in the midst of this it must be remembered that students are neither required to inhabit the public space nor have responsibility for its functioning. Rather, they are people who are in an intermediate state.

The tendency to occlude the voice of the other is particularly apparent with respect to the increasingly hegemonic claims of a globalised economy, which have an ever-increasing impact on the discourse that enfolds education. This is hardly a novel suggestion (see Ferguson 2001; Macedo 1993; Sullivan 1993), but what is increasingly apparent is the crushing force with which alternative conceptions of human flourishing are being squeezed out of the public spaces.[5] In order to understand the importance of liminality to education and consequently to the polity it is necessary to explore the nature of the educational contest. It is equally important to reclaim the notion of contest in the face of a growing consensus, especially among politicians and their officials, about equipping (training) the individual to compete on behalf of the country in the global economy (Tate[6] 1996, 11). Contests about human purpose need not be seen as limited to the *agora*; they exist within religious and other forms of community. And, in all such intra-community contests there inheres the possibility that they are reduced to little more than shadowboxing because there is no real difference to be maintained—a de facto closure. Thus, in this essay there are two intertwined elements, one formal and one substantive, which it has proved difficult to disaggregate. The formal one is discursive closure in a liberal democracy and the substantive one is the neo-liberal economic theories which have come to dominate the actual discourse and bring about a kind of consensus in education across liberal democratic polities. It is possible that discursive closure may take place with respect to a variety of issues, say sexual mores, political protest, certain rights of recognition and the dispensing of justice. In education, it may be testing, accountability, quality assurance, mission statements, performativity, competences, benchmarks and management strategies. It is equally clear that in contemporary politics in liberal democracies, economic considerations are rarely far from the trajectory of closure. For this reason many of the shibboleths of late-industrial educational discourse have their origins in and echo the discourse of industrial and commercial management.

The increasing degree of difficulty in sustaining a creative linguistic openness in the spaces around politics and education is commensurate with the extent that the language of economics and the language of education become one. In order that any community sustain discursive openness it is necessary that certain material conditions prevail. Among these are the conditions that there should be different kinds of explanatory and operational metaphors for different kinds of activities—there should be spaces wherein those who do not wield power have a range of opportunities to have their voice heard and properly considered in political and social questions. This latter condition should not, however, be confused with telephone and television polls, focus groups and the like. But individuals and groups can only avail of such formal opportunities if they have actually had continuing exposure to the different kinds of discourse. For example, my ability to critique television advertising (a particular set of metaphors) may well depend on whether or not I have been exposed to, nay, nurtured in a language of the self as an acting, independent subject (a quite different set of metaphors).

Exposure to alternative languages is vitally important since it is easy enough in a liberal democracy to entertain a certain free-play of ideas that masquerade in the world of *as if* where those who are in government act as if the views of this or that group, this or that person counted, but continue to shape their own discursive practices and policy according to an entirely different agenda: for example, where government speaks of the dignity of the person but resources the "training of such persons explicitly for their *role* within a global economy." The containment and domestication of protest, hardly a phenomenon exclusive to late-industrial liberal democracies but one which is subject to quite particular inflexions. The en-massing of the individual, and the concomitant erasure of the self, represent such inflexions. They also include the emergence of patterns of conspicuous consumption as a kind of connective tissue, where a conjunction of interest lies not in certain principles of justice or voice or representation but resembles nothing so much as a shared enthusiasm to acquire things. But, while the pattern of acquisitiveness is shared, the objects consumed have no shared meaning in the way that principles of justice have. This individualised world eschews a shared interest in the political or, for that matter, the educational, substituting forms of collective identity mediated through the purchase of mass identifiers.

The impact of this en-massing has resulted in the absence of a genuine critical awareness. Liberal democratic citizens have been unwitting participants in the masking of this absence. It might be thought that the power of the individual to criticise (and therefore have a voice) has been enhanced through the exponential growth of regulatory bodies, ombudsmen, television complaints shows, consumer groups and, in education, parents forums, school governing bodies, parents representatives, educational pressure groups and student councils. But herein lies the central contradiction of rights and accountability talk, and one that must perforce impact on what we understand critical awareness to be. It is true that there are increased forums for criticism but, like patterns of consumption, while appearing to represent a collective public undertaking, these criticisms are fundamentally private and, to some extent, trivial and pathological. Bauman articulates this particularly well:

> One can think of the hospitality to critique characteristic of present day modern society as having the pattern of a camping site. The place is open to everyone who has their own caravan and money to pay the rent. Guests come and go, none taking much interest in how the site is run, providing they have been allocated a plot big enough to park the caravan, that the electric sockets...are in good order, that the passengers in nearby caravans do not make too much noise.... Drivers bring their own homes attached to their cars.... They pay and they demand.... If they feel they are being short-changed...campers may complain and demand their due—but it won't occur to them to challenge and re-negotiate the managerial philosophy of the site (Bauman 2001, 100).

If ever there was a time of "critical reflection" evident in the public spaces of liberal democracies, then it has been largely supplanted by a "culture of criticism." It is important that these two are distinguished lest it be imagined that being afforded the right to criticise is the same thing as embracing critical awareness. In the first case the culture of criticism comes wrapped up in a cloak of desires and demands masquerading as a language of rights. Thus the individual assumes that being able to complain about the quality of teaching in her child's school or the tardiness of public transport represents the exercise of control over one's circumstances. Because she is one among many, and because her complaint is broken down into the en-massed individual, redress is minimal.[7] This illusory facility of criticism obscures the need for critical reflection if liberal democracy is to be maintained. The facility for complaint and the faculty of scrutiny are not the same thing. If the "public sphere" (Taylor 1995) is to be more than a forum where people are allowed to air their grievances then it has to operate according to a principle of the uniqueness of the person as being. This uniqueness, as I argue throughout this essay may not be confused with en-massed individual (though it frequently is in practice).

Some Conditions for Discursive Openness

So far I have suggested that globalisation endangers the capacity for critical reflection by doing at least two things. First, it generates the notion of process as its own end, which undermines any serious discussion of purpose and ends. Second, it ensures the en-massing of the individual while simultaneously presenting consumer criticism as political critique. In all of this the notion of the self as embodying the surplus that comes from the singular uniqueness of having been specifically born is itself obscured. But of course to accept this would be to accept practices that diminish the person, and concomitantly the diminishment of liberal democracy. And, Žižek's articulation of the ambiguity of democracy not withstanding, a belief in the virtue of liberal democracy remains, to date, the best possibility for securing certain fundamental freedoms. The task then is to see what conditions such polities need to secure and promote.

What then are the kinds of conditions that large socio-political entities need to have in place so as to ensure the continuance of discursive contest and the existence of liminal voices? Put like this, the question may apply to any extant or putative socio-political organism that, in some meaningful sense, underscores the desirability of a strong formal conception of human flourishing. In this way, even if the prognosis of some of the theorists of globalisation is accurate and the forms of our governance and social organisation do change, we may still retain a clear conception of the discursive conditions necessary for human flourishing. One way of doing this is to explore what conditions would need to subsist in any socio-political entity—not necessarily a liberal democracy—but does publicly (through its stated philosophy, with all that entails in terms of aims, intentions, dispositions and practices) espouse a developed notion of human flourishing. The Catholic Church offers one such interesting heuristic site for at least five reasons. First, it lays claim to a coherent understanding of and desire to support the meaningfulness of the individual life. Second, there is a formal requirement that Catholics, in common with many other religious groups, be good citizens in and for the development of the good society (Bishops of England and Wales 1997). Third, Catholicism may be regarded as an alternative form of global communication, which, if it is to be coherent, must maintain a critical distance from the globalised communication that is the commodity economy. Fourth, it shares with Rousseau of the *Social Contract* (1968) a deep ambiguity about the relationship between the rights of the individual and the good of the whole—an ambiguity that is at the heart of liberal democracies. Finally, and not the least important, there is much dispute about the credentials of the Catholic Church as an agent of discursive freedom. Like most religious communities it is not a democratic institution in the classical liberal sense and, as we shall see later, is not infrequently characterised by liberal philosophers (Hirst 1974) and other academics (Bruce 2002) as inherently closed and without a serious or significant internal contest and consequently with nothing significant to offer the public deliberations of the polity.

The central concern here is not whether or not the Catholic Church, or indeed any other religious institution is de facto "open," though no doubt that is an important question in itself. Rather, it is whether or not it offers some insight into the necessary conditions for the maintenance of discursive contestation that is at the service of human flourishing. This Church claims, in its core documentation, to uphold the dignity, primacy and freedom of the individual's exercise of conscience within a communal setting (Flannery 1975, Ch. 64: 1, §§15ff.)—a tacit acknowledgement of the surplus of being which is not self-evidently contained in the term "being a Catholic." The examination of the conditions necessary for contest within a particular church community together with some of the impediments to their successful instantiation may offer some insight into the way in which a community may broadly share the aims of a particular form of life while embracing significant differences as to the manner in which such aims are to be realised.

This in turn opens up some formal principles about freedom and closure for consideration.

In its general documentation, and in its specifically educational pronouncements, the Catholic Church claims to support the principles of freedom of choice and "genuine dialogue" (Sacred Congregation for Catholic Education 1988, §§96). It further maintains that the relationships between human beings, individually and as groups, are to be configured *justly*. Despite this apparent liberal concern with freedom and flourishing it is clear that the Catholic Church does not offer a similar kind of open-ended endorsement of a range of views as may be found, rhetorically at least, in a liberal democracy. In the period since the loss of the Papal States, the Vatican has attempted to centralise and control the freedom of its members to openly discuss theology and social philosophy. Indeed, it might be argued that it expects its members to eschew certain features of liberal democracy, such as the freedom of the individual to choose to live in extramarital sexual relations and to have an abortion, on the grounds that such practices are not conducive to human flourishing. The most recent attempt to curtail discursive freedom has been the attempt by the Vatican (Pope John Paul II 1994) and subsequently Cardinal Ratzinger (Allen 2001) to end theological and political speculation about the possibility of the ordination of women by invoking papal authority. To put matters crudely, Catholicism appears to embody contrary instincts, advocating the freedom of the individual while maintaining that certain exercises of freedom are objectively wrong. Given the contradictions inherent in this polity whatever conditions are necessary to protect discursive openness in such a circumscribed context are indeed likely to be the minimum necessary to sustain any intellectually and ethically healthy community.

The attempt to quell speculation on matters such as the ordination of women would appear to have been unsuccessful. Why, in a centrally controlled culture, has Ratzinger's injunction failed? It would appear that Catholicism is, in some important senses at least, open to plurality and discursive contest. This claim to vital discursive openness may be seen elsewhere such as in a very public exchange at the Jesuit-controlled University of Georgetown about whether or not crucifixes (the central icon of Catholic faith and worship) should be hung in classrooms. The discussion took place against a backdrop of ecclesial attempts to close it down (O'Hare 1999).

Given the ambiguities at the heart of this particular communicative form, what conditions would it need to sustain a discursive openness? Here I intend focusing on six key conditions that appear to emerge from a scrutiny of Catholicism. These conditions have relevance I think for other, more ideologically multivalent and complex polities. First, the development of Catholic theology is deeply embedded in Greek philosophical thought with the result that it readily recognises (even where it fails to admit) the provisionality of its own truth formulations. Consequently, its historic pedagogies were rooted in the dialectical method and the reasonableness of argument. Second, its theology and "justifiable" practices are inescapably founded on an identification with the powerless. Thus, even where there have been despotic individuals and groups, and undoubtedly there have been sufficient of those (see de Rosa 1988), the hegemonising tendencies of many prelates have always been subject to alternative and ideologically legitimate voices. Third, because it is geopolitically and historically—hence not just rhetorically—a world religion, its doctrines have been subject to countless modifications and diverse influences. Fourth, subsidiarity (see Komonchak 1968) is a deeply rooted principle in Catholic theology that it had drawn from social life in the first place and made its own.[8] It is a principle whereby the smaller or lesser communities may not be imposed upon by the larger or greater. In an address to newly named Cardinals in 1946, Pius XII, drawing on the earlier encyclical of Pius XI, *Quadragesimo Anno*, suggested that "what single individuals, using their own resources, can do for themselves, must not be removed and given to the community. This principle is equally valid for smaller and lesser communities in relationship to larger or more powerful communities" (see Quinn 1996).[9] Thus, Catholic institutional and administrative structures are always subject to the countervalent forces of centralisation and local autonomy, which gives rise to a certain creative tension. Even where, at one time or another, one of these two forces may come to dominate, the other one remains at the threshold. While it may be pushed as far as the doorway it cannot be excluded.

The fifth condition, tangentially related to the fourth, is particularly pertinent to the conditions of globalisation. The Catholic Church, while certainly a global entity, is not universally strong in the context of the local. Whereas in some countries that have been traditionally Catholic it appears to be at the political centre, a de facto national or civic church, in yet other places its influence appears marginal and the experience of the community is indeed one of marginality. Finally, its members owe allegiance to and are inserted into a range of external communities and groups, states and organisations so that they can bring to bear certain independence in their dealings with the institutional church. Equally important, they are economically independent of the church. Nowhere is this more clearly or poignantly seen than in the decision by middle-class Bostonian Catholics to withhold funding from the Church until the Archdiocese dealt with the issue of sexual abuse. It is undoubtedly access to a pluriform world that has allowed these Catholics to see, to understand and to act accordingly.

Now, it might be argued that the six conditions suggested here as necessary for discursive openness are historically contingent, but arguably they are no more so than the conditions that govern the discursive needs of any community. In any event, discursive contest appears to have been very much a part of Catholicism up to the first Vatican Council. In her evolutionary study of Catholic education, Sawicki (1988) charts both the continuity and the changes in the discourse from the early Church to the post-Vatican II period. These changes arise out of the need for communities to reassess the relevance and efficacy of their approaches to particular social goods at particular moments of history. Of course, were there not a reasonable claim to a historical continuity and connectedness then it would be impossible to maintain that there was any internal renegotiation of the purposes of education. Rather, there would be different conversations about education as between different communities that perhaps merely shared a label or title. In the light of this it can be reasonably claimed that third-century Christian educators and late-twentieth/early-twenty-first-century Catholic Christian educationalists share some irreducible common purpose in as much as they both continue to ascribe some foundational value to a belief in the *Parousia* and, in view of such a belief, regard Christian education as playing a formative role in preparing the individual and the community for their death and afterlife (Carr 1999; Haldane 1999). However, beyond this irreducible minimum there is a contest as to (1) what such a claim might mean in respect of the ways in which Christians are to deport themselves in the interim and (2) given some shared eschatology, the manner in which the individual relates to particular social and cultural structures. It is at this point that the contest moves from being one about the historic identity of the community to one between contemporary groupings or factions within a community.

There appear to be certain conditions, either structural or epistemological, that conduce to discursive openness. But behind these, the notions of singularity and surplus re-emerge in a yet more potent form. Those hegemonic impulses that the Catholic Church might harbour are ameliorated by the existence of a theology of singularity and the recognition that the person is neither described in, nor contained by, the epithet "Catholic." This surplus is not a part of her personality that is not Catholic; neither is it to be found, as it were, outside her being a Catholic, another part of her or another descriptive label. Rather, it is the determination that her being is possessed of a singularity hinted at in the acknowledgement of the primacy of conscience. Catholicism (in common with other Western religions) theologically acknowledges this in its teleological assumptions about the individual. Each human can think teleologically with regard to their own being without its being reduced only to the general will or again as Santner puts it, "the self pertains to that which in some sense persists beyond an individual's teleological integration into the life of the genus" (Santner 2001, 76f). But the self is not to be found in the acts of obedience to doctrine or the acts of confession or in the conversations about contest, all of which would impound it within the bounded space of this or that discourse; it lies rather at the threshold—neither at the interface of the self with the world nor as some ghost that lurks in another world behind or beyond this one. Ultimately, it is the acknowledgement of this singular self that provides (without being) the condition for other conditions of discursive openness. This comes about because the capacity to critique (not complain or criticise) depends on bringing my uniqueness to bear on the situation. As we have already seen, critique tends to be ensnared and neutralised by the simultaneous creation of mass identity and isolated individuality that result only in complaint and criticism. Where the unique self recognises that she is free she holds the possibility of actualising her freedom. This is the beginning of standing in a unique interrogatory relationship to the social, cultural and political conditions in which one is located. Similarly, in education the evocation of the uniqueness of each student stands against the very notion that education can be authentically represented as primarily concerned with a mass identifier like "the economy," or indeed the "global economy."

Education and Contestation in the State

Are there any principled conditions to be adduced from this brief analysis of contestation in the Catholic Church that might be applied more generally with respect to the state? Here I wish to apply each of these in turn and in doing so wish to discuss (1) whether or not such conditions are applicable to the liberal state and (2) what obstacles there might be to their effective instantiation. Arguments for or against a particular view or course of action in a liberal democracy are generally held as being dependent upon what may be reasonably asserted. The foundations of modern liberal democracies arguably reside in the principles of reasonable dialogue, grounded in the Greeks and mediated by the Fathers of the American Revolution and *Les Hommes des Lettres* of pre-Revolutionary France (see Arendt 1963). And, given that both revolutions were occasioned, in part at least, by the desire for representation in the public spaces then, it is not unreasonable to assume that the public spaces should be open to reasonable dialogue and that decisions about the well-being of the polity should themselves be reasonable and to some extent influenced by the conversation in the public spaces. However, it is not clear that choices in the public domain are always, or even predominantly made in accordance with reason if we take this to mean that decisions are made on the basis of empirical evidence and/or coherent argument, and the application of the same kinds of consideration to all. On the contrary apparently public choices are not infrequently predicated on ideological, political or economic attachments that may themselves become articles of faith but that are not necessarily reasonable. Arguably, the attachments that emerge in such choices are emotional rather than rational; much contemporary discourse is one thing masquerading as another.

Let me take a very practical example of what is meant here. Suppose that a Board of Studies in a university (no doubt a haven of common sense and bastion of liberal democracy!) is in session, looking at the need to generate greater income from research and consultancy activity. Proposals are tabled by that new breed of late-twentieth-century academic—"senior managers"—that require their colleagues to work more efficiently, cut some of their contact hours with students ("because," after all, "we are *all* over-teaching!") and re-design assessment procedures ("because," after all, we over assess!"). Colleagues around the table are invited to respond and one person (let's call her, Mary) vociferously makes the not entirely unreasonable point that even where such changes to working practices may be established as desirable the resources to establish them do not exist. Further, she explains, it is neither just nor reasonable to place an increasing workload on those who have already produced efficiency gains of the order of 30 percent in a matter of a few years and no longer feel that they have the necessary time or energy reserves to continue to effect such "savings." In any event, the argument goes, the educational justification for such changes is, at best, unproven. Mary's objections to the management strategy may, on the application of the canons of rationality, be deemed "reasonable"; that is, there are good reasons for the protest.

Suppose then that one response from senior managers is to apply their newly discovered pop psychology for management "techniques." Outside the meeting, one manager inquires after Mary's state of health. Sometimes directly, on other occasions obliquely, questions are directed to others in the group: "Is Mary working too hard?"; "Is everything okay with Mary?"; and "Mary seems to be under some pressure lately?"

It might be suggested that these intimations of managerial concern demonstrate an admirable sympathy for a colleague suffering from stress; exactly the kind of caring management style that we should expect from those who have traded in a neo-liberal economic outlook for "caring capitalism." If we apply the same canons of reasonableness already applied to Mary's objections, we might deduce that this is a reasonable concern. But, in directing attention away from the argument and onto the protagonist the substantive arguments against the proposed course(s) of action are lost. These, in effect, have been marginalised or trivialised, reduced to a function of their progenitor's stress. The language of care and concern has effectively subordinated the central issues raised in the critique, that the original proposals to change academic practices were or might be deemed inappropriate, unhelpful or misguided. The move is to reclassify the criticism as an *ad femina*. Mary has become pathologised as one in need of rest or support or some other form of help.

While this illustration may appear to be easily dismissible by philosophers as itself a product of the pop psychology chastised, it is actually more than first appears. The central issue is not the deployment of psychology to person management but the manner in which a particular discourse supplants criticism by linguistically pathologising the critic. The language is turned away from the content of the criticism and towards the state of mind/disposition of the individual or group, giving voice to the criticism. While appearing to cherish the individual, the manager strangles the unique self who brings her critical perspective to bear on the issue. So, whether it is the new breed of caring mangers, new labour or the neo-liberals the pattern of pathologising criticism is much the same. In using language in this way there is also an interesting and important desensitising of the original import of a language of concern—but that is a different essay. The veneer of reasonableness actually masks a commonplace act of closure and the avoidance of engagement in a reasonable discursive contest. When such "articles of faith" are inscribed into the political discourse they can tell against the actual exercise of democracy. When governments suggest that those who stand in opposition to its policies are "backwoodsmen," lacking in vision, for instance, it is important that we remain alert to the dangers of *ad hominem* displacement.

The second condition was the institutional identification with the poor or powerless, which as a central tenet of Catholicism mitigates some of the dangers of power. Thus, Sobrino (1978 and 2001) and his radical theology in defence of the poor and dispossessed is as much a part of the *communio* as Ratzinger and his impulse to control. Certainly, the French Revolution does carry in its wake what Arendt (1977) refers to as the "social question" of poverty and, in modern democracies, universal suffrage is intended to convey the sense that all are to be treated justly. The evolving provision of universal education did carry, along with a range of less noble desires, a concern for the welfare of the poor and dispossessed.

It is not at all clear, however, that either the American or French Revolutions, which are seen to be the cornerstones of modern democracy, were fundamentally based on a concern for the poor. And, as we shall see later, many governments in late-industrial liberal democracies appear relatively unconcerned about the role of the poor and/or marginalised in the institutions of democracy. Despite its rhetorical attachment to an inclusive doctrine for all citizens, certain tendencies in modern society can leave liberal democracy susceptible to the dangers of exclusion and declassification. The continued existence of significant numbers of poor and dispossessed (neither wholly inside nor wholly outside) is a liminal reminder of sorts that the claims to justice and fairness that rhetorically distinguish liberal democracies can fall far short of their aim in practice. The danger is that the democratic challenge that inheres in the voices of the economically and/or culturally liminal is so discomfiting that they are, in the political imagination, placed not at the boundary of society but outside it with the consequence that there exists an empty set in modern democratic discourse.

The third condition of discursive openness is related to the fluidity of ideas and influences. Liberal democracies depend on the free exchange of ideas. If people are not free to express their opinions without fear of either sanctions or reprisal then they are not free; and if the *demos* is intended, as it is, to denote all people, then all the people must be both formally and actually free to do so. (Once again we find echoes of the importance to such a project of a clear conception of the unique self.) Again, however, it is not entirely self-evident that liberal democracies provide the actual freedom for the individual or group to express their opinions. Even if they are formally permitted to do so, the actual conditions of their public life may inhibit, or indeed, prohibit them from realising the formal possibilities. The actual conditions of modern liberal democracies may, for example, be so circumscribed by, and in thrall to, a somewhat truncated conflation of economic success and human flourishing that the formal conditions are not operative. The preeminence of an economic discourse can itself, in such circumstances, contribute to discursive closure and lack of contestation.

Again, one or other versions of the will of the people—or "the general will" that, following Rousseau (1968, 61), holds that organised religion itself represents an illiberal challenge to the freedoms that accrue to the citizen— can militate against the free flow of ideas. As Schama (1990) demonstrates, adherence to the general will can too readily become a religion in its own right, displacing traditional religious forms with its own religious fervour, and turning the *Champs de Mars* into a temple to the general will wherein the general will itself is both reified and deified. It is not possible to have a rich and complex manifestation of liberal democracy without a robust and diverse "public sphere." Those who enter into this public sphere must do so not as the en-massed who see this as their comfort zone of compliance, but as someone who is a little estranged. To think of oneself and one's community as "strangers" is in some way to acknowledge our pilgrim status and with it the need for the ongoing search to find our fit. Such wandering must perforce bring us up against the thresholds of our own experiences and perceptions; it must also facilitate our recognition of the strangeness of those forms of discourse that would alienate us from our sense of self and other.

Subsidiarity is the fourth condition for the maintenance of discursive contestation. In the liberal democratic state this is intimately tied into the health of the public sphere and to the ways in which power and authority are distributed between various sites. In a liberal democracy, decisions that affect communities and individuals should be taken as near to the need as possible with authentic conversation playing an active role in the final decision. Thus, on the principle of subsidiarity, local communities should have an active voice in the development of, for example, their educational provision. Late-industrial liberal democracies, however, have developed a number of obstacles to the effective cultivation of such a principle, not least of which is bureaucratisation. In *The Origins of Totalitarianism*, Arendt distinguishes several versions of bureaucratisation. Two are of particular interest here. The first is where the administration, as in France, "has survived all changes…entrenched itself like a parasite in the body politic, developed its own class interests and become a useless organism whose only purpose appears to be chicanery and prevention of normal economic and political development" (1951 and 1973, 244). The second, typical of totalitarian regimes, and consequently more troublesome, is the creation of a multi-sited and multi-layered bureaucracy where the centre of power is not clearly visible. Indeed, the "only rule of which everyone…may be sure is that the more visible the government agencies are the less power they carry, and the less is known of the existence of an institution, the more powerful it will turn out to be" (ibid, 403). In the case of the former, the instinct to protect one's position can have a detrimental effect on the development of actual subsidiarity where the local is denuded of any real voice in case it would damage the centre. This is most apparent in modern public institutions such as schools and universities where there has been a staggering growth in the numbers of consultation processes and committees whose function appears to be to confirm the predetermined policies of the centre while creating an impression of democratic participation. Meanwhile, there has been a concomitant loss of autonomy for those who work in such institutions. Whereas pedagogic approaches and the distribution of activity time were once the domain of the professor/teacher in the classroom, they are now part of a centrally dictated format. These creations in their turn give rise to an ever-increasing bureaucracy that, by virtue of its expanded numbers, becomes ever more powerful and in a vicious cycle creates instruments to maintain its power. Such a state of affairs is hardly conducive to the flourishing of the principle of subsidiarity.

As to the second condition, while I do not wish to suggest that modern liberal democracies are somehow crypto-totalitarian cultures, there are structural similarities worth attending to. Governments in modern liberal democracies have, in recent years, established a wide range of bodies to oversee different facets of our social life. Education has been one of the key sites for the establishment of such bodies, which have included quality assurance agencies, funding agencies, qualifications agencies and training agencies. Such agencies are given a range of powers ostensibly intended to create the perception that they are independent of government, but this is not the case: their policies and finances are centrally driven. Added to this is the growing propensity for central government to establish advisory groups that stand outside the "normal" structures and, on the basis of their advice, make decisions over which the substantive body will have little or no control. In such circumstances it is not always clear what the lines of responsibility and authority actually are, and so obfuscation precludes the development of subsidiarity as a principle for engagement and decision-making from taking hold.

Penultimately, liberal democracies need to see the boundaries of their own existence as neither coextensive with some other global form of communication—say the commodity economy—nor out of communion with other communities. The cultivation of a rich conception of the liberal state as, on occasion, being the major force in the life of its citizens and in its relations with other polities, and at other times being marginal to but interested in the concerns of some international and transnational bodies, is key to a sense of proportion. Not to have these multilateral realities is to open the liberal state up to the hegemonising tendencies of the commodity market, making it little more than a conduit for the communication of the market.

Finally, there is the existence of overlapping communities of affiliation and allegiance. The liberal democratic community should indeed welcome in its citizens a range of overlapping communities, some of which are contained within its borders and some that overlap with other political, socio-economic, religious and cultural entities. For example, if an individual belongs to say a religious community, she will be within a particular state and may have allegiances to entities other than the state. In the case where these allegiances do not directly and self-evidently express themselves as contrary to the principles of liberal democracy, and where they bring a voice to bear on the deliberations of the political centre that may enhance and support a "foundational" claim in support of the flourishing of all citizens, then they should be welcomed. But here again there may be obstacles in the modern liberal state. Paramount among these is the gradual closure of the gap between the liberal democratic state and the corporation. Habermas opines that as "markets drive out politics, the nation-state increasingly loses its capacities...to ensure the essential foundations of its own legitimacy" (Habermas 2001, 79). These capacities are lost not because the "corporation" is an ineluctable force over which human beings have no control, but because political leaders have collectively abrogated their primary responsibility to continue to promote the flourishing of citizens. Again, Habermas succinctly sums up this tendency. 'Clinton or Blair,' he argues, "relying on empty formulas...pitch themselves as efficient managers for the reorganisation of failing business ventures. The truly programmatic vacuity of a political platform that has been whittled down to 'political change' corresponds, on the side of the voters, either to informed abstinence or the thirst for "political charisma....If the desperation is great enough, a little money is all that is needed for right-wing slogans and a remote controlled engineer from Bitterfield, a complete political unknown with nothing more than a cell phone at his disposal, to mobilise nearly 13 percent of the protest vote" (ibid, 79f). Habermas' anxiety is that the more the traditional liberal democratic state is assailed by corporate and ideological globalisation, the more readily is the conversation truncated.

Yet again, this is not quite the final word; underpinning all these basic considerations required for the maintenance of liberal democracy are two further conditions. First, there is the need for recognition and acknowledgement of the surplus of the self. Second, there is a need for a rich multivalent, untamed and untameable metaphorical language. Regarding the first point, part of the legacy of Rousseau and Paine (and to some extent Aristotle) on the one hand and Marx and his disciples on the other has been the loss of a sense of this surplus. As we have already noted, for Rousseau the will of the one had to be subordinated to the will of all thus squeezing out the surplus. The will or conscience or *daimon*—that which configures the self as a first person singular—has been transformed for them, as it was for Marx, into the third person thus losing sight of the "self." Nor is this difficulty adequately dealt with in the postmodern turn where multiple selves are posited since, even were we to add together all the possible multiple selves— parent, consumer, worker, boss, feminist—this would only offer a finite sum of descriptors still leaving untamed the singular self. Paradoxically, this self lies at the heart of the political since, to take but one example, freedom is not simply a general specification of politics but is incarnated in the particularity of the singular self. It is the self who is politically free. Even in a totalitarian regime the disruptive power of the free self always poses a threat.

Perhaps more than any of these conditions—or, more properly, as a consequence of securing all these conditions—we require a rich, complex and multivalent language that can counter the linguistic closure that arises as a result of the occlusion by the global economic language of the distinctive aims, obligations and discursive practices of the state.

In the course of this section I have tried to elucidate some of the structural conditions necessary for the maintenance of liberal democracy and some of the difficulties that such democracies have in upholding them. Moreover, I have suggested that these structural conditions depend, in turn, on the existence of the surplus of self that is not to be contained by physiological, socio-political, cultural or economic accounts of the person. The purpose of drawing these conditions from the experience of the Catholic Church is, in part at least, a practical demonstration of how, given the increasingly liminal position of religious communicative forms, the liberal state might draw on alternative perspectives to enhance its self-understanding. In the final section of this chapter I wish to suggest that the metaphors that lie at the heart of this study offer a positive set of responses to the incorrigible temptation to closure. In doing so I am sensible of Habermas' view that the liberal state can neither run away from economic globalisation nor embrace it warmly.

Suggestions for a Way Forward

If my diagnosis of some of the difficulties of liberal democracies is reasonably to-the-point, nothing is to be gained from simply rehearsing laments for a by-gone age. As an educationalist, it is important to at least chart a constructive response and I believe that an educational provision that cultivates the liminal as both space and disposition offers one way of maintaining openness so that we and our students can learn and develop as citizens. This response is rooted in the elucidation of a variety of metaphors that offer an alternative way of making sense on one's position in the world, and indeed of the world in which one finds oneself. Liminality is the key that unlocks a range of other metaphors. While there may be a range of attempts, conscious and unconscious, to bring about closure, in the liberal democratic polity these may be resisted not by a confrontation but by the maintenance of alternative ways of describing the self and the relationship between the self and the world. These alternatives may not be found at the heart of the polity, in the corridors of power or in the bureaucracies that, perhaps unwittingly, sustain closure. They are to be found in the interstices of our being together, in the excesses and surpluses that are not "taken care of" in and by the centre. Such interstitial places and opportunities are particularly suitable for teachers—adults who stand at the interstices of life—between adulthood and childhood, between the sphere of private growth and development and the "public sphere." between the realisation of individual potential and communal necessity. As such they have the responsibility in a liberal democracy of preparing children/adolescents to take their own responsibility for both the democracy and their role within it. The development of a liminal perspective in education supports the desirability of having contesting voices and challenges presented to the children. But it does not demand, as we shall see in the next chapter that they, the children, be engaged in a confrontation in the public spaces. Rather, the work of the teacher is to equip them with a language commensurate with the complex topography of their lives in late industrial society. This will entail the development of language and disposition, the creation of hermeneutically interesting and heuristically challenging perspectives. In fact, it will entail what we used to think of as *education*. That is, an intentional activity of assisting students in wresting back some control over their lives.

In arguing for this I am suggesting that the teacher is not to be summed up in a series of claims about her competencies or a statement of the benchmarks she is to attain. These contemporary approaches to the being and role of the teacher turn education into a racecourse, the teachers into horse trainers and children into steeple chasers. Teachers and students alike succeed only if they can jump the next hurdle. But on the account here, the teacher is a more complex and fluid figure who has to undertake to play many roles, some of which represent the centre and some the liminal.

Notes

1. Values may be seen here to be a form of communication to the extent that a polity communicates its priorities, sense of itself and so on by way of what it values.
2. Such claims are usually made on behalf of the individual or collections of individual citizens by the state, though increasingly these are paralleled by global corporations.
3. Fukayama, of course, wished to argue that history is at an end as the contrary forces that gave rise to events have been resolved by the collapse of contesting ideologies leaving Western liberal capitalism as the *telos* (though he has subsequently revised this assessment as a consequence of the events of September 11th, 2001). Baudrillard offers a competing analysis when he

argues that the end of history has not arrived in that sense of a final resolution, rather what we are witnessing is "the dilution of history as event; its media *mise en scène*, its excess of visibility. The continuity of time is less and less certain. With instant information, there's no longer any time for history itself" (2001, 277). In both cases, each regards what has gone before as no longer determinative of the present or future. Certainly, if the conserving function of education is regarded as referring only to the attempt to retain and maintain cultural shibboleths rooted in the past, then the suggestion that education continues to perform such a function would hardly be legitimate. However, if conservation refers to the maintenance of power and control at the centre a la Foucault, then education remains securely conservative.

4.   In any event, knowledge is not accessible online since, even at its most primitive level, to know something requires a knower who has already made a series of judgments.

5.   Here, and throughout this essay, public spaces refers to the sphere of the social and political where adults meet and wherein they act.

6.   At the time of his writing Nick Tate was Chief Executive of the Schools Curriculum and Assessment Authority for England and Wales. His comments on the overtly economic nature of education were subsequently echoed in a public speech by Douglas Osler (Her Majesty's Chief Inspector of Schools for Scotland) who suggested that "education for work should be the chief end of education." His speech was reported by Neil Munro in the *Times Educational Supplement* in 1997.

7.   In Britain, the redress for poor service is laid down by the relevant regulatory body. In the case of late trains (including those significantly behind schedule) the redress is a 20 percent refund of the original fare for which the complainant has to apply in writing. This hardly represents a significant disincentive for companies who charge some of the highest fares in the world.

8.   The term subsidiarity derives from the Latin *subsidium*, meaning the reserve troops who would come to the aid of the front line troops if, and only if, those troops were seen to be incapable of doing the job on their own. Pius XI first articulated the concept as a reaction to the then-recent totalitarian experience of Nazism and the then-fully emergent experience of Stalinist totalitarianism.

9.   This quotation is taken from a lecture by Archbishop John R. Quinn given on June 29th, 1996, at Campion Hall, Oxford, on the occasion of its centenary.

Chapter 2

Liminal Places and Possibilities in Education

The Child's Toys and the Old Man's Reasons
Are the Fruits of the Two Seasons.

William Blake "Auguries of Innocence," (1997, Ln.91f)

Introduction

The previous chapter elucidated the problem which discursive closure poses for a liberal democracy. It also describes and delineates a set of minimum conditions necessary for the maintenance of openness. Specifically, closures hasve arisen in the political—and as a consequence, educational—displacement of a perfectly reasonable concern to secure an individual and collective livelihood with the fetishistic economisation of being itself. In light of this, the present chapter endeavours to articulate the minimum conditions necessary for the maintenance of discursive openness in a liberal democratic polity, grounding these in the notion of the surplus of the self. This entails the exploration of an approach to education that is likely to cultivate and nurture these conditions. It would be naïve to suppose that any approach to such a complex problem can offer more than a partial solution with respect to the sphere of the political per se; it would be even more naïve to imagine that somehow the answer is to be found in some particular manifestation or transformation that might take place within the sphere of school education. Indeed, some would argue that education is no place for the overtly political; though frequently, as we shall see, such protests can be a little disingenuous. Yet, schooling in a liberal democracy clearly has some connections with the way we choose to live as well as our forms of governance. The growing interest in and emphasis on education for citizenship is testimony to a concern about a perceived deficit in our public spaces. The first question to arise here, then, is whether or not education is the appropriate forum for politicising young people and, if it is, how might this be properly approached.

To Politic or Not to Politic?

Blake's aphoristic litany on innocence (and experience) throws into sharp relief the problem of seeing schools as strategic sites for the remediation of a democratic deficit. Play and exploration are to childhood what politics and economics are to adulthood. In the confusion of these categories a certain balance is lost with respect to both child and adult. In relation to the child a certain unburdened dimension of growing up is compromised when she is expected to fulfil someone else's aspirations or make up for their deficiencies. Generally, we tend to think that the frustrated career ambitions of a parent should not be transferred to the child. Surely when such a thing happens we are wont to say to the offending parent, "Take responsibility for your own career and do not visit your own sense of failure or incompleteness on your offspring." We might wish to say of the parent that their failure to assume responsibility for their own career and desire to fulfil their frustrated ambitions through their child not only diminishes the child but herself, as someone who has, at least putatively, responsibility for her own life. Why then, should we not apply a similar principle to the polity? Adulthood requires an assumption of a healthy responsibility for "how things are." The inappropriate displacement of some of this into the realm of childhood and adolescence may only serve to make adults less than they should be.

The child-self emerges as a first-person subject in an evolving series of affiliations, attachments, displacements, discoveries and traumas. These involve projections and introjections, distance and belonging. It is hardly new to suggest that this complex process of learning to be in the world is precisely the state of being a child. It is a world potentially rich in metaphor and symbol, flights of fancy and imagination, but one that is also fragile because of the ineluctable strangeness of one's own self. Where we disrupt, or, more correctly, impede development within this complex web through the introduction of pedagogies and discourses that have as their intention the assumption of perspectives and responsibilities for which the subject has not the requisite background or experience, we are likely to undermine the state of childhood itself. Of course, there is always a danger that childhood appears to be some kind of temporary condition (a state of naïveté) from which children need to be liberated. And, it might be argued that part of this entails their preparation to assume adult responsibilities. I would suggest that it is true that childhood is a temporary condition as is all human being, but that does not preclude the possibility of seeing it as a discrete state of being, its own present (Conroy 1999a). Being its own present we should look on childhood as a place of exploration and enthusiasm-making, of interest and excitement where the play of language and ideas carries its own import. It should be regarded as a time and space where children are encouraged to see that this stage is more than a prelude to their *real* life. We often ascribe unruly classroom behaviour to student disaffection. Perhaps it may more readily be seen as a consequence of disenchantment.

It was, I think, precisely such a concern that motivated Arendt to pen her short essay on *The Crisis in Education*, where she opined, "The role played by education in all political utopias from ancient times onward shows how natural it seems to start a new world with those who are by birth and nature new" (Arendt 1977, 17). She questioned the validity and advisability of an education that failed to distinguish between the worlds of childhood and those of adulthood. Arendt was writing as a political scientist and one irrevocably committed to an expansive view of the political process. Equally, she believed that the political process was properly conducted in the public spaces of a liberal polity, and that it be so conducted by adults with adults, sorting out their differences and working together to foster the conditions of an open ethical polity. Children as students were not properly equipped to deliberate on or offer much to the political process, since they had neither the requisite experiences, nor were they in a position to carry the burden of responsibility for any decisions that might be made with respect to the conduct of the polity. Her belief that children lacked the necessary experience and should not be condemned to be responsible for the failures of adults expanded into a trenchant criticism of industrial and post-industrial pedagogies that, she argued in an ironic twist, were premised on a profound error—that of experience. The claim that experiential education was flawed rested on her belief that it placed too great a burden on the resources of the student, implicitly ignoring the real limitations of and on their experience as well as on the richness of the world to be known.

Ranged against Arendt's views are a formidable if somewhat disparate and complex set of arguments, advanced by a range of discrete protagonists joined together only by the belief that education is an explicitly political endeavour and must be treated as such. This does not mean that they all overtly promote "political education" but, as I shall show, they all wish to substantively politicise children in particular ways. These protagonists and their arguments may be placed in three or four main groupings depending on the nature of the analysis.

First, there are neo-liberals who have their roots in Hayek's view of markets as representing the highest form of social organisation, and consequently providing the only moral framework within which human beings can effectively operate. For Hayek (1983, 42ff.) a market-organised society is the only feasible modern society—that is, Adam Smith's "Great Society"; one which transcends local and national boundaries and which, in so doing, subordinates its social institutions to the politico-economic needs of the market. Here too we may find confirmation of the view that markets are to be seen as coextensive with the geopolitical limits of the earth. In Britain, neo-liberals found voice in the work of such think tanks as the *Adam Smith Institute* (Butler, Pirie and Young 1985), which claimed that the professional interest groups of Local Education Authorities (LEA's), teachers and civil servants represented the singular obstacle to parental, and therefore, social freedom. If parents were given free choice, then schools would be more effective than they otherwise can be. Parents want their children to succeed because the individual largely desires personal success not baseline equality. Such is the stand taken by Milton Friedman who argued, in *Capitalism and Freedom* (1962, 91), that parental choice must be restored in education so that the failures attendant on central state planning and control may be reversed. The loss of social cohesion is a small price to pay for the liberation of talent and self-determination that choice and control affect. Friedman, Butler and, in Britain, the authors of the *Black Papers* (see especially Cox and Dyson 1969; and Cox and Boyson 1975) believed that the organisation, structure and practices of education were political and that the appeal to collectivism embodied in the socialist (and social justice) doctrines of the left were historically dislocated and properly regarded as relevant only to an earlier stage of human evolution where survival itself depended upon co-operation. The old politics of post-war educational consensus and liberal political concern should therefore be replaced, they argued, with the new politics of the self. It may be suggested that all that is being affirmed is an extracurricular doctrine of free choice, and that consequently neo-liberal economics does not create or necessarily support a particular form of political education in the classroom. This is, I think, to adopt an overly naïve position. If, for example, I wish to shape political preferences in the population at large and think that the provision of education has a key role to play, then it is difficult to see how the practices of education themselves are not to be informed by the philosophy that drives the system. We might as well ask if it is possible to conceive of a situation where parents wish their children to be caring but have no concomitant expectations that such a view might inform the practices of the classroom.

Alongside the more strident political voices of the neo-liberals a second, conservative voice may be heard to offer a different but not totally unrelated view of the place of the political in the educational. Among their voices are philosophers such as Scruton who hold to the belief that schools exist to transmit a very particular view of society, its cultural accretions and traditions. Ironically—and despite his feelings of repugnance at government intervention in almost any area of public life—Hayek shares the deeply entrenched attachment of the more governmentally minded conservatives (Scruton 2001, 32) to tradition, and this for the rather straightforward Burkean reason that institutions, customs and mores represent some accumulated wisdom.[1] As Gamble points out in his study of Hayek, Hayek believed that "those who created the institutions are not necessarily wiser than the present generation; nor may they have the same knowledge. But their creations were not from nothing; they reflect the experiments of many generations and are therefore likely to embody more experience than is available to any individual or group of individuals in the present" (Gamble 1996, 34). Interestingly, the "New" and the "Old" Right found common ground in sustaining the totemic status of tradition. And such traditions were important, indeed more important than socialist notions of redistributive justice. How can this be? Burke, Hayek and Scruton, in their different ways, accepted rules as evolutionary markers laid down by successive generations as a consequence of communal living. These rules themselves provide the substance for tradition(s) and the traditions provide both a framework for understanding human purpose and engagement and the content of human aspiration. For Scruton meaningful educational provision embodies such traditions. As he observes, "precisely because its aims are internal, education may be a point where the values of people are formed, elicited and sustained. Education is essentially a 'common pursuit,' formed by traditions, and directed towards recognised ends. To engage in it is to envisage a form of community, and to desire it is to desire that community" (Scruton 2001, 141). Despite the oft' heard claim to take politics out of education, what was really desired was the erasure of one kind of politics and its replacement with another. Scruton wished that the politics of redistributive justice and its concomitant classroom discourse and pedagogies be replaced by a politics of traditional belonging and participation.

The third group comprises those traditional liberals who, like Bernard Crick (1990;[2] see also *Speaker's Commission on Citizenship* 1990; and *Qualifications and Curriculum Authority on behalf of the Citizenship Advisory Group* 1998) give voice to a deep-seated anxiety about the perceived loss of political literacy or, more importantly, political interest in the adult population and belief that this lacuna needs to be addressed. Having abandoned hope of change in the adult world they have turned their melancholy gaze on childhood, maintaining that the future of liberal democracy is indeed in the hands of children and that consequently we should develop programmes in citizenship education and create cognate pedagogies so that children will take their rightful place in future political developments and deliberations. It represents the attempt to create education as an instrument of democratisation. The clear expectation laid on children is that they become politically literate from an early age, and that they come to terms and be burdened with political questions and their concomitant anxieties before they are ready. There is here something of a hint of nostalgia.

The final group, which includes Giroux (1992), McLaren (1995), Peters and Lankshear (1996), (Giroux et al. 1996), draw their inspiration from the thought of Friere and Foucault, among others. In doing so they adopt an altogether more radical and combative view of the politicised nature of education as a social and cultural activity. A mirror image of the neo-liberals, their analysis of the depoliticising of the individual is complex and multivalent but may be broadly summed up in McLaren's view that what is required is "a critical pedagogy in our colleges of education that can problematic schooling as a site for the construction of moral, cultural and national identity, and emphasise the creation of the schooled citizen as a form of emplacement, as a geopolitical construction, as a process in the formation of the geography of cultural desire. He asks, dare we transform teaching practices in our schools into acts of dissonance and interventions into the ritual inscription of our students into the codes of the dominant culture: into structured refusals to naturalise existing relations of power; into the creation of subaltern counter-publics?" (McLaren 1995, 21). I shall take up in detail some of the difficulties posed by this challenge in a separate section, but at this stage it is worth pointing out that the kinds of "structural refusals" sought by McLaren are not unproblematic for any meaningful conception of childhood. On the one hand he appears to wish to protect childhood from the exploitative influences of adult culture, while at the same time liberate them from some kind of perceived imprisonment.

Clearly, each group takes up quite a distinct position on the political analysis of educational practices, with radicals on the right and the left seeing education as a kind of battleground upon which to wage cultural war. In the middle are those who see schools as the natural place for the retention and sustaining of a certain view of democracy with its attendant cultural practices. From their different perspectives, each group would demur from

Arendt's view, presumably regarding it as somewhat naïve. Yet matters are rarely as straightforward as they appear and the danger to which Arendt alerts us is no mere chimera. Her claim stands as an interrogatory yardstick by which to measure the intentions and attitudes of those who would promote schools as political playgrounds. None of the four groups can escape the dilemma to which Arendt alludes.

Children are not responsible for adult political, economic and social problems and adults should try to address their anxieties with adults as adults, rather than confront them through their work with children. In each of the four cases discussed the protagonists appear to demand, overtly or covertly, more than a school can reasonably be expected to deliver. Thus, the right-wing libertarian wants to construct schools as if they were spaces only for the negotiations between the private individual and the market. In doing so, she advocates a politics of the private and, consistent with this, would, intentionally or otherwise, undermine any sense of common being. The traditional conservative wishes to use schools to promote a particular, slightly nostalgic political sensibility that arguably would undermine the student's capacity to live richly in a complex, multivalent world. The liberal on the left is equally nostalgic, imagining as she does that the democratic deficit that has arisen for varied and complex reasons of disenfranchisement, poverty, collapsing social structures and so forth may somehow be overtly remedied by schooling. The final group, regarding schooling as essentially political in any event, wish to make overt what they deem to be covert and, in doing so engage in a cultural war.

It is difficult to see the two more extreme positions as particularly helpful in the school context. On the one hand, the neo-conservative position turns the child into little more than a marketised chip in an economic board game, failing to meet either their human or developmental needs. The child and their parent(s) are consumers and education is merely one more product to consume rather than a discrete, if interstitial, space that facilitates a certain degree of exploratory freedom. On the other hand, the critical pedagogues position raises some fairly basic questions about the level at which such an approach should be adopted. Moreover, it is not at all clear that children who inhabit the borderlands (or the wastelands that lie beyond the borders) are to be helped by the claim that power is asymmetrically distributed in society, however true it might be.

But all are, to varying degrees, mistaken because they fail to understand the nature of both childhood and schooling. With respect to childhood they fail to make sense of the ambiguity and interstitial nature of childhood. Later, in the same work from which the opening epigram of this chapter is drawn, William Blake observes:

Every Night and every Morn
Some to Misery are Born.
Every Morn and every Night
Some are born to sweet delight.
Some are born to sweet delight
Some are Born to Endless Night.
                    (William Blake 1997, "Auguries of Innocence," Ln.120/125)

The double refrain of "sweet delight" and "Endless Night" emphasises
the chances, indeed the chanciness, of life and, in an interesting twist, the
condition of "Endless Night" is capitalised whereas "sweet delight" is not,
leading to more than a suspicion that Blake perceived the former as a rather
more pervasive and pungent condition than the latter. Moreover, it is not
difficult to adduce from his reflections that a state of innocence was rather
easily maintained in the world of lace petticoats than in the "dark satanic
mills."[3] While it may be true that for Blake innocence is a provisional (or in
my terms, an interstitial) state that gradually gives way to adulthood, it is also
to be seen as a state in its own right, and as such, one of delight and
imagination. This very state of delight stands as a kind of admonishment of
those forces; economic, cultural and political that would diminish childhood,
making it nothing more than a prolegomena to adulthood.[4] That children
occupy this deeply ambiguous space means that on occasion they can appear
very worldly and are thereby often and inappropriately miscast as worldly
wise, when in fact this may be far from the truth. Indeed, like the trickster,
they can almost simultaneously manifest the dark and troublesome spaces of
human being as well as its airy aspirations. But even were this not so the
interstitial condition of being a student should make us wary.

   Located, as they are, in the traffic between innocence and experience
schools may be regarded as the site for a fundamental *rités de passage* in
late-industrial society. They occupy neither the world of childhood nor the
world of adulthood and should consequently be seen as a different kind of
space. This distinctive space of the school is compromised where its
particular characteristics and concerns are occluded or extinguished by the
encroachments of the bounded spaces on either side—that is, childhood and
adulthood. Schooling is essentially a public structured space, whereas
childhood, as such, is primarily domestic. Thus, those distinctions that mark
different backgrounds and family circumstances, such as wealth and position,
should have no place in the classroom. That these distinctions are frequently
not observed in practice may indeed be a cause for regret, but increasingly in
late-industrial societies the more serious intrusions are likely to come from

the public world of adulthood—that is, particularly the world of economics (Munro 1997). These encroachments are increasingly seen not just in the ever increasing applications of the discourse of performativity to teachers and schools (see Gewirtz 2000; Merson 2000) but in the obsession with preparing students for work from the beginning of schooling. Increasingly, education is cast as the preparatory phase for "making one's living" and not as a separate and transitional phase. UNESCO has, for example, suggested that "literacy programs should preferably be linked to economic priorities" (1996, 97). Or even more pointedly, in their document on the structure and balance of the curriculum for 5 to 14 year olds in Scotland, the *Scottish Executive* and *Learning and Teaching Scotland*[5] reflect on the "new educational context." This is seen as being delimited by four claims to growing performativity; the need to expand I.C.T., a revised curriculum for 3 to 5 year olds; and "a strengthening commitment to ensure for pupils aged *3–18...learning that prepares them for the world of work* and is based on an inclusive ethos of achievement for all" (2001, 3).[6]

The apotheosis of such economic considerations is the increasing tendency to turn schools over to commercial corporations on the grounds that business delivers education better than the professional educational cliques. Again it should be stressed, my primary concern is the manner in which such strategies communicate the view that there really is one important public discourse in liberal democracies, an economic one (Klein 2001).[7] It might be imagined that students and their parents see education primarily in terms of securing employment and that, since this offers a certain set of satisfactions, it is to be welcomed (see Winch 2002). Further, it may be argued that there is nothing very new in the present circumstances. After all, the extension of mass education from the mid-nineteenth century onwards has been driven largely by economic considerations. Moreover, schools have always been subject to the pressure of preparing students for work and, in any event, it might be argued that youth in pre-industrial societies were subject to the concerns of the community that they be able to sustain themselves, their family and their tribe. One response, and one that runs somewhat against Winch's view, is that parents' and students' perspectives on education are merely testament to the success of the discursive limitations that valorise economisation above all else, most especially in late-industrial polities. Moreover, pre-industrial cultures were interested in creating a space so that their youth could be initiated into a way of life—quite a different conceit from "making a living." In any event, however nostalgic it may now appear, educational discourse towards the end of, and immediately after the Second World War period, clearly embodied the view that education was a good in its own right to be offered to the offspring of those who had done so much to protect the very existence of liberal democracy (Conroy 2000).

On the one hand, children are not adults, and as such should be allowed their childhood without being overly burdened with the worries and woes of being an adult. On the other hand, innocence is a much-vaunted notion in need of tempering by an acknowledgement of the complex and, at times, ambiguous relationship between childhood and adulthood. Moreover, education requires that children be nurtured over time with the capacity to understand, question and evaluate, and that schooling,[8] being a somewhat different enterprise, shapes the socio-political context within which education (if it be allowed) takes place. So it is that the question changes from whether or not children should be "politically educated" to what approaches and pedagogies are most likely to enable them to remain as children/adolescents/ young adults while developmentally satisfying their affective, intellectual, social, cultural and political needs. Education must take account not only of children's present, but also that they have to create a future for themselves. Arendt remains right, I think, that education is not appropriately seen as the site for *burdening* childhood, but its very fabric is charged with political considerations and it is virtually impossible to consider schooling outside the realm of the political. Thus, the question is not whether children should be educated politically but "how?" And, "in what forms of the political is this to take place?" A balance is to be struck in educating children in and for liberal democracy. Such a balance may be achieved by the subtle exercise of the art of engaging the imagination rather than promoting an overtly rationalist and, more or less, axiomatic account of how things *are*. The development of the liminal as a normative metaphor may help facilitate those insights and abilities that will enable the student to become a politically thoughtful person in her own right without transforming her qua student into a surrogate agent in a political war or a quiescent worker. I have chosen such a metaphor in the belief that it is sufficiently robust to be used in classrooms of all kinds in liberal democracies including both the country parish in Dorset and McLaren's inner-city wastelands of Los Angeles, California. It is complex and multi-layered, subtle enough to be useful in both primary and secondary schools as well as across disciplinary boundaries.

Liminality

Liminality may both describe and develop an approach to education that will cultivate an awareness in students of the discursive closure emanating from the growing symbiosis of state and corporation, while doing so in a fashion commensurate with both the present and future needs of those same students. Since such an education is a matter of concern to all in a liberal democracy any normative metaphor should, by extension, be capable of application to the provision/system as a whole. Liminality and the derivative metaphors explored here have this capacity. Liminality derives from the Latin term for threshold and is closely allied to but different from the notion of borders. Transformed into an effervescent metaphor in the thought of anthropologist Victor Turner, it has emerged as a tool in understanding a range of complex social forces that are not easily identifiable in the social structures of organisations and societies.

For the purposes here, liminality may be thought of in binary terms. It can be seen in particular circumstances to be cognate, but not coterminous, with borders, a term that is also used in educational and anthropological discourses. The threshold is to be regarded as the entry and exit point between zones of experience or understanding. In this sense it is on the edge of "things": a point of entry and/or exit. Indeed, Donnan and Wilson (1999) tend to use the terms interchangeably. In their anthropology of borders, they recognise that state borders are places where identities can be both brokered and broken, and where inhabitants are generally configured differently from those who geographically, culturally and epistemologically inhabit the centre. Thus, borders or those areas attached to borders carry their own particular sets of meanings, which can, to quote Donnan and Wilson, "transcend the physical [and ideological] limits of the state and defy the [monolithic] power of state institutions" (ibid, 4). Those on the border or at the threshold perceive culture, social relations and politics quite differently from those at the centre. Again, as Donnan and Wilson have it, "border people may share a sense of belonging, and thus have much in common with each other that distinguishes them from the residents of other places in their national societies. But borders also shape relations between borderlanders and people and institutions beyond border regions, and these relations form the basis of differential access to wealth, status and power" (ibid, 79). An acute awareness of these differentials is what gives rise to the borderlands pedagogies of such thinkers as Giroux.

The liminal position, which sits on the border, is always in a relationship of tension with the political or cultural centre to which it is attached. It is more or less determined by the centre in that the liminal-border position is, inevitably in some significant respects, at odds with the centre position. If, for example, the poet Seamus Heaney's (1995) claim that poetry acts to redress, among other things, cultural, social and ethical imbalances is deemed true by the majority of poets then this may be deemed the centre position per se, for the poet (or other artist). There may then emerge those poets who regard their art as no more than a form of dilettante delight. These latter may then be regarded as giving rise to or occupying a liminal position with respect to those purposes adumbrated at and by the centre of the poetic establishment. In this sense they are or become marginal.

At or on the border, the liminal may offer a contact zone—a space where disparate cultures, ideologies and frameworks may meet without the constraining force of the centre's attachments. Such contact zones have been thoughtfully explored by Pratt (1992) and are to be seen in cultures as disparate as Northern Ireland and South Africa. In such places, Catholic and Protestant, black and white might come together outside the trammels of oppressive cultural expectations. Outside the transactions of everyday life these zones emerge in the midst of what is seen as taken-for-granted normality. Thus, while urban Catholics and Protestants in Northern Ireland largely lived culturally segregated lives—going to different entertainment centres, pubs and churches—socially mixing only with their co-religionists, there were certain spaces (e.g., a restricted number of occupations and sporting events such as horse racing) where they might "rub shoulders" and affect a kind of normality. Here, traditional antinomies would, however temporarily, evaporate. These contact zones were not to be found at some geopolitical border but in the heart of civic life. Their emergence "in the midst" rather than "at the edge" signposts a fundamental feature of the liminal as understood by Turner; that is, its interstitial condition. Moreover, it is this capacity for emerging in almost any space or location that distinguishes the liminal from the border position.

Turner (1967; 1969 and 1995; 1974) was concerned to understand and explicate those periods in traditional societies that marked out the passage between one social state and another; that is what van Gennep, in his early twentieth century writings, referred to as *Rités de Passage* (see van Gennep 1960). These transitional states prevailed where an individual or group was in the process of moving from commoner to king, from childhood to adulthood; in other words, those in the liminal state were to be seen as neophytes, in transition from one kind of structured existence to another and as having to undergo certain rites in order to effect the change. This could also be a negative transition from a "higher" to a "lower" state.[9] In any event, all of those in the liminal state would be in-between or outside "normal" structures. Turner suggests that this involves the loss of status:

> In so far as they are no longer classified, the symbols that represent [the liminal personae] are, in many societies, drawn from the biology of death, decomposition, catabolism, and other physical processes that have a negative tinge....They are at once no longer classified and not yet classified. In so far as a neophyte is structurally "dead," he or she may be treated, for a long or short period, as a corpse is customarily treated in his or her society" (1967, 96).

Accordingly, all traditional denominations of status disappear and those in the liminal state are equal in a manner unimaginable in that structured life, which, on either side, hems in the liminal. Further, in this state the standard laws and modes of conduct no longer pertain and liminal personae are hedged around with ambiguity, "since this condition and these persons elude or slip through the network of classifications that normally locate states and positions in cultural space" (1969 and 1995, 95). What we get then from Turner is a conception of an ontological space where the normal rules of structure and status do not apply and where those in such a space may be drawn together, for their time there, through a congruity of interest certainly but, more importantly, through their equality as people shorn of power, position and location. In such circumstances the liminal is conceived as eruptive, emerging out of those interstices that exist inside bounded spaces as well as at and across borders. It is not limited to the marginal interests of a particular society or indeed particular interests on the margins. Nor is it limited to those overlapping interests, ways of thinking and discourses that meet at cultural and political borders. Rather, the liminal moment may arise *within* the bounded spaces of a given society while at the same time not being *off* it. The Buddha Gautama Siddharta emerged as a liminal figure in Northern India not as an outsider—a border-crosser, a harbinger of insights from a different space—but as one who erupted into the heart of the bounded polity in which he lived. Both the liminal person and space are open to many different possibilities; located betwixt and between, they are not easily categorised and, consequently, not easily domesticated. The Buddha's liminality, however, may also be seen as shaped by the before and after. Before his liminal encounter the kingdom of his father existed in one form. After, it had changed. The liminal transition then represents that eruptive force wherein particular changes take place—in consequence of which the past and the future are both joined and separated.

As Turner indicates, however, the liminal does not offer us an unalloyed space for good given that those in it may find themselves vulnerable and isolated. Thus, in some traditional societies it was not unknown for someone occupying a liminal space to be attacked, killed or subjected to particularly dangerous ordeals precisely because they were without the protective layer of their normal social structures.

Yet more characteristic of the liminal space is what Turner terms *communitas*. In the status system, he argues, certain rules and regulations, distinctions and social ascriptions, values and attitudes and asymmetries of power structure, the relationship between different groups and individuals. In the liminal state these distinctions are suspended or negated. They have no purchase on the individual person as long as she is in the liminal state. In tribal societies this evocation of the individual self as a *tabula rasa* in common with other *tabulae rasae* is seen to be important largely because, as we have already seen, the liminal state is transitional wherein one has moved out of one fixed state and is not yet in another. In this non-state, one cannot have authority over another or see oneself as superior—all are equally stripped of their badges and labels. Here, Turner argues, "we are presented...with a moment in and out of time, and in and out of secular social structure, which reveals, however fleetingly, some recognition...of a generalised social bond that has ceased to be and has simultaneously yet to be fragmented into a multiplicity of structural ties" (ibid, 96).

Turner has argued that in this condition abnormal bonds of fellow feeling and friendship appear to be generated because the normal rules and rivalries do not apply. Here then, he observes, communitas arises and does so precisely because those in the liminal space have equal status and, having equal status (which is no status), find themselves drawn together in bonds of fellowship. At least implicitly, he is arguing that status consciousness is a significant barrier to the cultivation of communitas in structured social settings. Though Turner's main focus was on liminality as a state or condition within pre-industrial societies—where circumstances are significantly different from the highly differentiated and fissiparous social settings that are to be found in late-industrial societies—there are significant applications of a modified conception of it in our own time. In *I and Thou*, Martin Buber (1970) distinguishes two relational word pairs: "I–It" and "I–Thou." In doing so, he is not concerned primarily or exclusively to distinguish relations between people from relations with objects. Rather his interest lies in distinguishing a way of *being* in the world. The "I–Thou" way of being captures the idea of encountering another self[10] in his or her own surplus so to speak, not as "Dr. So and So" or "Professor This or That," but as a self who is without categorisation. The encounter has no other purpose than itself. This is distinguished from other kinds of relations that happen in the day-to-day engagements with others, which govern most of our normal lives. These two relational word pairs may be likened to the states of the liminal on the one hand and the status system on the other. Buber acknowledges that life in the world of the encounter is not the life of one's everyday transactions—it would be impossible to constantly live such a life since both its intensity and its lack of structure would fail to support some fairly basic features of survival and social engagement. However, he argues that the life of everyday structured existence—including education—may be configured in the light of the encounter. Liminal communitas is not to be regarded as a utopian wish but as that relational encounter that emerges in the midst of everyday life, and that can, in turn, inform that everyday life.

The exploration of anthropological and philosophical theories offers three interrelated aspects of liminality: borderlands, contact zones and communitas. Together they offer some possibility of challenge to that discursive closure that hovers over liberal democracy. They do so by opening up alternative heuristic possibilities to the structures of the centre, by offering a way of conceptualising otherness. Too much is made of modern political and educational rhetoric in the pursuit of the common. Frequently the common may be little more than the reduction of the self to sameness and from there to consumer, worker, citizen; an evacuation from the public spaces of those difficult but perennial questions about selfhood and otherness, choice and decision. Liminality on the other hand recognises otherness for what it is, even in the very heart of the common. Communitas is built not on extinguishing otherness but precisely in recognising strangeness as an inherent condition of all. What the transitional figures in the liminal period or space have in common is their explicit estrangement from the normatively structured environment of everyday life. The bonds that arise in this space are not necessarily, or even predominantly, predicated upon sameness but, let me suggest, upon the commonality of feeling like an outsider and as one estranged. In this liminal space there arises the possibility that I might be able to acknowledge that I am always, to some extent, a stranger, even to myself. If I am, so to speak, a pilgrim—a stranger in a strange land—then there is always a bit left over, either that of which I am not aware, or to which, in the normal course of my everyday transactions, I do not have access. My strangeness is implicated in that surplus of being that I have discussed earlier. If this strangeness is authentic then I have no difficulty in acknowledging that of the other since it is the same condition within which I myself live. Having outlined the nature of liminality as a political and social metaphor the next step is to explore what it might mean in an educational context.

Liminality in an Educational Context

Liminality lends itself to a variety of uses and interpretations. First, following Turner's anthropological usage, it may be deployed as a heuristic metaphor allowing us to delineate particular kinds of ontological spaces in and around the school. For example, the space between the privacy of the home and the engagements of public life might be one; the point at which a particular tradition or subaltern community (religious or cultural, for instance) might make its presence felt in the broader polity; that point where the voice of the child is first heard among adults. Thus it may be used to illuminate the point of transition from no felt presence to a felt presence or as "an interstitial condition, a journey from one state of social being to another" (Donnan and Wilson 2001, 66). Another example may be found in the work of McLaren who draws upon Turner's model in order to delineate and describe the functioning and "significance of youth culture outside the boundaries of classroom life" (1986, 1). In my own youth this space was physically located behind the handball alleys, a place where teachers rarely ventured despite knowing "what was going on." It is what McLaren calls "the street corner state" (ibid, 84); a state that is likely to arise in such places as the playground, the coffee bar, the bicycle shed, a set of attitudes and, increasingly common in economically prosperous countries, the shopping mall. It is important, however, not to confuse the place for the state—the former is merely location, the latter a form of consciousness or awareness. For McLaren, the liminal place is one that is removed from the direct supervision and control of adults, somewhere that the students can adopt distinctive, different personae and where certain bonds and affiliations may be developed. Here, as elsewhere in his analysis, McLaren explores how children informally develop sites of resistance to the practices and policies of schooling.[11]

Descriptive uses of the notion of liminality may be important in opening up particular lifeworlds that stand outside the normative structured existence of the school, and we may draw on any ensuing insights in order to understand our students better. More importantly for this study however liminality may be used as a normative metaphor for mounting a challenge from within the pedagogical and relational possibilities of the school to the dangers of discursive closure. Moreover, as a normative metaphor it may be drawn upon in a manner that avoids the danger of turning schooling into the site of an overtly political culture-war and confusing education with political literacy.

In all of this, and in the classroom, we must also confront the darker side of the liminal experience alluded to earlier. But this may not be as problematic as might initially be thought. Indeed, this darker side may be regarded as a necessary corrective to the rhetoric and fiction of whole-child philosophies of education with their denatured views of education; views that, for example, imagine that all education has to do is offer the pathway of enlightenment out of the dark. And, if only teachers were sufficiently technically competent then education would unquestioningly provide the key to inexorable development into something better, quicker, wiser, fuller, more consistent. As Egan (2002) points out, there are certain assumptions held by educational protagonists on both the right and the left that are nowhere near as self evident as is often imagined. For example, the proper nurturing of children is imagined to follow a developmental schema characterised by a movement out from the sensorimotor self to the world of concepts and abstractions. Thus, we should build education on what we can do. And, from there it is a small leap to argue that utilitarian considerations should dictate and shape both curriculum content and pedagogic practices, and hence to the doings/workings of the market. But as Egan points out, such a conclusion "seems so patently false that it is bewildering to see it constantly repeated.... Before, and after, we can walk or skate, we know love and hate, power and powerlessness, the rhythms of expectation and satisfaction of hope and disappointment" (ibid, 109).

It is for this and allied reasons that we might want to say that education should be subtler in its dealings with young people, recognising as Haldane (1999) does, that death and life are intimately bound to each other. Or again, we might want to acknowledge, as Golding (1954) does in *Lord of the Flies*, that childhood and adolescence are riven with contradictions where love and hatred sit side-by-side in a nexus of community and power. The rhetoric and fiction of the whole child and her treatment in education with its excessively happy denatured view of experience and trivialising of cultural complexity is likely to produce little more than a denial of the self configured in the midst of the hope that arises out of our natality, and the anxiety—and sometimes despair—that emanates from our death. Indeed, it is an irony of most versions of whole-child approaches to education that they have excised whole regions of child (qua human) experience, sense and feeling. Attempts to deal with "growing up,"—a leitmotif of whole-child approaches—have been unable to address this gap precisely because the intractability and ambiguity of life too often yields to the superficiality of more effective consumption.

Yet hope lives on, and there are significant numbers of teachers who have a growing though as yet somewhat inchoate sense of the structured vacuity at the heart of much educational discourse, content and practice. It may be for this reason that in my own department and elsewhere an ever-increasing number of in-service and Continuing Professional Development programmes are being provided for teachers in education for grief and loss. Dislocation, fragmentation and loss have emerged as important tropes for a significant number of educators with their concomitant practices and pedagogies that draw precisely on story, drama, rites of passage, confrontation of the self; in short, the imagination. While a late-industrial society's loss of belief in the imaginary construct of the child striates the flattened surface of the classroom, in the bumps and crevices the repressed and uncomfortable returns.

I now wish to develop three ways in which liminality can be deployed as a metaphor of three interrelated sites. First, we may speak of *liminal education*, the pedagogies and practices of education as manifest in the classroom. Second, we may speak of a *liminal disposition* on the part of the teacher. And third, of education in *liminal communities* and its relationship to the political centre of a liberal democracy. Each of these will be dealt with in turn because each provides a particular lens on the shaping of an education that can, within the reasonable expectations we may place before children in the institution of schooling, counteract the tendency to discursive closure. In the case of the first two the interrelationship is quite intimate since the creation and exploitation of liminal pedagogies depends on the teacher having a sense of the liminal, the eruptive and the interstitial. It is no more possible to conceive of a funny play without a playwright who is open to *seeing* the world with wry amusement, and consequently interpreting it as such, than to see liminal possibilities without, so to speak, the *eye* for such things.

Liminality can take two related forms in pedagogy. The first, somewhat akin to borderland pedagogy, which I will discuss in the next section, is the planned introduction of students to that which is liminal and marginal, to experiences, insights and perspectives that stand outside the everyday, accepted ways of viewing and making sense of things. In opening up alternative positions critical of or running counter to the centre it enables students to adopt a critical position themselves. By engaging and exploring with them insights to be garnered from the periphery and deployed in their own education, children will enjoy richer and more varied experiences. What is on offer here is the cultivation of an authentic reflective pedagogy that is open to the peripheral. More than offering students the possibility of developing a critical perspective it opens them up to otherness—the realisation that standing outside the mainstream is not the same thing as being alien. As I have already intimated, this sense of alterity is paradoxically tied not to the encounter with the one who is, as it were, over the border but with the recognition of one's own estrangement. Awareness of one's own strangeness can emerge through the occupation of a liminal position. A small pedagogical strategy may serve to illustrate this. Some years ago, a colleague taught an introductory course in world religions to first-year undergraduate student teachers who were mostly Catholics. Many, if not most, of his students were "cultural Catholics," raised with a set of taken-for-granted assumptions about the nature and content of their beliefs. He wished to dislocate these "normal" frames of reference by inviting them to move outside their comfort zone and into a place where they might indeed recognise their estrangement even from their own religio-cultural beliefs and icons. With this in mind, he would begin his programme with a PowerPoint image of Shiva in full iconic splendour. The student response was, more often than not, one of amusement and a certain dismissiveness. He would then gradually cross-fade the image into one of the Sacred Heart (historically regarded as one of the most potent images of Catholic Christianity). With the visual transition from the strangeness of the other to the strangeness of the self, recognition emerges. Such "seeing" is not only, or even primarily, concerned with religious iconography but the disclosure of one's own suppositions and estrangement from those very images one holds as central to identity. Hindu and Christian iconography are not the same, nor are believers the same, nor are their creedal claims the same. Yet, it is in the recognition of their own estrangement that students may begin to appreciate and identify with the strangeness of the other. This in turn may offer greater possibilities of children developing an authentically critical perspective as they grow into an increasingly complex world that demands ever more subtle judgements of the practical intellect.[12]

The second manifestation of the liminal, which is closely related to communitas, is rather more spontaneous and arises out of a disposition to the openness of possibility. It is a pedagogy of spontaneity and of the moment. In this it is intimately related to the dispositions of the teacher, but I shall pursue this a little later. In this second sense liminality and its correlate—communitas—are embedded in the possibilities of anti-structure. Used here, "anti" may be regarded as a strategic move and not, negatively, as an exclusively oppositional category. Rather, it may be seen as "something positive" and "generative" (Turner 1974, 273). Structure is an inescapable feature of schooling especially within a public system where there is a degree of accountability. It is not necessary to be a thoroughgoing structural-functionalist to admit of the necessity for structure in a system that has responsibilities for and towards students from 4 to 18 and that involves large numbers of adults. One has only to think of the potentially chaotic alternatives to see the difficulties. In any event, traditional arguments about pedagogies are not fought over the existence or non-existence of structure but about the kind of structure operative in the classroom. For all its determinative power, however, the structured space of the classroom does have significant limitations with respect to learning and should therefore not be regarded as solely determinative of education. I may organise students along particular lines; I may decide that a particular investigation may take this or that form, that the conditions for a given study may be "a" or "b," but I cannot determine precisely what learning may take place within these structured parameters. This is largely because much of human thought, reflection and engagement with the world emerges out of the cracks and fissures of our personal and social relations and not in the wide-open structured spaces.[13] These fissures open and close in the course of the daily transactions of the classroom but are not self-evidently manifest in any kind of easily predictable manner. Too often their existence is entirely missed in the conduct of education, precisely because the teacher is overly preoccupied with the maintenance of the structures and structural progress of the classroom. Such preoccupations appear to be related to the increase in performative evaluations of schooling and these, in turn, to the discursive closure around the dominance of economic values in the classroom. Hence, the greater the emphasis on economic outputs the greater the emphasis on assessment of both student and teacher, with a corresponding emphasis on the central structured experience of the classroom that perforce must facilitate "hitting the target." The more this happens the more likely it is that teacher and student will miss—and miss out on—those liminal possibilities that inhere in the classroom. The more they miss out on these the narrower is their perspective likely to be; the narrower their perspective the greater the danger to the *agora*. These possibilities are not to be confused with the well-planned, intentional creation of interesting diversions for students so that they might better understand some particular aspect of geometry—say Pythagoras' theorem. The liminal stands apart from these considerations precisely because of its unpredictability and its openness to breaking down the structural barriers between student and teacher. In the liminal moment both are equal in the face of this or that encounter with an idea, a creation, comprehension or insight. No longer is there a separation between teacher and student—each learns, each encounters. Of course this does not preclude the possibility that the teacher may establish those conditions that are conducive to the emergence of the liminal moment, but I shall return to this in exploring the nature of the liminal disposition.

So what might a liminal encounter with respect to pedagogy and/or disposition entail? Central to Turner's account of liminality is its *modus* as a transitional state found in the midst of cultures where it appears in contradistinction to normality. As a state of being it is to be configured in terms of binary oppositions between "transition and stable state, absence of status and status, no distinctions of wealth and wealth" (Turner 1969 and 1995, 106). Let me pursue this a little with an example. In 2002, the journalist John Pilger (see also Pilger 2002) mounted an exhibition in the Museum of Contemporary Art in Sydney. The exhibition comprised a small number of video presentations and a large number of photographs taken by Pilger himself and the many photo-journalists[14] who accompanied him on his travels around the world for more than three decades. These captured some of the seminal moments in the history of the twentieth century, from the Civil Rights marches in the American South through the horrors of Vietnam and Pol Pot's Cambodia to the tragedies of Central Africa. Not all the images were of horror but they all told a story. Accompanied by a group of students, I walked into the museum on a bright, sunny afternoon. The exhibition halls were full, yet there was a quiet meditative atmosphere as people of all kinds, shapes and cultures, of all colours and no doubt creeds, followed the photo narratives Pilger had laid out. After some three hours we emerged back into the sunlight.

Of course, people go in and out of exhibitions and museums all the time and not all are moved. Sometimes, however, there are moments that stand outside or in-between our ordinary structured experiences. This may be counted as one. What enables us to think of this space as liminal? It cannot be its physicality (though no doubt the construction of appropriate physical space can conduce here) nor that it was an exhibition hall, nor that it was in a museum since in all these cases there are many exhibitions and displays that certainly do not fit either Turner's conception of communitas or Buber's of encounter. It cannot be because people went in and out of the sunlight per se since people do this all the time without wishing to claim any special status for it. So if its liminal status lies outside its physicality where is it to be found? Three things are necessary for the creation of those liminal spaces, all of which are central to education. First, and akin to the dispositions of the teacher to which I have alluded earlier, there is the intentionality of Pilger and his confederates to create the conditions of *possibility*. It is not that they know that people are necessarily going to respond in this or that way but they are alive to possibility when imaginatively conceiving of the exhibition. Second, the moment must have an inherently democratic aspect. And third, the viewer must be receptive and open to whatever possibilities might emerge in such a space. We can see all three aspects working together in examining a single black-and-white image—a photograph of a schoolhouse that had been turned into an interrogation and torture centre in Pol Pot's Cambodia. The photograph, taken by Eric Piper, frames an old iron bedstead in the middle of a sparse room with flaking plaster; the bed and the surrounding floor are heavily stained with blood. There is nothing else but the caption explaining that here the Khmer Rouge tied people on the bed and tortured them. The photo and the caption are what might be described as minimalist but in their very minimalism they communicate much about pain and suffering. Not just pain and suffering as generalisations but the pain and suffering of individual after individual being; thus after all the generalisations are exhausted there remains the particular, unique suffering of each. The picture carries a surfeit of meaning. The creators of this collection set out to weave a story or stories about human being in general, but also human being in its singularity. Photography is potentially one of the most democratic arts; it offers access to all, but only those so disposed can actually see the singularity of the suffering.

What such "works" offer is an intentionally created space which opens up the possibility of our standing aside from the stream of our everyday structured being; a place that allows a certain kind of democratic entrée with the individual retaining choice. Consequently, those who entered the exhibition were opened to the possibility of "encounter". It is here that we can see an in-between emerging in the midst of the ordinary everyday, even, we might say, banal, existence. While it is not possible to *live* in that (ontological) space it is possible to return to the "sunlit day" and have our daily experiences inflected with the insight from the encounter. How we conduct ourselves is related to the possibilities that such encounters offer us. In such a space teacher and student are one; traditional structured differentiation is, at least in that moment, suspended. *Communitas* is, as I have suggested earlier, primarily a relational condition and Turner prefers it over the much vaunted contemporary notion of community (and by implication, communitarianism) since communitas distinguishes a "modality of social relationship from an 'era of common living'" (Turner 1969 and 1995, 96).

Second, and crucial to all of this, is the cultivation of particular dispositions in the teacher. It would appear that the particular kind of discursive closure associated with the economisation of public life has favoured a technicist conception of teaching and conversely downplayed any notion that it might be an art. This being the case, the structured spaces of the classroom have increasingly been dominated by pedagogies for the production of measurable outcomes. It matters little whether these are driven by education defined as a process or straightforward didacticism since both may be deployed quite easily in the service of an outcomes-based education. What matters is that the teacher is increasingly construed as a purveyor of techniques rather than someone with particular insights and the capacity to make subtle judgements about the complex relationship between subject matter, student and the forms of engagement. But if my earlier supposition that schools are, or should be, to a significant degree liminal spaces then it might be argued that the teacher is, to some extent, the guardian of those spaces, adopting a transitional position between not only childhood and adulthood, but also between the centre and the periphery. The kind of education proposed here is significantly dependent on the existence of teachers who can and are prepared to inhabit the liminal "space." To do so is to embrace a particular kind of ontology, one that recognises that surplus of the self considered in the previous chapter. Practically, this entails the willingness to take chances, the capacity to let things take their own course, the patience to hang back. More than technical skills it demands "insight." This is no Luddite faith eschewing technological advances as aids to pedagogy. Rather, it is an expression of the wish to place these in the context of perceptual acuity and sensitivity. In his poem "Seeing Things," Heaney (1993) evokes "the dry-eyed Latin word" *claritas* as being perfect for gazing beyond the stone façade of a church, with its hard stone lines, to see the sinewy being out of which its carvings issue. Drawing the analogy with the banks of a river, he goes on to meditate on how transparency may itself hide much.

> Down between the lines…
> in that utter visibility
> The stone's alive with what's invisible

(ibid, 19)

This capacity for "seeing" will be revisited in the penultimate chapter.

What Heaney alerts us to is the need for continual adjustment of our vision; yet given their common perception that the world is, in Wordsworth's words, "too much with us" many teachers, teacher educators and policymakers have chosen to conduct their professional lives in the world of "as if." What is meant by the world of *as if*? Ironically, many teachers continue to operate in the classroom and beyond as if the epistemic and cultural changes associated with globalisation on the one hand and postmodernity/structuralism on the other had not taken place—as if the neo-liberal economics, political philosophies and discursive closures that bedevil education were in some way anterior to the classroom, school and system. While this may appear to be a harsh judgement there is little doubt that teachers function much of the time in this world of *as if*: as if there remained extant models of educational management that retained vestiges of collegiality; as if there existed a genuinely dialogic classroom environment supporting the exchange of perspectives between themselves and learners (Conroy and Davis 1999; Hull 1985); as if they, and the children, were engaged on a mutually enriching journey; as if the world of economic rationalism had not utterly transfigured the language and nature of the classroom. Standing over and against this is the vision of the teacher who is open to cultivating, both in herself and in the other, the life of the imagination. Such a vision entails the recognition that the liminal is not, by definition, the main fare of the day, rather that the day is configured in the light of it.

Finally, the third site of liminality mentioned at the beginning of this section is education within or with regard to liminal communities. Now this expression or mode of the liminal differs from the first two but is nonetheless important for the configuration of education as a whole. It differs because the focus rests not on the classroom, or even the school, but on the system. It has two quite discrete manifestations: first, state educational provision that acknowledges and makes space for liminal communities, such as religious communities, migrant communities and second-generation groups; and second, education within such communities. Here I am primarily concerned with the first of these.

Liminal communities may be thought of as those that adopt philosophies and practices that are regarded as marginal with respect to the structured life of the mainstream or alternatively have chosen to withdraw to the fringes of socio-political and cultural engagement. It is quite a shift from talking about the liminal experiences and dispositions of individuals and small groups to those of organised groups, and one can only do so by extending the metaphor. However, such an extension is entirely legitimate because the liminal experiences of the individual, the class group and the community group or organisation share certain family resemblances. For example, the liminal community sits, at least psychologically, at a remove from the normative demands of the centre but is not detached from it. It experiences itself as at the threshold and is generally so construed by the centre. This condition is most clearly seen in migrant groups such as the Irish Diaspora of the late-nineteenth and early-twentieth-century or late-twentieth-century British immigrants from Pakistan. Turner puts it thus: "What is interesting about such marginals is that they often look to their group of origin, the so-called inferior group, for communitas and to the more prestigious group in which they mainly live...as their structural reference group" (Turner 1974, 233).

Additionally, just as in the case of the classroom, the liminal is not a fixed condition—the liminality of a given community is not fixed with respect to the political centre. Such a community may exhibit varying degrees of liminality over time and with respect to different normative features of society, which also incidentally may set it apart from the position of an outsider group. This may be seen where the beliefs of a particular community, with respect to education for justice, may be in complete accord with those promulgated by the political centre. At the same time, there may be substantial divergence on the underlying philosophy and consequent practices of education for human relations. The liminal community may hold its views on such matters precisely because of its commitment to human values; a possibility which underscores the view that the liminal as anti-structure is not to be regarded as a negative stance. Rather, it (re-)presents a different ontology.

Of course, not every group may be regarded as liminal. For example, if a group were to wish to challenge the very foundations of liberal democracy they might well be regarded as dissident outsiders but not as liminal. Their influence may be felt, not as a threshold experience but as enmity camped outside the citadel. Destruction and disruption are not the same thing as challenge and eruption. Equally, there may be communities that exist within the bounded geopolitical space of a polity but that have no meaningful traffic with the polity. In such cases the adjective liminal hardly seems appropriate. This distinction is entirely in accord with Turner's original conception of the positive salience of liminality.

If it is necessary for education—as opposed to the many other things that may be transacted in the school—that the liminal, "shining like shook foil" (Hopkins 1972), keeps the classroom alive and charged with questioning, reflection and discernment, then surely a similar kind of energy is required for the maintenance and practices of democracy. The liminal energies of schools such as those out of a religious or Steiner-Waldorf tradition are, as I hope to establish in the final chapter, conducive to the maintenance of a certain discursive freedom. Of course, a religious school—or system—may realise that its influence will not (and maybe should not) be extensive. But that its voice should at least be allowed to emerge from the wings or erupt into the centre—that is the important thing! Given the gradual, but clearly perceptible, discursive closure in late-industrial liberal democracies, liminal education at the level of systems assumes increased importance as a countervalent force to the centripetal tendencies of the centre that currently might be even more powerful because, as Spinner-Halev states, it is burdened with few restrictions (2000, 204).

In the context of a liberal democracy this opens the question about the extent to which liminal communities are themselves required to offer liminal education. This is indeed a complex question precisely because it involves an almost intractable paradox. On the one hand, liberal democracy requires certain epistemological, conceptual and expressive freedoms. On the other, these very freedoms can serve to undermine any authoritative claims that a community might make, and in doing so shatter its liminality. I will not dwell on this here except to suggest that, given the weight of sociological evidence (Bruce 2002) that points to the almost overwhelming power of the forces of liberal secularisation and market-driven consumer consciousness, my sympathies lie with those communities where a different epistemology and ontology may be manifest.

Borderlands Pedagogy

There are substantial areas of agreement between the kind of pedagogy that is to be developed in the light of the liminal metaphor and other educational traditions including, on the one hand, the liberal pedagogies of Peters (1973) and his inheritors such as Hirst (1974) and, on the other, the critical pedagogies of those who draw on the metaphor of borders. (Although it is clear that Peters saw himself in the tradition of promoting critical reflection in education (ibid, 51). While both are normative accounts of education, the approach here may be distinguished from that of liberal education on several grounds, most notably that liberal education places a much greater emphasis on knowledge and intellectual understanding as initiation into a largely determinate and fixed culture; that is, "into a public world picked out by the language and concepts of a people" (ibid, 52). Liberal education more easily accommodates itself to the view that the centre and its concomitant discourses are not only the most appropriate, but really the only ones to be adopted in a liberal democracy. Again, as Peters observes, "the cardinal function of the teacher...is to get the pupil on the inside of the form of thought...with which he is concerned" (ibid, 53).

The differences with liberal education are not intended to be construed as fuelling a contestorial approach, but as illuminating some blind spots in the traditional liberal discourse on education. It is not that these considerations are entirely eschewed in the liminal approach, rather the emphasis is quite different, pressing, as it does, for a more complex relationship between the self and culture. While interpretation and engagement with the home or dominant culture may be vital this has to be modulated via a more critical, distanced set of perspectives. In *Ethics and Education*, Peters consistently dematerialises the body (ibid, 34) and subjugates the emotions (ibid, 32f), controlling them by means of a cognitive mastery. Why are the only reflections on these centrally defining features of human being so treated? Could it be that the body and the emotions contain anarchic elements that disclose something about who and how we are that discomfits the liberal-rational mind? Take, for example, laughter. Why is it that laughter is so rarely in evidence in the formal life of the school, except as an expression of superiority? Could it be because, as I shall argue later, it is a manifestation of the eruptive force of both body and emotions; an eruption that might call into question some of the pomposity of the liberal approach. Again, the Peters and Hirst version of the liberal approach may be seen as having the effect of ensuring a certain docility and acquiescence in, as Peters states, the "working-class man" (ibid, 52). The proponents of liberal education enjoy little or no sense that the centre may or should be altered by its encounters with the periphery (and clearly working class men were regarded as peripheral to liberal education).

Or, we might look at the trickster figure (dealt with in detail later). The trickster has never been far from the heart of human education (his appearances have constantly teased and played with groups of human beings across cultures in order to teach, challenge and invert our taken-for-granted categories). This he does as a consequence of his capacity to simultaneously embody light and dark, reverence and fun, insight and obscurantism. Yet he has played no part in a liberal description of education, because on its own account such a description cannot admit of those deep contradictions and indeterminacies that lie at the heart of human being and that the trickster so pointedly exposes. Finally, in this connection it is the absence of any deep sense of the ubiquity of the dark in the liberal account of education that most distinctly marks its differences with the liminal. Here, as I have argued above, there is less faith in the light of education. Rather, as the author of St. John's Gospel has it, "The light shines in the darkness and the darkness has not overcome it" (John 1:7). If it is true that the light of Enlightenment and its consequent theories have not been consumed by the darkness, it is equally the case, as Pilger, among others has illustrated, that such darkness has not itself been banished from our engagements; a complexity that is more or less absent from standard accounts of liberal education.

In some ways the more instructive similarities and possibly the more interesting disagreements are with the critical pedagogies of those who have adopted the metaphor of the borders. Giroux (1996), for example, draws on the notion of borders as way of addressing the failure of modernist ideology, especially in education, to come to terms with—and adequately deal with—notions of otherness in multicultural education. He argues that modernist approaches have failed because what is missing is "any attempt to either critique forms of European and American culture that situate difference in the structures of domination or reconstruct a discourse of race and ethnicity in a theory of difference which highlights questions of equality, justice and liberty as part of an ongoing democratic struggle. Multiculturalism is generally about Otherness, but is written in ways in which the dominating aspects of white culture are not called into question and the oppositional potential of difference as a site of struggle is muted" (ibid, 117). McLaren has also developed the notion of the borderland as a metaphor for education in late modernity[15]. His purpose is congruent with Giroux's, yet more focused in its emphasis on the use of border pedagogy as a method for the liberation from the snares of the dominant corporate consumer culture, which is heavily implicated in the discursive closure explored in chapter one. Both authors are drawn to the world beyond schooling where youth are not students but consumers, producers, creators, providers of services and so on in a fissiparous, hybridised world.

Others such as Egéa-Kuehne (1996) have advocated a yet more heteroglossial approach to border pedagogies, believing that nothing less than a complete disruption of present patterns of pedagogical engagement will challenge the hegemonic powers that shape our patterns of being. In their different ways, each wishes to adopt the notion of border pedagogy as a means of challenging the structural displacement, marginalisation and discrimination experienced by non-white students in claimed post-industrial liberal democracies. Of course, their mission is goes beyond addressing the structural asymmetry in white/black or Chicano/a relations since they hold that students need, more generally, to be exposed to, and equipped to engage with, critiques of the forces of globalised production, which they believe have further instantiated this asymmetry. Ultimately, their radical education has at heart the "public mission of making society more democratic" (Giroux 1992, 10).

This study has little argument with the advocates of a critical pedagogy with respect to their desires for the realisation of social justice, increased public-political participation and enhanced social and personal empowerment. However, there are three quite fundamental differences between the approach advocated here and that of Giroux, McLaren, et al. First, there is the distinction between liberal democracy/education and critical democracy/education. In seeing knowledge and power as being "joined at the hip," they tend to eschew any conception of a literary, cultural and epistemological canon. Their resistance to a particular view of conservative public philosophy, which they see as "having reduced democracy to gaining access to an unproblematic version of Western civilisation and defined learning as the training of good citizens" (ibid, 95), has blinded them to the import of drawing on particular cultural traditions for insight into the very difficulties with which they are so concerned. Culture, whether elite or popular, is to be regarded as a "mobile field of ideological and material relations that are unfinished, multi layered, and always open to ideological contestation" (ibid, 99). Pedagogically, culture is to be regarded as a stratagem in and for the creation of subjectivity. Once again, this can seem quite unobjectionable from a politically left-wing perspective. After all, the creation of subjectivity may be construed as a form of empowerment. However, the danger is that culture becomes no more than the reduced utility so valorised by Rorty (1999); a pragmatic remainder embodying insights of no value beyond the particular use that we wish to make of them at any time.

While it is perfectly possible to recognise that culture and cultural canons are always in some sense contingent, it is not necessary thereby to evacuate them of a certain kind of *transcendent* status (let's not say objectivity). Such status relies on an acknowledgement that there are more or less adequate manifestations and interpretations of literature, art, design and architecture and that considerations about their goodness, adequacy, worthwhileness and efficacy in producing certain kinds of responses are not merely arbitrary. It is simply neither helpful nor credible to imagine that the worth of a particular creation or work is to be assessed only in terms of one's subjective engagement. If I were to interpret the literary corpus of Seamus Heaney as eulogising the militant republicanism of the Provisional Irish Republican Army, I would quite simply be wrong, irrespective of my subjective engagement with the texts in question. Neither the words themselves, nor the intentions of the poet, nor indeed what might be described as canonical interpretations, would lend themselves to such a view of Heaney's work.[16] Of course, the advocates of subjectivist accounts may wish to argue a more nuanced position, asking, for example, why Heaney should be accorded a place in the classroom over and against a performer such as Eminem. It is the case that judgements on the relative merits of two "artists" may wish to take account of a host of considerations, such as emotional depth, tonal quality and revelatory capacities, but these are not simply arbitrary—not any old proposition about these will do. In a liberal democracy it is important that people read texts in the light of their own experiences, but such readings should also take cognisance of wider readings. Education is concerned with more than oppositional centre-periphery dialectic. Centrally, it offers children a complex set of relations, understandings and interpretations that may enable them to become adults in this or that culture. Affecting complexity, critical pedagogy, like the neo-liberalism it challenges, actually offers an over-simplified conception of the relations between student, teacher, culture and polity. It is for this reason that I draw on the notion of *Verstehen* in some earlier reflections (Conroy 1999b).

A second difference is that a liminal approach to education can take more seriously the liminal status of students themselves. As a defining approach, critical pedagogy tends towards that danger to which Arendt alerts us because it demands that children somehow be full actors in the political drama through which it is intended that we shape our liberal democracy. As I have suggested earlier, this places an unfair and unreasonable burden on children. It is not that critical pedagogues are unaware of student liminality, but see it as concerned with the nature and location of those spaces where students develop their own associations, relationships and friendships outside the strictures and structures of the adult world in school. In contradistinction, the use of liminality adopted here has a different ontological and normative impulse, addressing, as it does, the in-betweeness of childhood; not by turning children into cultural warriors (one way of denying their liminal status), but by pedagogically acknowledging the necessary ambiguity of the interplay between the structured and the unstructured in the practices of the classroom and the school.

Finally, there is the notion of the border itself. While the border metaphor appears prima facie to be very attractive and well suited to the post-structuralist/postmodern turn, inviting perpetual transgression, on its own it is not sufficient for schooling. Unlike liminality, it is limited by a general conception of its fixity (see Conroy and de Ruyter 2002a). Despite claims about their growing permeability and fluidity across a range of fronts (Habermas 2001), borders are more or less fixed, encapsulating particular languages, discourse, rules, habits, mores and values. Liminality, on the other hand, is more properly seen in terms of the in-between. Liminal moments and insights are not necessarily confined to spaces between borders but, as I have already pointed out, may erupt into the world within the border. To construe the liminal only as a border position runs the risk of misrepresenting it as an either/or—a kind of position that one can occupy on a permanent or semi-permanent basis, or a position or state of being that is always related to the two sides divided by the boundary line in the same way. The continued existence of the liminal requires borders, its emergence does not. By way of contrast to this more fluid notion, where the border is dependent upon the emergence of the limen, it is instructive to reflect on the Iron Curtain, the building of a giant, reinforced concrete wall between the Palestinian homelands and Israel, or the "peace line" between Catholics and Protestants in Belfast. In these cases, walls act as fixed barriers, de facto borders, offering no actual or imagined possibilities for liminal engagement. Whatever merits such structures may or may not have they are not hospitable to ambiguity; an ambiguity that opens up the possibility of trafficking in new perspectives and changed relations. Of course, they invite transgression but that is hardly liminal engagement.

While I find myself in some instinctive sympathy with the critical pedagogues' desire for a more obviously participatory democracy, I am less than persuaded that the direct oppositional practices that they propose for education either work or are desirable. It is for this reason that I have turned to the notion of liminality as offering both a structural and a pedagogical metaphor for the creation of a particular kind of approach to education—one that first nurtures a sense of the importance of perspectives, ideas and artefacts that are not wholly under the control of the dominant and powerful; second, respects the distinction between childhood and adulthood; and third, recognises the potential for healthy liberal democracy in the cultivation of institutional difference.

Conclusions

So far I have argued that a key distinction between liminal education and border pedagogies is the latter's almost exclusive and direct focus on the overtly political. Further, I have noted that the political is a particular representation of the world of adults—the public world—and if children are overexposed to it, the glare of this public world makes their growth to maturity difficult at best. Arendt suggested that "everything that lives, not vegetative life alone, emerges from darkness and, however strong its natural tendency to thrust itself into the light ... nevertheless needs the security of darkness to grow at all" (Arendt 1977, 186). For previous generations, the security of darkness may have been provided in the domestic space of the family, but radical changes to patterns of family life and, more significantly, the ubiquitous intrusion of the public-political world into the home via the media have made it increasingly difficult for the family to maintain the sphere of the private. This carries the danger that children are overexposed to political and other forms of violence, and to the political corruption to which Arendt has alerted us. Schools cannot substitute for the family, though; they are, after all, indelibly public spaces. However, they are public spaces whose function is to nurture and promote the flourishing of both individual and community. For such flourishing to take place children need not be exposed to the full glare of our adult political anxieties. Increasingly, the school curriculum is required to embody every adult anxiety from poor civic participation through deficient workplace skills to the rise in sexually transmitted diseases. Despite appearances, this is neither a conservative stance nor a call for the critical pedagogues to retire. Rather than precluding the political, it expresses the intention to place it in a more comprehensive pedagogical context alongside other forms of discursive engagements rooted in play and laughter, literature and music, art and photography. Liminal education embraces, but is not coterminous with, education about politics.

Rather than see the response to discursive closure in terms of a full frontal assault, it might be more apposite and effective to continually be open to the possibilities of creating different spaces, which then emerge into the structure of the classroom. These should be configured so as to create a more subtle and nuanced account of the eruptive possibilities of the imagination, manifest in play, in poetry, in religion for certain, but also in mathematics, geography and history. Lessons may be learned from the attempts to develop religious education in Britain, Australia and elsewhere. As students have become increasingly uninterested in religion, attempts to interest them in some quarters have become more intense and more overtly religious. According to almost all research, this frontal assault has had no appreciable effect (see Flynn and Mok 2002). Again, this is because adults imagine that a lack of interest in religion is a matter of poor pedagogy or an absence of clarity about the nature of the territory. In truth, it is more likely that the type of religion that adults use to attract children is only applicable to adults. An approach to the discursive closure of late-industrial democracies that relies too much on the overt engagement with cultural politics is likely to face similar difficulties. Better to allow the liminal to emerge, like the Aboriginal *Songlines* visible to those who are prepared to engage with its subtleties and able to move back and forth between the structured space of the classroom and the interstices at both the margins of discourse and within the heart. Such an approach requires teachers to be educated in a richer vein than is currently the case. If they cannot develop the capacity to transcend a vision of education dominated by the surface phenomena of schooling, such as quality assurance, assessment and the other calculations of performativity, then it is unlikely that they will be able to educate children to "see to the heart" of liberal democracy.

From here I wish to move on to explore what I believe to be some important sites of liminal possibilities.

Notes

1. Many on the left, including Giroux (1992, 93–96), argue that traditional conservatives, whom I think Giroux wrongly labels neo-conservatives, have denied the political in the educational. But this is not quite correct since what these conservatives wish for is a different kind of political outcome and engagement than that advocated by Giroux.
2. See his essay entitled "Education and the Polity," first published 1979. (For a further discussion of Crick's views, see Conroy 2000.)
3. Of course, the discussion here is limited to the conditions of late-industrial liberal democratic societies and does not take account of those children living in other cultures whose economic and social burdens are beyond imagination.
4. There are deeply conflicting and confused attitudes to childhood with the elongation of economic dependence upon parents and, at the same time, its construction as a particular "independent" site for consumption. This confusion is seen clearly in the creation and marketing of Barbie dolls, play

make-up; vanity cases and other "grown-up" toys aimed at very young children—the same children for whom teddy bears and baby dolls are also manufactured.

5. An arms-length agency largely funded directly and/or indirectly by government.

6. My italics.

7. Governments can, of course, delude themselves that the kinds of strategic changes that see schools being built and owned by private companies and leased back to education authorities (under the euphemistically titled "Public, Private Partnerships") is anterior to the actual "stuff" of education, but some practices in Scotland would suggest that this is not so. A recent case exemplifies the damaging effects of the conflation of a business and an educational discourse. In this instance, children at a new, privately built state school wished to establish a tuck (sweet) shop to raise money for a development charity but were refused permission, not by the Principal, but by the owners of the school, on the grounds that there was a franchise for supplying food on the premises that forbade competition.

8. For a helpful, if brief, discussion on the relationship between education and schooling, see Carr (2003a, Ch 1).

9. Turner (1974) points out that "ritual degradation occurs as well as elevation. Courts martial and excommunication ceremonies create and represent descents, not elevations. Excommunication rituals were performed in the narthex or porch of a church, not in the nave or main body."

10. Buber does not limit the "I–Thou" only to person/person encounters, but sees it as extending downward into nature and upward to the heavens. However, for our purposes the emphasis on the human encounter will suffice.

11. McLaren subsequently develops the notion of border pedagogy as a response to what he sees as these liminal conditions. In doing so he clearly comes down on the side of those who might see the liminal as a border condition.

12. For further discussion on the liminal in this context, see Conroy and deRuyter (2002b).

13. For an interesting discussion of the effects of the relationships on students' learning, see Day (1999).

14. These included such luminaries as Marion Kaplan, Eric Piper and Ken Regan.

15. McLaren uses the term "late modern."

16. For an interesting left-wing challenge to the post-structuralist/modern attempt to relativise all cultural creations, see Eagleton (1996). See also on the political Right, Scruton (1983, 22–31).

17. Songlines are tribal memories held in song that guide Australian aboriginal peoples across large wide-open distances without encroaching on others' Songlines.

Chapter 3

Laughter as a Liminal Activity in Education

Above all, above all horrors, I saw accepted the notion that conscience was no longer a private matter but one of state administration. I saw men handing conscience to other men for the opportunity of doing so.

(Arthur Miller, *The Crucible*, 1968, 4)

Introduction

In the development of sites[1] in and for liminal education in a liberal democratic polity, laughter pushes itself to the fore largely because it has variously been regarded through the ages as dangerous, deviant and subversive (Townsend 1992; Jenkins 1994; Isaak 1996); yet equally, as refreshing, challenging and constructive. In order to establish its credentials as a liminal site, particularly in education, it is necessary to map out some understanding of the personal and socio-political ways in which laughter has been and continues to be deployed. This coupling of the personal and political dimensions of laughter is important because, as shall become evident in the course of this chapter, action in the world is dependent upon the personal, otherwise it may be seen as no more than a set of behaviours prescribed by someone else. It is also important to develop some understanding of how laughter might relate to an understanding of human action, as distinct from behaviour. And finally, to see how it may serve as both a context shaping and pedagogic device in modern education.

There have been many attempts to offer summary accounts of laughter, some of which are touched upon in the course of this chapter. Broadly speaking, these fall into three categories. The first, and for a long time the most common, were theories of superiority, seen early on in Western thought in Plato, who, especially in *Philebus* (1982), decries laughter as something rooted in derision. Hobbes (1651) and Descartes (1911/12) take up this theme. They both dismiss joy as the source of laughter, preferring to believe that it arises out of a sense that the one laughed at is in some way beneath the one who laughs. Hobbes in particular felt this was to be avoided as it was a form of "sneering" and would only encourage a kind of ungodly pride. The second variety of explanations may be summarised under the heading of incongruity an finds early expression in Aristotle who, in the *Poetics* (1952b, Ch. 5, 1449a), appears largely to agree with Plato's fairly negative assessment, but moderates his antipathy in the *The Nichomachean Ethics* (1976, Bk. 4, Ch. 8, 167f), distinguishing between the well-bred and the vulgar with respect to laughter. The incongruity thesis became popular with Kant who regarded laughter as "an affection arising from the sudden transformation of a strained expectation into nothing" (1952, Pt. 1, Div. 1, 54 and 538). It could not be a transformation from one thing into its contrary since that would, in fact, be into something "and may frequently pain us" (ibid). Incongruity theories may be said to typify laughter as a reaction or response to the sudden change in our expectations with respect to some object, perception or idea not occasioned by direct falsehood. The third class of theories might be generically described as relief theories seen primarily, but not exclusively in the work of psychologists (see Chapman and Foot 1996). There are various ways in which laughter may be operative as a relief. For example, when children run into the playground laughing and playing it is, at least in part, because they have been released from the constraints of the classroom (which requires them to learn the "art" of suppression). Pre-eminent among the relief theorists is Freud, who, while limiting himself to a discussion of wit[2] as a particular form of laughter, regards it as a form of release that saves psychological expenditure. Such expenditure is a derivative of psychic repression where a great deal of energy may be expended on, as it were, keeping things under control.

These three major explanatory schemas and their many variants all appear to have important elements to contribute to our understanding, but none of them individually could be described as a comprehensive theory of laughter precisely because laughter is so many-faceted. Some modern treatments of laughter have attempted to synthesise these various elements into a comprehensive theory. Monro (1963) suggests that laughter emerges out of inappropriateness; such inappropriateness can take a variety of forms but all of them depend on the inappropriateness itself containing an element of appropriateness, since inappropriateness on its own would hardly be a sufficient condition. I might, for example, walk onto a stage and slap an actor across the face. This could well be deemed inappropriate for there are many circumstances in which it would not be funny or occasion laughter among the audience. On the other hand, say the play was a comedy and the actor on stage had just spent the first act being, as one might say, "a cad and bounder": a pompous bully and misogynist. We might think that the act of hitting, while normally inappropriate, might in this context, have an element of appropriateness.

Morreal offers an alternative comprehensive theory, which claims "laugher results from a pleasant psychological shift" (1987, 133). Presumably, in both these general theses laughter is but a species of a more general class of conditions. Thus, it is quite possible to have pleasant psychological shifts that do not necessarily entail laughter, or again, have appropriate inappropriateness, which similarly does not necessarily entail laughter.

While it is difficult to reject such theses (though the first may be said to be focused on what gives rise to laughter, whereas the second is concerned to explain the source of laughter in the self) given their level of generality, it is equally difficult to deploy them exclusively as heuristics. I am not concerned here to offer a critique per se of such definitions but as I grapple with the role laughter plays in personal and social action, and therefore in liminal education, I attempt to follow the "things-in-themselves." Insofar as my concern is to disclose the manner in which laughter as a site for the liminal may make a contribution to keeping discourse open, I draw upon the different cadences that emerge out of the various theories touched on here. In doing so I am indebted to Plessner's phenomenological stance, which requires that "we entrust ourselves to everyday experience [which indicates that] we must put up with uncertainty. [And that] loyalty to everyday intuition is paid for only with an elasticity in linguistic usage" (Plessner 1970, 18).

Laughter may be regarded as an interesting and important site for the evocation of liminality in education because, as Plessner would have it, its ground is that ambiguous terrain of the embodied self. This ambiguity arises because the body is both the self and not the self. In looking at or observing myself (my body) I perceive an object but that object—my face or my hand– is no object among objects, but is me. Despite this ability I have to see myself, the psychological and the physiological are not to be equated to two selves and it is precisely the propensity of human beings to laugh and cry that undermines any recourse to such a Cartesian dualism. Plessner argues that (what he refers to as) these "eruptions," challenge the simplistic responses to the dualism of both the monists such as Spinoza or Russell and those who would simply dismiss the issue of mind/body difference as illusory. Laughter and tears open up an altogether more complex relationship between human beings and their bodies. Plessner argues that:

> Their form of utterance, whether expressive or expressionless, whether full or empty of meaning, reveals as such no symbolic form. Although initially motivated by us, laughing and crying make their appearance as uncontrolled and unformed eruptions of the body, which acts, as it were, autonomously. Man falls into their power; he breaks-out laughing, and lets himself break into tears. He responds to something by laughing and crying, but not with a form of expression which could be appropriately compared with verbal utterance, expressive movement, gesture or action. He responds—with his body as body as if from the impossibility of being able to find an answer himself. And in the loss of control over himself and his body, he reveals himself at the same time as a more than bodily being who lives in a state of tension with regard to his physical existence yet is wholly and completely bound to it. (ibid, 31)

This quotation offers a summary of Plessner's belief that our uniqueness resides in the relationship to our bodies, a relationship where the balance can be disturbed without our conscious volition. The use of the notion of "breaking out" is important in indicating the physiological existence of the self even though this may be only fleeting. However, it is not my body that laughs, but *I*. This ambiguity may be summed up as a recognition that human beings both have and are bodies—a position that Plessner denotes as eccentric. Plessner's insights are helpful here in so far as they open up the realisation that human beings are eccentric with respect to the world they find themselves in. The body, so to speak, inserts us into the world; it is the surface that appears in the world. This eccentricity itself embodies something of the very notion of the liminal; laughing and crying may be deemed as liminal activities—activities that momentarily lie at the threshold that opens the self to the world. Let us imagine a student in a classroom who is sitting quietly when a friend whispers a derogatory and amusing nickname for their teacher. Immediately the student bursts out laughing and has much difficulty controlling herself. Her laughter has erupted into the classroom but it doesn't do so without the student; she too erupts into the classroom and has instantaneously changed the space.

Or again, suppose there is a school assembly where the principal, being somewhat pompous and officious, has decided to demonstrate new "keep fit" exercises because of concerns about obesity among the young. However, his efforts are somewhat less than professional and he falls on his bottom. Immediately students (and some staff!) burst out laughing and in doing so have radically changed the dynamic of the gathering. Their collective entry into the space as bodies no longer controlled, however briefly, has changed that space. In these particular instances it might be argued for the better. Of course, there are those who might suggest that such a lack of control is to be deplored, but that is merely to misunderstand the relationship the self (or collective selves) has to the body. When applied to education, Plessner's view discloses the kind of category mistake made by teachers when they, for example, command students to "stop laughing," thinking that the neurophysiological eruption of laughter is somehow under the control of the will. In any event, the assembly has been changed, though most likely with respect to its atmosphere and not its structural components. (In education sometimes all that is required is a change of atmosphere.) This eruptive moment of laughter is itself a liminal signal of the embodied, eccentric self. Even though it may be speedily transmuted into another kind of thing—for example, if all in the classroom were to burst out laughing—at the moment of eruption it is a kind of transition at the threshold of the self in the world. The hidden self emerges, however briefly, into the public space, influencing and changing it but without being encapsulated by it. Laughing at the limit is not containable in the way certain intellectual capacities might be, which is why it is paradigmatic of the liminal. While Plessner's insight is important here it is nevertheless incomplete—laughter may not be directly sourced in the will but, as I shall argue later, the will is not unimportant in the matter.

It is in some sense the unpredictability of laughter that places it at the heart of this excursus into the liminal. Yet it is possible—indeed, I would argue, desirable—to create the conditions wherein laughter is likely to flourish, and to understand that the creation of such conditions may make a significant contribution to the evolution of a site or sites for liminality and for reflective, discursive contest. The remainder of this chapter is concerned not with the development of a typology of laughter, of which there are sufficient already, but with exploring particular features of laughter that may be utilised in the development of an approach to education that encourages the liminal and, in doing so, discursive contest. This discussion focuses primarily on laughter as a kind of self-activation whereby one can effect change in one's attitude in the world, which can in turn lead to laughter as a politico-educational act. Again, it needs to be re-emphasised that this self-activation is not exclusively a function of an internal movement of the mind but is directly related to the eccentric position that one holds with respect to one's body in time and space. Nevertheless, the kinds of morphological distinctions discussed briefly above do re-emerge in subsequent reflections and I will return to some of these issues in the final section.

Laughter: Good and Bad

It might be thought by those familiar with Arthur Miller's *The Crucible* that

the play hardly represents the acme of comic theatre, nor does it offer much
by way of raw material for Scottish comedian Billy Connolly. Nevertheless,
it provides a useful starting point for the structure and argument of the
remainder of this chapter for three reasons. The first is that, even in
adversity, human beings have developed a capacity to laugh. Second,
particular forms of laughter may be seen as *acts*, which are appearances of
the conscious individual self in the world even where this may take place
within the ambit of a group or collective. Finally, laughter is a political act as
it has the potential to subvert the claims exercised over the individual by
those who occupy more powerful positions in the public—or indeed, the
private spaces. Given the claims throughout this work that education is
central to any conception of human flourishing and that the state has a
primary obligation to further the well-being of its citizens, laughter will be an
important "site" not only in a general socio-political context but perhaps even
more so within education.

There are many (largely those defenders of some version of the
superiority thesis) who would regard laughter in the *polis* with a combination
of anxiety and disdain—as something to be avoided, at least as a public
phenomenon, because it is disruptive of peace and order. Brother Jorge, in
Umberto Eco's *The Name of The Rose* (1983 and 1984), is emblematic of
this view. Even Bergson (1913), somewhat swayed by a kind of attachment
to the superiority thesis, is at best ambiguous about laughter. He is not
entirely convinced as to its efficacy, claiming that laughter and joke making
are often conducted at the expense of some infirmity or deformity in the
other. He proceeds to illustrate this with examples such as the sight of
someone tripping and falling as they run down the street, or again, that of a
hunchback. (Clearly, some examples of laughter are more conditioned by
time and place than others!) Drawing on Bergson, Kuschel (2000) suggests
that jokes about minorities, the disabled and other disadvantaged people may
be classified as macabre; they deal with death, darkness and cruelty. The
"macabre," he observes, "means treating death, sickness, human handicap
mockingly, making jokes about them" (ibid, 115). He goes on to disparage
such laughter, claiming that it has been commodified in modern life and used
as a means of submerging human beings' anxieties. In this, I take it that he
means that whereas laughter once emerged spontaneously between groups of
people, or in communities, as a response to the particular exigencies of life,
in late-industrial culture it has been packaged and domesticated by the media,
thus functioning as a kind of narcotic. In *Leviathan*, Hobbes—the pre-
eminent and most notorious proponent of the superiority thesis—embodies
the archetypally negative characterisation of laughter when he opines, "those
grimaces called laughter" serve to offer a kind of confirmation of their

superiority where people can "by apprehension of some deformed thing in another, by comparison whereof suddenly applaud themselves" (1651, Pt. 1, Ch. 6, 63). Earlier yet, Aristotle regarded the kind of macabre intent expressed in laughing at someone with a disability as issuing out of base emotions—the sense of one's superiority over another or of one's contempt for the other—and therefore to be avoided as vulgar and coarse. Thus, the negative characterisation of laughter has a long history that is summarised by Glasgow (1995, 306ff), who observes that it is frequently deployed to ridicule what may be categorised as "ugliness" or being a misfit. And indeed, it is hardly necessary to be an overly observant teacher in order to see instances of this in the average school playground, where children who are a little awkward, diffident or different from the crowd may be subjected to the ridicule and scorn of their peers. Laughter can be cruel, often deployed as a mask to avoid acknowledging one's own frailty and alterity. However, even the macabre face of laughter is not unequivocal and Kuschel's analysis, in this respect at least, is lacking in subtlety and nuance.

It would be naïve to suggest that certain forms of laughter are not characterised by the disdain for and the diminution of the other, but this is not necessarily its most important form even where, prima facie, it may appear to be in bad taste. Let me explore this a little more fully. Despite the trauma of the events of September 11th, 2001, in the United States—where airplanes were hijacked and used to attack civilian and government buildings—it was a matter of only a few days before jokes about the attacks abounded. This phenomenon is hardly new, and indeed Connolly and other comedians have drawn much on the traumas of their childhood in the development of their stage personae (Stephenson 2001). Even in the most adverse of circumstances—pain and suffering, stupidity and obduracy, death and oblivion—human beings make jokes. It is reported that on his deathbed Machievelli was visited by the pope, who entreated him, "Machiavelli, will you now renounce the devil and all his works?" Machiavelli made no response. The pope again asked, "Machiavelli, will you now renounce the devil and all his works?" Machiavelli produced no more than a flutter of one eye. A third time the pope entreated him, "Machiavelli, for the sake of your soul, will you renounce the devil and all his works?" Machiavelli now opened his eyes and looking up at the pope muttered, "This is no time to make enemies." The making of jokes, even in the face of death, would appear to offer a significant strategy for coping with adversity. The Irish tradition of "waking" the dead has long offered an opportunity for those in mourning to assuage their suffering through a kind of playful laughter. Here the bereaved gather together not only to mourn their loss but to remember and recount stories and tales where the deceased may simultaneously appear as both perpetrator and victim, hero and villain in the conduct of some mischief that would induce nods, smiles and laughter among the assembly. As a small child at my grandfather's funeral, I remember both the sadness of his parting and a story told about himself. My grandfather was a cattle dealer and he and his brother were at a fair in Donegal in the west of Ireland when a farmer arrived with six bullocks that were untidy, shaggy and unkempt. My grandfather bought the bullocks for £1/7/6 (old currency) and paid the man who went off to the pub. He then set about giving the livestock a coiffure, cleaning and clipping them. In the afternoon he went into the pub and asked the same misfortunate farmer if he was interested in buying some stock. He then took him out and sold the poor man back the very cattle he had brought to market that morning—this time for £2/10/6!

Such stories are legion and legendary at the Irish wake and, in another story, my grandfather might have been cast as victim rather than perpetrator. Such stories allow us two key insights into the nature and function of laughter: the first is that it frequently arises out of our observation about the misfortune of the other; the second is, that even where this is the case, even in death, humour cannot (and perhaps, should not) be suppressed. It is the interchangeability of architect and victim that gives rise to the ambivalence with which laughter has been treated down the ages by philosophers going back to Aristotle and beyond.[3] One of the key issues in the wake story that is often overlooked by those who harbour too much suspicion about laughter, is that while we may well laugh at the naivety of the farmer our mirth is equally, if not more occasioned, by the dexterity and sharp wit of my grandfather. Laughter in the face of the most terrible misfortune can have a redemptive quality, as Connolly's biography or Brian Keenan's (1993) tale of his captivity illustrates. Controlling one's deepest, primordial fears by laughing at them may well issue in the macabre, but this alone does not make the act wicked or bad. The laughter that emanates from the comical stories surrounding the deceased may be one way the living have of dealing with the recognition of their own finitude. The conception of laughter as exclusively or primarily a physiological function emanating from some wicked, evil, sneering or pernicious disposition raises a fundamental anthropological question: What view of human being and relations do such thinkers hold? Further, and equally importantly, what is their conception of human flourishing? A Hobbesian view of human exchange (albeit primarily, though not exclusively, mediated through his conception of political economy) was largely governed by a combination of self-love and fear (Hobbes 1651, 60–63). The human richness of ambivalence completely bypasses Hobbes and is entirely captured by Plessner. In any event, despite the dominance of Hobbes' legacy, his analysis was subject to critique from the outset. The

Scottish philosopher Hutcheson took an entirely different view of laughter and observed about Hobbes that "by some bad fortune he has overlooked everything which is generous and kind in mankind; and represents men in that light in which a thorow [thorough] knave or coward beholds them, suspecting all friendship, love or social affection, of hypocricy, or selfish design or fear" (1750, 6). In contradistinction, Hutcheson welcomed laughter as an essential ingredient in our humanity. Whatever might be adduced with regard to the sources of laughter like many before and since, including Aquinas (Conroy 1999a), he regarded its expression as a necessary feature of both personal and political flourishing.

Among those who explored the physiology of laughter there was, from the outset, some ambivalence though most tended to construe laughter as good for the health. Early on this tended to acquire a certain metaphysical character. For example, in his treatise on laughter, the Renaissance scholar Laurent Joubert (1560 and 1980)[4] developed a physiology of laughter that strayed into the metaphysics of personality. Physiologically, laughter had its source in the alternate dilations and contractions of the heart. These movements were, in turn, the result of the alternate pulls on the heart of joy and sorrow. Given that he was writing at a time of great social and intellectual ferment, with the contrary forces of the school-men on one side and Erasmus and Rabelais on the other, it might also be argued that his metaphysiological description was a kind of personal metaphor for the contrariness of his socio-political world. Having weighed up the competing claims as to the efficacy of laughter, Joubert opts for the positive view that laughter needed to be cultivated for reasons of personal and social well-being. In a reference to Cleomenes, King of Sparta, he remarks that it was important that the "citizens have a good time among themselves, jeering and mockery all of which sharpen the mind" (ibid, 17). Here Joubert is pointing to a recognition that laughter (and, I would suggest, its concomitant, play) are to be regarded as constitutive of the well-rounded individual who can laugh not only at the infelicities of others but also at her own. This in turn, I will argue later, is a necessary requirement of education in and for a liberal democracy.

Before proceeding to deal with the arguments with respect to the role of laughter in our public spaces, it is necessary to further ground the claim that the default position should be that laughter is to be construed positively, both personally and educationally, since one route to effective and positive critical engagement with one's political culture may be found in a laughing disposition. In their study, Martin and Lefcourt (1983) discovered that while the appreciation of and ability to accurately perceive humour was not in itself a sufficient condition for the reduction of stress, the production of humour was nevertheless found to moderate its effects. In a later study, humour was seen to moderate the stress levels of those exhibiting signs of depression, but not for symptoms of anxiety (Nezu, Nezu and Blissett 1988). This is at least suggestive of the psychological need for the "waking" stories so popular at Irish funerals. The making of jokes provides one strategy for coping with present psychological or socio-psychological difficulties. Nowhere does Plessner's notion of the eccentric attitude become more manifest than at the threshold between comedy and tragedy, where the comic will intrude, evoking laughter, irrespective of the solemnity of the occasion; I might stand as one grieving when something happens that momentarily dislocates my body from my grief.

Other recent behavioural (Fridlund 1998) and neuropsychological studies (Provine 1996 and 1998) have demonstrated how laughter is both physiologically and psychologically related to the individual's social well-being; that play and laughter take us to the perimeter of our knowledge. Further, Fried (1998) has demonstrated that the laughter function is located in an area of the brain adjacent to that which controls social and moral synthetic functions. In his work, Damasio (1994; 1996) has established the physiological link between the emotional centres of the brain and effective socio-moral decision making. When the ventromedial sectors of the frontal lobe are damaged, so too is the individual's ability to make morally synthetic judgements of the practical intellect. If laughter can be said to have positive effects on my emotional well-being and my emotional well-being appears to affect my moral well-being it can be proposed, at least tentatively, that in neurophysiological terms, laughter is a necessary concomitant to moral well-being. It is worth taking a moment to explicate this a little more. If I am not emotionally stable,[5] then it is unlikely that I will be in a position to make genuine moral choices. I may of course do things with positive consequences but that is not the same thing as making moral choices. For example, I might be periodically delusional, imagining one day that I have access to the alchemical formula for gold and consequently give away all my money to the indigent in the street. In fact, I have a family who needed the money and who now do not have it. On one account, the giving away of the gold had positive outcomes for the indigent but, since I was emotionally unstable and incapable of making a rationally and emotionally synthetic judgement (taking into account all the necessary features of the situation), it could not be described as a moral act. This is but one of a wide range of issues connecting laughter and our emotional lives. In this chapter, and somewhat later, I will deal with these in the context of fear and anxiety.

In observing that laughter assists in the overcoming of morbidity we can begin to see that its ubiquitous character, even in the face of the most appalling circumstances, is at least indicative of its importance to our humanity. The making of jokes provides one strategy for coping with present psychological or socio-psychological difficulties. It may also be concerned with confirming the appearance of one's insider status, but I will return to that later. These observations on recent neuroscience are not the end of our reflections on the moral importance of laughter for the individual in their social education, but the beginning. If we are physiologically programmed to use laughter as a means of self-integration and as a way of interrogating the boundaries of our world, then a central function of schooling should be the provision of the opportunity to laugh and play. In supporting students as they move into adulthood, we should be assisting them to live in a democracy, which implies a certain kind of ludic distance from the stentorian claims of the political centre about education for economic well-being.

Laughter and Action

In the previous section, I have attempted to analyse some of the claims and counterclaims surrounding laughter and to suggest that it may be important for our personal well-being. Here I wish to extend this claim to embrace our social, cultural and political well-being. In doing so, I will draw on Arendt's analysis of the distinction between action and behaviour in order to better understand the role of laughter in the cultivation of the acting self and the reflexive community. According to Arendt, action is to be distinguished from behaviour. Whereas the former is an attitude of taking hold of and acting into the world, thereby exercising some power with respect to it, the latter indicates passivity wherein one is subject to the condition of being part of the mass. Behaviour is the negation of action.

In a closing passage of *The Human Condition*, Arendt opines:

> The last stage of the labouring society, the society of jobholders, demands of its members a sheer automatic functioning, as though the individual life has actually been submerged in the over-all life process of the species and the only active decision still required of the individual were to let go, so to speak, to abandon his individuality, the still individually sensed pain and trouble of living, and acquiesce in a dazed "tranquillised" functional type of behaviour. The trouble with modern theories of behaviourism is not that they are wrong but that they could become true, that they actually are the best conceptualisation of certain obvious trends in modern society. It is quite conceivable that the modern age—which began with such an unprecedented and promising outburst of human activity—may end in the deadliest, most sterile passivity history has ever known. (1958, 322)

Drawing on her analysis of the rise of totalitarianism, Arendt (1973) recognised the dangers inherent in the loss of individual action. There is no suggestion that acting as an individual represents some kind of solipsistic retreat. Indeed, being myself necessarily requires the engagement with the other. It is only in action that we appear to each other (Arendt 1958, 168) and can become ourselves. Action then is tantamount to Buber's (1970) "encounter." As encounter, it is freighted with danger and uncertainty. As we have already noted, to encounter some being is to meet her on her own terms and not within the predetermined limits of my experience. It is to recognise her fundamental otherness or alterity. Again, as we have noted earlier, much modern philosophical and educational thought assumes that what conjoins human beings is their similarity and that the task of education appears to be to "get to know the other" so that those apparent differences that divide us will evaporate. Of course, we do not really get to know the other because the other is fundamentally a stranger to us; indeed arguably, we are a stranger to our selves. Action is also, *par excellence,* that which truly makes us human, giving shape to our individuality. To act or speak[6] (speech being itself an action) is the means by which we distinguish the self from the other and assert our individual being. It is the *hoi logos* of John's Gospel, a kind of self-initiation borne out of neither physical "necessity like labour...[nor] prompted by utility, like work" (Arendt op cit, 177). In contradistinction, behaviour is indeed a mass activity and, as such, cannot be creative. It may be taken as a synonym for behaving oneself. When a parent wishes to admonish or otherwise control a child they are unlikely to say, "act yourself," preferring instead, "behave yourself," precisely because behaviour is something that may be regulated. Again, in the context of the classroom, teachers require that children "behave themselves." In other words, they should conduct themselves like the others thus incipiently contributing to the notion of the en-massing of people.[7]

But, if Arendt's distinctions hold true, what can laughter do to promote action and dilute behaviour? If, as Plessner believes, laughter as an expression may not be interpreted as "purposive actions whose goal is mutual understanding and signalling" (1970, 58), then how is it to assist in promoting action over behaviour? As well as raising the question, Plessner also provides a kind of answer. "Sometimes," he suggests, "the body serves as a sounding board and emission surface for emotions pressing for relief, sometimes as an organ of speech, sometimes as a means of signalling and an organ of gesture.... Everywhere the nature of the situation permits man, indeed compels him to find an unequivocal relation to the ambiguity of his physical existence as body in the body in the light of this very ambiguity" (ibid, 67). He goes on to suggest that, where this ambiguity cannot be resolved, disorientation arises. This can take different forms from the kind of pathological collapse and capitulation attendant on life-threatening situations to the eruption of laughter or tears in situations where life itself may not be threatened but where there is the disorganisation of "normal" expectations. Laughter opens up this ambiguity that we have with our bodies in time and space. In doing so it also, however momentarily, draws back the veil that cloaks the ambiguity of all human being. Behaviour, of course, radically depends on this veil remaining firmly in place. The cultivation and development of particular patterns of behaviour emanate not from the recognition of ambiguity but out of a claim to unequivocal surety. Indeed, it might be argued that the emergence of undemocratic forms of governance in all kinds of contexts, from families to educational institutions to political systems, is a consequence of the inability or failure to live with our own ambiguity writ large.

Action, on the other hand, is much more amenable to ambiguity because it is sourced in the self, which is already deeply implicated in its own ambiguity. It is "I" who acts precisely because action has a teleology, some goal towards which it is directed, and teleology in its own turn is predicated on intentionality. The "I" must consciously intend something. But in acting as body, I am, consciously or unconsciously, embroiled in my own ambiguous relationship to this body that faces into and engages with the world. And, as we have already seen, laughter occupies the same territory even though it is not self-evidently directed towards some goal emanating from the will.

At this stage, it is also important to distinguish the self who laughs from, as one might put it, occasions of laughter. It may be that while the eruption of laughter itself is not an act of the will and therefore not a deliberate choice of the self, the cultivation of laughter or the cultivation of openness to laughter can be. It is quite possible to cultivate and establish the conditions where the individual is likely to be confronted with the range of ambiguities, contraries and unexpected happenings that give rise to those discontinuities (and here at least Morel's general definition is apposite) that occasion laughter. It is also clear that—Plessner's reservations about laughter as a social signal notwithstanding—laughter does indeed have a socially binding function through mutual playfulness (Provine 1998, 41). It is in the recognition of its social nature that we come to terms with another aspect of laughter's ambiguity in human reflection. On the one hand, its socially binding function ensures that the self may not feel too strongly its alterity and can, consequently, derive a certain strength from the group identity. This in turn may facilitate the possibility of withstanding oppressive situations and cultures, most especially when these are manifestations of the dominance of the centre over the periphery. On the other, it can have the effect of creating a kind of false consciousness wherein no one in the group feels themselves sufficiently strong to move outside or critique or challenge the group. It is this that opens up the second reason for beginning with Miller. It is precisely because he recognises that individuals too easily, and too often, fail to act in Arendt's terms—being too scared or too indifferent, or lacking the requisite individuality to do so. Laughter may simply reinforce inaction when it serves to negate the other or to reinforce the sense of "us." This is seen in the everyday relations an established group will have when a stranger enters their midst. Take a group of high-school students who spend a lot of time following the latest fashions as mediated by television programmes aimed at mid-adolescents. They may have an inkling that what they spend their time and money on is a set of largely vacuous behaviours but will admit it neither to each other nor to themselves. A new student arrives in class who has, for whatever reason, self-evidently turned her back on the "temptations" of television and dresses in a way that calls into question the values of the already established group. Are her fellow students likely to embrace her with open arms as one who brings a fresh perspective on their "fashionable follies," or are they likely to laugh at her as being different? If we assume that they will respond by shutting her out, we can see that what might appear as an action is actually inaction. To laugh at the difference is one way of reinforcing the status quo.

Reminders of this are to be found everywhere. For instance, in the Monty Python movie, *Life of Brian*, Brian tries to dismiss the crowd by telling them that they are all individuals and to go away. The crowd remain, chanting, "We are all individuals," when a single voice, that of the actor, Spike Milligan, shouts out, "I'm not!" The paradox, that the only acting person is the one who claims not to be so, is disclosed. The freedom to act, which the individual enjoys, is not a necessary consequence of any rhetorical claim. During the rise of National Socialism, people were rhetorically persuaded that they were taking into their own hands responsibility for the future economic and social well-being of Germany. A central feature of this "power" this was the putative "freedom" to laugh at the Jews. Of course, such laughter was not really an act at all but a response, and one that was a prelude to the annihilation of Jewish communities all over Europe. Jews were created as a "them" over and against an "us"; the rhetoric also embracing the claim that here was a people rising up in action to liberate themselves from the tyranny of a pernicious group of outsiders. In actuality, there was no action, merely behaviour. Like the exhortation to the crowd in *Life of Brian* that they are all individuals the claim that all were called to act is bogus. But, while recognising that laughter can be deployed to encourage social, cultural and political complacency, my concern here is to explore the obverse of that coin—that is, the ways in which laughter serves as a critique.

The laughter that may arise in the observer of the Monty Python sketch is two-edged; on the one hand she may wish to laugh at the sheep-like behaviour of the crowd and the dissonance between what Milligan says and what he is. On the other, this laughter at "the other" (embodied in the crowd) is also laughter at herself and her own potential impotence. It is here that the crossover emerges between the largely personal (including social[8]) senses of laughter and the more political sense in which I wish to use it here. The evocation of laughter, or participation in it, can be construed as an act of creation and one that stands in direct contradistinction to behaviour. (For a fuller discussion, see Arendt 1958; also Dunne 1992; Conroy 2003.) If the observer recognises that the cameo is not directed outwards to "them" but also inward to herself and can laugh at her own complicity in the world of "behaviour," then she may have begun a process of recognising her own need to act.

As I have suggested earlier, there are occasions when laughter may take the form of mass behaviour where, for example, it is deployed as a weapon in determining and subsequently distinguishing the insider and the outsider. Glasgow puts it thus: "At one level affirming ourselves as moral representatives of the social order in the face of deviations from that order, the act of laughing—an act that always has the potential to get out of hand and turn subversive—may at another level be regarded as a release from that order, an expression of the body transcending social control" (1995, 243). In this sense, and in that discussed by Bergson, it may be construed as, at best, deeply ambiguous and at worst, malevolent, and therefore as having no place in the education of children. It is worth reiterating a couple of points here. First, even where it can be argued that laughter may be characterised by wickedness or meanness, this does not negate its status as a creative act.[9] And second, it is this very act of creativity that provides a necessary but, at this stage, an insufficient condition for seeing laughter as important to the processes of education. By this, I mean to suggest that laughter may be deployed as a force for either good or evil and that its importance as a resource for a critically reflective education is dependent upon other features of the endeavour, most especially intentionality.

In this section I have attempted to address the relationship between laughter and action. In doing so I am too readily aware that laughter does not lend itself unambiguously to an exclusively ethical explanation or to the kind of action that is so vital to the maintenance of a discursive contest. Against its deliberate deployment in an intentional environment such as education, a kind of Hobbesian view might be taken that sees it only as a group mechanism for inflicting psychological pain on the unwary. Or again, it can be used as a form of teacher control where a miscreant is deemed a suitable candidate for some sardonic comment intended to invite the other students into a co-conspiracy with the teacher. It is true that laughter can be and often is so used. Such a misanthropic view would tie laughter to behaviour—the movement of the crowd, and no doubt laughter is frequently used in schools in this manner. Alternatively, I have attempted to demonstrate that this view of laughter is, at best, partial and have made a prima facie case for arguing that, in its very ambiguity, laughter emerges out of the same impulse as action. This alone would, I suggest, make it a propitious site for the liminality required in an era of political, social, cultural and educational uncertainty. I have rooted this positive conception in a consideration of both the neurophysiology and the psycho-philosophy of laughter. In the next section I expand these discussions of laughter's relation to action and in doing so elucidate its importance for both the self and the community.

Laughter, Fear, Dissensus and Education

Having proposed that the kind of laughter I am alluding to here may be related to action, I wish to explore what obstacles to action might exist and how these might be confronted and challenged by laughter. Earlier, I suggested that laughter has some locus in the healthy emotional life; here I wish to explore its contrapuntal relationship to fear. I do this in order to establish that engagement in the life of a liberal-democratic polity is dependent upon the individual having the capacity to act, and that such action cannot take place where fear is overwhelming. The capacity to dissent is directly related to one's freedom not to be intimidated either by one's own psychological predispositions or by external political and social forces. And so, back to Miller. In the introduction to *The Crucible* he inveighs against a kind of subservience that emanates from either an inability to do otherwise or collusion in one's own powerlessness. Miller is writing in the context of the McCarthy purges that aimed to eradicate the perceived threat of difference through the creation of a climate of fear where laughter and the comic was all but extinguished in American public life. It was in this context that Charlie Chaplin, at the end of his career, was refused entry into the United States (Jenkins 1994, 3). Fearing laughter as ridicule, the attempt to extinguish it is a significant feature of those governments who seek to exert overwhelming control of the polity (Townsend 1992). It has to be remembered that the particular political closure of action in favour of behaviour as executed by McCarthy and others was done in the name of freedom. It is here that word and deed part company, ruptured by the dissociation of initiation (*archein*) from completion (*prattein*).[10] As Marshall has it, "promised independence and liberty masks the ways in which we have been made unfree and docile, according to Foucault, in the march of modern power" (1996, 81).

In addition to this dissociation of word and deed the most potent weapon yielded by McCarthy and his aides was fear, a deeply debilitating and corrupting emotion, and one that I shall argue is most susceptible to the challenge of laughter. In a short essay on fear, Aung San Sui Kyi discusses the Buddhist concept of *a-gati* (corruption)[11] and points out that the most potent form of corruption is *bhaya-gati* (fear), "for not only does bhaya, fear, stifle and slowly destroy all sense of right and wrong, it often lies at the root of the other three kinds of corruption" (1991, 180). For example, it is not unreasonable to maintain that the corrupt desire (*chada-gati*) to arrogate increased power to oneself, and the possible concomitant willingness to engage in bribery and other forms of chicanery, may be said to be borne of the fear of not being number one; the fear of not being in control. It is the fear that if someone else was in power they might treat me as badly as I have treated others. Such behaviour may be seen to reside more deeply in the fear of one's own freedom to be and to act. Many fear the aloneness and anxiety that may accompany action and so resort to a kind of submissiveness (or behaviour) in the hope of maintaining attachment to some mythic centre but, as Fromm points out, this is not the only alternative available to human beings; indeed the only positive alternative, he argues, is to be found in the "spontaneous relationship to man and nature,"[12] a relationship that connects the individual to the world without eliminating his individuality. This kind of relationship—the foremost expressions of which are love and productive work[13]—are rooted in the integration and strength of the total personality and are therefore subject to the very limits that exist for the growth of the self' (1942, 24). For both Fromm and Aung San fear is debilitating, obstructing the attainment of personal integration at the level of the individual for the one and stultifying collective action for the other. As suggested earlier, given the importance of laughter in the integration of the personality, it is not unreasonable to see it as an important response to individual fear. Once the individual has controlled or dissipated her fears, she enjoys an enhanced possibility of joining with others in overcoming their collective fear(s). If I am able to laugh at my fears, first as an individual and then with others in a group, those objects that give rise to fear, be they psychological insecurity or physical harm can at worst be ameliorated and at best evaporate. In circumstances of political, economic or cultural fear, laughter can both challenge internal and external sources of fear *and* nurture solidarity with the other without the need to posit love.

Two well-loved children's stories serve to illustrate how laughter, construed as a positive force can, on the one hand, address those internal fears and anxieties that prohibit the individual from acting and, on the other, those powerful centripetal forces that can diminish collective action. With regard to the first, Frank Muir's story of a nervous dog entitled, *What-a-Mess and the Hairy Monster* (1987) assists young children in dealing with the ubiquitous fear of the dark/upstairs. The young pup goes up the stairs backwards to avoid having to look into the darkness. He bumps into a number of things and believes them all to be monsters. Eventually he is accompanied by his mother who good-humouredly shows him that his fears are within. Following his antics, children can also come to term with those internal fears which can be barriers to their acting out of freedom. *What-a-Mess* and the children who read the story are enabled through laughter at the absurd to confront their own fears. This absurdity is no accidental feature of the situation. As Berger points out, "absurd comedy releases a curious dialectic. It puts before one a reality that is both strange and familiar, and that evokes the response that it is impossible. But as one exclaims, "That is absurd!"—that being the magical counterworld one has just entered—another exclamation immediately suggests itself, "This is absurd!"—and this, of course, is the world of ordinary, everyday experience" (1997, 182). Through her attention to such a situation, the child gradually comes to recognise the dialectic of everyday experience. Just as *What-A-Mess* is absurd, so too are her fears. Gradually, the external sources of fear are seen to be no more than shadows and the internal response disproportionate to the threat. Once this source has been so diminished, the acting subject has the opportunity to claim back power and control.

This dialectic of the absurd is even more the case with respect to individual's joining together. Roald Dahl's book *Matilda* (1998) illustrates this particularly well. When a lizard lands on Miss Trunchbowl's (the villain of the piece) chest during one of her excessively abusive tirades, the children in the story roar with laughter. In doing so they have confronted the object of their terror; in their laughter they have not acted individually but in concert. In the wake of their laughter Miss Trunchbowl becomes decreasingly menacing. This comes about not because her experiences have ameliorated her viciousness but because the children have taken control of their fear through their laughter. Miss Trunchbowl has become increasingly absurd and this recognition again brings the cognate realisation that their own fears of such a ridiculous creature are themselves in some way absurd. Once the children laugh at her this dominant force no longer holds centre stage. Perceptibly, the balance of power shifts from the centre to the margin. For the child who reads the story, the messages about acting in concert and laughing are powerful indeed; more importantly, the story allows children to see that the control and dangers that the centre can exercise in respect of those on the margin can be assuaged through communal laughter. Of course there are particular issues related to the nature of childhood and the transitions in and out of laughter that mark it. I will return to these in the final section.

If education has a concern to release students from fear it is because, properly conceived it is at heart about human flourishing. And, in turn, such flourishing is impossible if the individual is practically constrained and debilitated by fear. For the individual to flourish she must be enabled to engage in self-creation. Such self-creation is aided and abetted by the freedom that comes from conquering one's fears. Laughter can act as both a catalyst for and a sustainer of the process of growth and self-creation that emerges out of "taking a different view" from the dominant one. In this context of self-creation, laughter constitutes an act. That is, it is an act, which brings into being a change in perspective or understanding. When I laugh at the source of my fears this constitutes an act; a taking control. The story of Matilda and Miss Trunchbowl is a story where the child, in solidarity with other children, breaks free of the inappropriate control exerted by the centre, and in doing so establishes her credentials as an actor. In her joining together with others, Matilda moves the process outwards so that it is no longer a matter of only conquering individual fear but is also a step towards evening up the scales in an asymmetrical relation of power.

Let me move from a consideration of laughter as embodying the possibility of personal and social action to a consideration of its place in the public space. In a liberal democracy the public spaces should be places where individuals and groups can attend to what might constitute the corporate well-being of both, within the boundaries of the state.[14] As I have argued earlier however, our public spaces too often represent an exercise in the foreclosure of meaning, where the centre retains power over both the nature and substance of the discourse and any of its concomitant strategies and behaviours.[15] In order that liberal democracy remains faithful to both its liberal and its democratic traditions and mandate, it must be subjected to acts of critique. In its positive guise laughter may offer a voice from the edge, which can challenge the centre.

The conditions of late modernity may exhibit very particular manifestations of the concern about the asymmetry in the relationship between the centre and the periphery, but the concern itself is neither historically nor culturally unique. An interesting example of what is meant here is found in the reaction of the eighteenth-century Scottish philosopher and logician, James Beattie, to the self-aggrandising tendencies of those either at or desirous of being at the centre of power. Beattie criticises the penchant of poets and other courtiers for paying undue homage to the king. In particular, he has in his sights the seventeenth-century poet, J.D. Blackmore, whom he regarded as meanness masquerading as self-importance and as one who turns his own words into a form of burlesque. The reasons for Beattie's animosity can readily be found on reading some of Blackmore's work through which he establishes himself as the guardian of all dignity and uprightness in the face of the perversions of many of his contemporaries in the worlds of poetry and letters. In his rewriting of some of the psalms, Blackmore offers a sycophantic rendering that is more concerned to ingratiate himself to the monarch than reflect the sentiment or content of the scriptures themselves (Blackmore 1700, 235). In critiquing him, Beattie deploys an ironic voice, claiming that "whatever may be employed as a means of discountenancing vice, folly or falsehood is an object of importance to a moral being; and Horace has remarked 'Ridiculum acri Fortius et melius magnas plerumque fecat re'" (1779, 299).[16] On this account, laughter offers the individual the space and tools to develop a sense of the absurdity of some of the more outrageous suggestions and ideas that emanate from the claims of politicians and educationalists, to understand the defects in much that we take as read and to recognise pomposity and self-aggrandisement for what they are. The positions adopted by Beattie and Blackmore reflect an ongoing struggle that goes beyond church and court to embrace educational and social thought, and a struggle that resonates with our own educational projects. The deployment of laughter as a means by which those on the periphery can critique the centre is thus not a modern or postmodern phenomenon. Public spaces in all ages need to be places where those in power are held to account. Beattie held that laughter offered at least one way of doing this.

The place of laughter as a liminal force for critique is perhaps expressed nowhere more effectively than in the plays on politics of Aristophanes who, through wit, irony and laughter casts a purifying light on some of the more grotesque practices of the state, committed in the name of the people. In his earliest work, *The Acharnians* (1961), Dicaeopolis is the liminal figure and the voice of laughter; the one who embodies a kind of *jouissance* and ridiculousness, but at the same time, the voice of trenchant critique. Dicaeopolis [17]sets about creating a private peace when his entreaties have no affect on bringing the Peleponesian war to a conclusion. He certainly adopts a liminal position with respect to the Spartans when he calls into question the claims that the Spartans were to be solely blamed for the war. In a typical tone-twisting tricksterish speech, Diceaoplois begins with a vitriolic attack on the Spartans whom he declares he hates. Thus, he begins, "I loathe Spartans, I detest Spartans. I abominate Spartans...I here implore Poseidon the Earthshaker, god of Tainaros, to shake, quake, shiver, and tumble their hovels into rubble, to rain destruction on those damnable animals" (ibid, 53). Then, in a complete *volte face*, and with a change of tone, he suggests that:

> They're only human, and we're too hard on them, friends/Why should we blame the Spartans for all our troubles? Specifically, the War? The cause, if the truth were known, was our own people/Note, I do not say Athens. Particularly note, Gentlemen, that I do not say Athens—It was our own men, a few corrupt men, be-based, mis-struck types, the bastard pinchbeck outpouring/of foreign mints, the all-too-common coins, the two-bit Informers the Co. of Kleon and Co. (ibid)

The humour and wit of Aristophanes lies not only in his words and in his wordplays, though these are plentiful enough, but also in his nimbleness in weaving back and forth through argument and counter-argument, exposing the gaps in the claims of his opponents. In his wordplay, laughter is play, is satire, is political commentary, is religious commentary. He moves back and forth between the categories effortlessly but not seamlessly, for his intention is to constantly startle and delight with sudden changes of pace, tempo, direction and language (an appropriate inappropriateness!). The delight that he takes in the word is to be seen in his play around coinage, which is how people are bought off as well as being that which continues to fuel the war. The pecuniary interests of the corrupt men are repeatedly brought to our attention. They are "mis-struck, pinchbeck" (mean); they issue from a "mint," they are "all-too-common coins," "two-bit." Central to Aristophanes' work and role (and indeed, old comedy in general) was the recognition that the continued existence of a healthy polity required those who sat on and viewed political life from the edge. In doing so they brought a new perspective to bear on the affairs of state. Further, they invited their audiences to laugh at what might be deemed the madness and excesses, the corruption and the inadequacy of the political centre. Of course, this should not be taken to imply that Aristophanes wishes the affairs of state to be banished. His attack is directed only towards their corrupt and corrupting forms. This can be adduced from the distinction he makes between banishing the traditional Gods from the stage of comedy while retaining them in reality. He wished to banish them within his plays because of the corrupt manner in which they were used and abused by those in power (see Riu 1999). So it is with the use of comedy in a liberal democracy—it is not that liberal democracy is to be banished, rather comedy is there to expose its abuse. Importantly for the argument here, we should note that Aristophanes does not sit at the margins of Greek society. His work is not banished to some desolate zone beyond the pale. Rather it continually erupts into the heart of the polity.

Dissensus or Complicity

To this point, I have argued against those who would regard laughter exclusively or primarily as a stratagem for confirming one's insider social status and in favour of the view that it is an activity that enables the self to come to terms with one's own ontological alterity. Allied to this, I have suggested that laughter may usefully be construed as a liminal site that gives rise to the possibility of subjecting the politico-educational rhetoric of the centre to a critical hermeneutic. It might be countered that, in this analysis, I have paid insufficient attention to a range of objections that countermand the central claim that laughter is an important site for active dissent or indeed that it is an appropriate site in and for education which reaches beyond the personal. In support of the first objection it might be argued that the observer of Aristophanic comedy, for example, was primarily in attendance to be entertained by the poet/playwrights' wit and linguistic dexterity, and to scoff.[18] Consequently, the disposition to action (in an Arendtian sense) is not present. This being so, the laughter that arises from old comedy or modern irony is passive. It might further be suggested that such passive observance of old comedy or, for that matter, the modern jester, fool or clown hardly constitutes *dissensus*, because dissensus assumes an act that cannot be passive. Indeed, Averintsev (2001) argues that laughter, far from being an act is merely the suspension of our will to act. "Personal will," he maintains, "is not consulted at all; it is irrelevant…. Laughter [rather] belongs to the class of states that in the language of Greek philosophical anthropology are called *pathe*—not what I do, but what is done to me" (ibid, 81). If Averintsev is right and the audience are just passive absorbers of the comedy to which they consequently respond, then laughter could not be deployed as an activity that perforce enables the individual or group to use it as a form of dissensus that in turn can act as a heuristic corrective in the polity. However, for this view to prevail, two things would need to be established. First, it would have to be demonstrated that laughter was always and for everyone a response and that no one, on ruminating about some feature of the play, did not notice or cognise a particular feature of its absurdity or stupidity or perverseness and, seeing it as funny, begin to laugh. The assumption that all perceive the play in the same way and respond accordingly partakes in the fundamental mistake of seeing the one and the all as interchangeable. It is true that some may simply "laugh" in the way he suggests, but it is not possible to make the grander claim that all do. This merging of the one and the many contributes to the belief that the en-massing, of human beings was somehow necessary. Second, it would also have to be shown that neither the individual nor the group were likely to change their views on or practices in relation to the object of laughter. And of course, some may be as Averintsev suggests and will laugh passively, but others will change their attitudes, beliefs or views on the basis of having engaged with Aristophanes' invitation to join with him in laughing at the absurd activities of the state and its "servants."

Let me explore these ideas a little further. It has become an axiom of late-modern philosophy (Rorty 1999) that we must all follow Shylock's lament that "he too bleeds" and that in consequence we are all the same. It is of course true that we all bleed but that, as one might say, is but physiology and our bodied self is testimony not only to some similarities but also to much distinctiveness. As I have already discussed in relation to Plessner's view, my body is that within which I simultaneously can both communicate and mask myself. It is our indebtedness to *The Enlightenment* with its (admittedly ambiguous) attachment to a common reason,[19] which has given rise to this masking of otherness and the development of the concomitant claim that we are conjoined by our sameness. But this masking has had the effect of dulling our sense of the strangeness of life. Laughter, because it is implicated in the disclosure of strangeness, opens this up for us once more. When I join with another in laughing at a joke or a parody or a satire I do so precisely because we both recognise this "oddness"; we share a sense of strangeness. In laughing at Groucho Marx making his entrance in *Duck Soup* when about to be installed as the President of Freelandia, we are laughing not at the stupidity of the people who are all facing the main entrance with fanfare and due pomp while he slides down a fireman's pole behind them, whips off his pyjamas to reveal a dinner suit and asks Margaret Dumont (1) if she'd like to marry him; (2) if she's rich; and finishes by asking (3) that she "answer the second question first!" Rather, what evokes laughter is of course the sheer delight that comes with the combination of the visual and the word play, but more importantly, it is the strangeness of the figure, the displacement of the crowd who one minute are central to the visual narrative in facing the supposed action, while the next, having been outflanked, they are suddenly outsiders. We recognise the strange situation, Groucho's strange behaviour, the suddenly estranged crowd and undoubtedly the disruption of the position of the powerful. The idea of strangeness and estrangement cannot be underplayed in our understanding of the role of laughter and in its use as a corrective in liberal democracy. Recent social philosophy and psychology has underplayed the role strangeness plays in our lives, preferring to construct us as basically "all the same." This has, I think, contributed to the en-massing, of late-industrial society with its claims to globalisation. Globalisation can only be effective where all are persuaded that their wants and needs are similar if not the same. Were it to be too successful this drive for sameness would pose a real threat to laughter as construed here.[20]

Allied to the notion that the evocation of laughter and its concomitant response is rooted in our alterity is the claim that the comic is fundamentally concerned not with en-massing, but unmasking. This is well illustrated by Stephen Poliakoff's (1999) television play, *Shooting the Past*, where the central figure, Oswald, is transformed from the bumbling, dishevelled, somewhat dissolute and down-right awkward photo-museum archivist who impedes progress, into the narrator of the personal in the midst of an impersonal world. The world in which he lives (a photo museum) is to be closed by its new owners in favour of a "modern," information-driven business school that has no room for the unreconstructed scholar. The business school may be seen to represent modern mass culture, the sacrifice of the individual to the project. On the other hand, Oswald is a comic figure from a by-gone era; like the fool, he is to be simultaneously pitied and laughed at. But, in an ironic twist, he is able to reconstruct the secret life of his businessman protagonist because his knowledge is not that of the mass-market but of subtle connections. He unmasks the "truth." He is the carrier of a vast store of knowledge, and because of this can make connections between photographs and stories that appear, prima facie, to have no links. He makes these connections because he *knows,* not because he is the possessor of information. Ultimately, however, this world of knowing is to be discarded for the high-technology culture of modern business where information is traded as if it were knowledge. In all this, Poliakoff invites the viewer to reflect on the loss of the idea of knowledge and its replacement with information. This is done not through a confrontational discourse but, obliquely, by offering a comic character as the vehicle of a form of rationality that illuminates the absurdity of the appearing rationality of the technologically advanced businessman. In Poliakoff's story, Oswald plays the traditional role of the fool or trickster (see Boston 1974). A truly liminal figure, he is the one who challenges and questions our assumptions about how the real world operates. As he says of himself when under attack from his director: "The extraordinary thing about me—shall I tell you what the extraordinary thing about me is?!...Despite what I look like...despite being a shaggy irritating prat...I know how the world works" (Poliakoff 1999, 61). In late modernity, "a shaggy irritating prat" is not supposed to know how the world works; that is the domain of the "sharp-suited businessman."

In neither of the examples offered here is the audience merely being entertained or invited to be scornful; rather they are invited into a hermeneutical relationship with the text (even where the text is televisual), and beyond the text into the social and economic discourse of the dominant centre. They are invited to consider displacement and inversion as categories by which they can interpret particular sets of relationships. This in turn raises the question as to audience passivity and whether or not laughter is merely conceived as reactive and having nothing to do with the will.[21] In this, and from the context of his work, it is reasonable to assume that he is laying claim to more than the fairly unexceptional and equally uninteresting physiological assertion that some thing, person or event stimulates me into a laughter response. In his essay on "Bakhtin, Laughter and Christian Culture," Averintsev (2001) challenges the Bakhtinian argument that laughter is about inducing or nurturing the transition from unfreedom to freedom (a view contiguous with that presented here) but then goes on to propose that the transition itself implies that someone has to be unfree in the first place in order to become free. "It is always harder," he says, "to make a wise man laugh than a simpleton because the wise man, in regard to a greater number of particular cases of inner freedom, has already crossed the line of liberation, the line of laughter and is already beyond the threshold" (ibid, 81). There are a number of things that might be said about his notions of freedom and unfreedom. There are also questions to be asked about the evidence for what is after all an empirical question but I shall have to pass them here so as to concentrate on his central thesis that laughter is passive; done to me and that, in turn, I need already to be intellectually unfree to take advantage of it.

Perhaps the best way of responding[22] is to draw on the work of Robert Jenkins (1994) who, in his discussion of Lithuanian resistance to Russian domination, demonstrates how, though externally stimulated, laughter need not be construed as a passive response beyond the capacity of the individual to influence. In 1990, when Russian troops were patrolling the streets of Vilnius on a holiday to celebrate the revolution, a clown with a mask of Brezhnev began to lampoon the former Soviet president and the empty propaganda of the Communist Party. As the soldiers, somewhat ineptly, attempted to catch the elusive clown, the crowd below began laughing thus heaping more scorn on the already discomfited troops. Laughter, in this instance, evokes a communal resistance to a centralist hegemony. As Jenkins goes on to suggest, "The relentless assault of laughter in theatres, parks and meeting halls helped to undermine the credibility of the Soviet system at the same time that it enabled Lithuanians to express common values essential to the survival of the cultural identity" (1995, 51). So, when it might be argued that the laughter of the crowds was a response, it was certainly not a passive consequence of the other but arose out of the initiating self who brings into being some word or deed. This is true whether the self in question is individual or conjoined with other selves in a collective.

That laughter may be seen as a corporate response does not negate the claim that it serves as an "act." Different though they are, the examples of both Matilda and the Lithuanian protesters exemplify the importance of laughter as a form of reclamation or self-empowerment by the individual or group with limited formal power or access to the power to shape the conditions within which they can determine and access choice. Here, laughter is an activity that, at one and the same time, protects the individual self and disempowers the dominant (even domineering) other. The objections to laughter as a political force do not, in the light of this analysis, seem to be sufficiently powerful to dissuade me from the claim that it can indeed act as a liminal voice of dissensus in the educational activity of a liberal democracy. Laughter on this account is not simply about maintaining the passive insider status, the better to ensure the complicity of the mass in the maintenance of inappropriate political, and cultural and economic strategies in and beyond education. It is rather a dynamic force, which may be initiated individually and developed collectively to challenge the dominant "political" or cultural insiders.

Laughter in the School

As I have argued throughout this work, the issue for education is not that the follies of the market are placed before children as if they provided axiomatic accounts of human flourishing, though that may be reason enough to be cautious about future developments. Rather, the concern is about the gradual closure of the public conversation as to what counts as such flourishing and the consequent understanding of education. This closure itself may be regarded as the necessary consequence of the growing congruity between the claims of the market, the claims of advertisers and the claims of government with respect to human well-being that "squeezes out" alternative conceptions within the public spaces. In turn, I have suggested, the not entirely novel idea, that liberal democracies need a certain degree of dissensus within their public spaces and that education, being both a public space and one where children are, putatively at least, nurtured within the public domain as future citizens needs to create sites where this may happen. These sites are not, I have also argued, to be found in the formal programmes of citizenship education, *de rigueur* though these may be, or in the transformation of schooling into a cultural war zone, but on the boundaries and in the interstices of school life. The maintenance of such a liminal quality is necessary to avoid the containment of the centre that tends to collapse all difference. Laugher provides precisely this kind of site as it is both beyond containment and holds the possibility of cultivating human action in contradistinction to behaviour. In construing laughter in this way, I have defended it against the charge that it is a more or less negative emotion. In this final section I hope to sketch out some of the implications for the school as an institution and for the conduct of the classroom.

It would be inappropriate to conceive of laughter as some kind of formal element in the curriculum. At best, such formal elements as there are might be regarded as parasitical upon and emanating from more general features of our culture. Laughter is not manufactured in a classroom; it cannot be made to order or according to a set of overtly prescribed social, cultural or educational representations. This is not to suggest that parodies and witty stories, anecdotes and even a certain amount of grobian laughter[23] should not find their way into the overt curriculum; rather, they should not be subject to those formal standards of inclusion that are the quickest way to negate their power. Nor is it to be regarded as a set of pedagogical techniques such that they might be taught in a teacher education programme. Laughter cannot be the subject of competences or benchmarks or mission statements. While this may appear to give laughter a quality too elusive to be of use within the educational frame of late modernity, it is nevertheless absolutely appropriate. It is not possible to offer such a definite or definitive construal of laughter in education because the evocation of laughter is not about rule following. If it were it would rather defeat its interstitial quality. In any event, I am persuaded by Charles Taylor's argument, in his essay, "To Follow a Rule" (1995), that we know the topography of lived, embodied engagements with both the world and the other, not in virtue of following a set of rules that are given either as brute facts to which the individual inner self attends in making judgements about how to think or act. Rather, in his view, much of our "intelligent" action is carried on in an unformulated way against a backdrop of what Bourdieu calls the *habitus* (1992). This habitus is nurtured, not by way of a map, where each feature is linked sequentially to each other feature as in the formalised curriculum in schools, but as a thing embodied in particular moments of time. Here, Taylor is not concerned with a general or abstract notion of time but its particular incarnation as a moment or moments in space. Those representations that manifest themselves in the curriculum of our schools are predicated on there being lots of explicated rules and procedures that students, and indeed teachers, should both attend to and follow. They are there to guide behaviour and to provide justifications for particular behaviours and activities. But this is not the way in which we learn to be and to do. I do not learn to give another her space in a conversation according to a fixed set of explicated rules, yet it is possible for myself or another to recognise when I have spoken for too long; or again, I do not need my host to don his pyjamas and come into the dining room yawning to tell me that the dinner party is over and it is time to go home; I do not realise that the joke I have told is inappropriate because there are a set of rules that I follow that, in turn, inform me that jokes in such and such circumstances are in bad taste. Nevertheless, I do learn to give the other space, I do learn when a dinner party has run its course, and I do learn that the telling of this joke was inappropriate. It is, as Taylor has it, that "rather than representations being the primary locus of understanding, they are only islands in the sea of an unformulated practical grasp of the world" (1995, 170). Laughter as a set of discursive and dissensus practices is, I would argue, the same kind of thing; that it is unformulated does not imply that it does not exist as an "activity" in the school and its curriculum.

To suggest that it is difficult, and probably inappropriate, to denominate a set of pedagogies or practices as "laughter" does not mean that it is not an activity of the classroom. Nor is it to imply that it is arbitrary or that there are not distinctions to be made between different kinds of laughter. Nor is it to suggest that we cannot assist students in discerning different kinds of laughter. It is just that, in our approach to it, we take care not to undermine its contribution to the evolution of the habitus. Laughter on this account contributes to and is a part of the practical grasp of the world. Indeed, for any such contribution to make sense we need to rely on a pluriform approach where the evocation of laughter is sometimes serendipitous and is sometimes refracted through the materials, approaches, conversation and style of teaching. Interstitially woven into the habitus of education, laughter is an activity.

Having suggested how laughter may not be approached in the school, it is now worth postulating some ways in which it may. The first is to recognise that just as laughter itself is to be seen as issuing out of varied, and sometimes contradictory impulses, so too children experience and engage in laughter in myriad ways. As Plessner points out, laughing and crying are closely related. Nowhere is this more readily seen than in childhood where, for example, a game of peek-a-boo with a young child can suddenly be transformed from a source of pleasure and excitement to one of intense fear and anxiety depending on the child's perception of the context. Shaping the context in school is, one might say, everything here.

Two approaches might loosely be taken towards some explicit (though not necessarily formal) treatment of laughter. The first, based on Berger's (1997) discussion of the expressions of laughter, is to establish contexts wherein the different purposes of laughter, some of which have been touched on earlier, might be explored. These could include humour as benign and diversionary, as consolation, as wit and intellect, as political, social and cultural satire and as folly. The second takes a more developmental view so that, for example, in early-years education, teachers (and the good ones already instinctively know this) need to understand the border between laughing and crying and play games that strengthen children's sense of appropriate inappropriateness. The next stage is to cultivate the delight children have in word play and punning. This, in turn, may lead to setting up particular comic situations, introducing students to witty texts and so on. A further development could be the introduction of a certain politico-educational dissensus rooted in the literary creations of satirists, clowns and fools.

Such approaches are likely to be effective to the extent that they are underpinned by a thoroughgoing commitment to the cultivation of discernment. As I have suggested elsewhere, people stand in asymmetrical relationships to each other with respect to the exercise of power, most especially in terms of the centre and the periphery. In schools there are a variety of centres, depending on the location and context. For example, the experience of some students is that they are on the periphery with respect to some centre created "behind the sports hall," where bullying is the order of the day. Such bullying can indeed be predicated on a destructive manifestation of laughter, which is of course not laughter in the sense advocated here, but abuse. Nor is such abuse the exclusive domain of students. Teachers can use laughter equally as a form of bullying but the task of education is to assist students in their discernment as to the differences between activities that may indeed lay claim to the same nomenclature but in fact have entirely opposing intentions. The cultivation of such discernment requires that students develop an understanding of the functions and applications of irony, parody and foolishness. This is done not—as the modern curriculum tends to—in the elision of those literary and cultural forms that gave shape to dissensus, but in embracing them as foundational in the habitus of the school, its teachers and its pupils. It is neither desirable nor possible that education in a liberal democracy embrace laughter as a mainstream curriculum activity but it is important than it facilitate its possibilities as liminal activities of what Aquinas might have called the practical imagination.

The justification for the approach being advocated here lies as much in our imagining the consequences of not embracing laughter as a liminal activity in education. Imagine a playground where the bully is not laughed at, or the school where a teacher who yields power inappropriately is not subjected to a host of "unholy" nicknames, or a polity, where the government with but a single voice, is not called to account by an Aristophanes, a Swift or a Chesterton. Such a world would be one dominated by the fears of

Brother Jorge in *The Name of The Rose* (1994), occasioned by the desire to protect the Christian world from the inherently dangerous ideas lodged in the second part of Aristotle's poetics; the ideas of comedy are responsible for killing his brother monks. These ideas about comedy are dangerous, Jorge believes, precisely because they come from the philosopher and not from the carnivalesque and saturnalian street plays and theatre of the peasantry. This latter could be tolerated because it allowed for a kind of catharsis and it was possible to "bracket it out" of the divine order. But Aristotle was another matter, because he had the ability to transform the comic from the ridiculous into an art form, to enable it to become what brother Jorge saw as "the object of philosophy and of perfidious theology" (ibid, 474; see also Conroy 1999a; Cooper 1922).

There are those who would argue that schools are not primarily or indeed at all concerned with laughter, or that such laughter as there is should remain as a feature of the underbelly of schools (students can call teachers nicknames, they can perform jokes in and out of the classroom, attempt to trick their teachers in various ways), but this should not be allowed to surface. As I have illustrated earlier, they would argue believe that schools are for preparing students for economic and social realities. Against this I would reiterate an argument that has been implicit throughout this chapter that laughter as conceived here is an imaginative form of cultural and political rhetoric that embraces action. This does not mean, as Jorge would have had it that laughter has a place as long as it was about keeping order among the "lower classes." Of course, there are "postmodern" forms of laughter, especially in the visual arts,[24] which represent a more robust cultural politics than that advocated here, but there laughter is the mainstream purpose; here it is at the *limen*. Nevertheless, poetry and prose, art and history should offer excurses into a range of forms of laughter the more effectively that students can act out of the laughing dispensation.

Nowhere is the power and importance of laughter as a part of education more evident than in Walter Benjamin's radio series *Aufhklarung für Kinder*[25] with which I will finish this chapter. Written contemporaneously with the prohibition laws, his story, told with wit and ingenuity, discloses the multiple deceptions at the heart of American government manifest in its laws. Those who wanted the law maintained were of course those that benefited from it—the bootleggers, the criminal gangs and the bureaucrats who received payments. The multi-layered lying that attends all bad law and dubious politics is unfolded in Benjamin's witty and evocative story, translated and recounted by Mehlman (1993, 8):

> Young black boys move alongside a train, which has just come to a stop, concealing
> beneath their clothes containers of various shape on which may be read in large

letters: iced tea [Kalter tea]. After signalling to a vendor, a traveller, for the price of a suit, buys himself one of the flasks, which he adroitly conceals. Then a second one, then ten more, then twenty, or fifty. "Ladies and gentlemen," the black boys implore, "wait for the train to leave before drinking your tea [trinken Sie de Tee erst wenn Zug fahrt]." Everyone winks complicitously....The whistle blows, the train starts up, and all the passengers raise their containers to their lips. But disappointment soon clouds their faces, for what they are drinking is indeed iced tea.

Notes

1. In this context, site is used to denote a particular location for liminal activity where that might be grounded in activities of the classroom, school or community as distinct from a geophysical space.
2. Of course, Freud is sensible of the many varieties of wit, which it is not my purpose to explore in this essay. (See Freud 1916.)
3. For an interesting and detailed analysis of the negative construction of laughter, especially in the Renaissance, Reformation and early-modern periods, see Skinner, 2000.
4. There is some dispute as to the original date of publication; the date indicated here is the one annotated in this translation.
5. I take this to mean that I am incapable of making balanced judgements because my attachments to particular ways of looking at the world are constantly shifting, having neither anchorage nor fixed points.
6. Here I wish to distinguish speech from talk or chatter or other forms of phatic communication.
7. For a fuller discussion of the role of the masses in political life, see Arendt 1973, Ch. 10.
8. The personal is allied to the social in so far as the social represents an encompassing space for both the public and private but is not political.
9. Even where destruction takes place there is an act.
10. Arendt lays the blame for this dissociation firmly at the feet of Plato whom she regarded as having reframed *archein* and *prattein*. Prior to his intervention the former signified the beginning or initiation of some action, activity or project and the latter its completion. When I initiated something it was with a mind to completing it. Beginning and completion were contiguous and complementary parts of a single process. Plato, according to Arendt, compromised this complementarity so that *archein* dissolved into rules and *prattein* constituted the activity of completion according to those rules (Arendt 1958; see Dunne 1992, Ch. 3 for an interesting account of Arendt's development of this notion). So it was that the creation of the rules governing activity and the activity itself came to be lodged in different hands; the rulers "speaketh" the instructions, the doers followed. For Arendt, the consequence of this has been the elision into behaviour. Behaviour is a feature of the social

realm, which she distinguished from the political or public believing that it was just such an elision that had made a significant contribution to the twentieth-century trauma that was the Holocaust.

11. The other forms of *a-gati* are *chanda-gati* (desire, which leads to deviation from the path; the desire to hold onto power can lead to the pursuit of bribes); *dosa-gati* (taking the wrong path to spite others); and *moga-gati* (aberrant behaviour is a consequence of ignorance).

12. Author's italics.

13. Fromm's definition of productive work here is not too dissimilar to Arendt's notion of action. Work is that activity where one unites the self with the world; "not work as a compulsive activity in order to escape aloneness, not work as a relationship to nature which is partly one of dominating her, partly one of worship of and enslavement by the very products of man's hands, but work as a creation in which man becomes one with nature in the act of creation" (1942, 225).

14. It is important here to recognise that the members of a liberal democratic state may also be concerned with the well-being and welfare of others outside their boundaries and with considerations of the general well-being of humanity. None of what is said here is intended to negate either the possibility or desirability of such considerations being central to a liberal democracy. Indeed, the "liberal" of liberal democracy may arguably presuppose a concern for the applications of universal justice and integrity.

15. In education, such acts may include public expenditure, curriculum planning and the regressive shift from teacher education to teacher training.

16. "Ridicule shall frequently prevail and cut the knot when graver reasons fail." For Beattie, "ridicule" was the adoption of the parodic stance with respect to the grand and verbose claims of the court.

17. The name Dicaeopolis (Dikaipolis), meaning "just city," is itself intentionally ironic since he spends his time wanting to be away from the polis that he regards as deeply corrupt and miserable. Hence, one speech goes as follows: "I loathe the stingy, greedy city./I long for my own ungrudging countryside, my generous village,/my open hearted home.../...and that blasted city word 'Buy'—/goodbye to that" (1961, 16).

18. Nietzsche clearly adopts this view of Aristophanic laughter when he observes in *Beyond Good and Evil* that "we are...prepared like no previous age for a carnival in the grand style...for the transcendental heights of the highest nonsense and Aristophanean derision of the world" (1966, 150).

19. This, I suggest, is true despite the claim that *The Enlightenment* has given rise to individual reason and the consequent individualized self. This is because individual reason was to be seen as reasonable only in so far as it partook in some greater rational process, which embraced both the thought and the rational will of all. This is particularly evident in Rousseau's *Social Contract* (1968) but is also apparent in Kant's *Groundwork of the Metaphysics of Morals* (1998).

20. The importance of recognising the socio-psychologically foundational nature of human "strangeness," the sense of which has been lost in the attempt to assuage some of the negative effects of difference, has been a fundamental feature of the religious impulse (see Santner 2001). Many of the world's religious traditions explicitly aver to this sense of our perennial strangeness (see Boys 2002). In the Jewish and Christian scriptures there are many examples of the importance of alterity to the self and to the community (Gen. 15:13-20). Further, it is refracted through those teachings, which predicate salvation, not on welcoming the friend but the stranger into one's midst (cf: Matt. 25:34-46). Thus comedy, while there to entertain and amuse, is also there to alert us to the strange otherness that is human being.

21. Clearly it is possible, on occasion, that one laugh, as Avertinsev has it passively but equally it is possible to laugh "actively."

22. Others such as Berger (1997) and de Sousa (1987) would also take issue with Averintsev, maintaining as they do that there is a robust ethical dimension to laughter.

23. These can include the plays of Beckett, the poems of Lear, the stories of Swift and Dahl. Context determines choice.

24. For a highly stimulating account of just such a view of the role of laughter, see Isaak 1996.

25. *Enlightenment for Children*. It is not without reason that Benjamin uses laughter as a form of enlightenment. The story was first recounted as "Die Bootleggers" read over Berlin radio 8 November 1930 and printed in *Aufklarung fur Kinder*, 151.

Chapter 4

The Teacher as Trickster

Fools, they are the only nation
Worth men's envy or admiration...

Ben Jonson, *Volpone*, Act 1: Sc. 1.ll. 156–57 (1962 and 1971)

Introduction

As we turn from the exploration of laughter as a generic quality of liminal education to a more specific incarnation in the person of the teacher, some of the themes of ambiguity, inversion and dissenus discussed there are here taken up again and further developed. Specifically, attention is turned on the person of the teacher as one who needs to embody some of the characteristics of laughter in order to open up the rich complexity of the world to students. Here and there the discussion on laughter touched explicitly on the character of the fool or trickster. Now I wish to suggest that the teacher who wishes to maintain discursive openness without being prey to an overtly political approach to education may don the mantle of the trickster. This is a particularly interesting and evocative, though somewhat ambiguous, metaphor for the teacher. In order to make sense of such a challenging metaphor it is first necessary to understand something of the identity and role of the teacher in late-industrial polities. As a child growing up in a small Northern Irish village, I had a vague sense of the local teacher as a kind of trinitarian figure, an earthly manifestation of a triune God that also included the clergyman and the general practitioner. His role was reasonably unambiguous—he was a learned man, an intellectual (however limited he might have been in actuality). No doubt this is a very peculiarly romanticised view of village life and the ruling pantheon but, even with its romantic overtones, it hints at something long gone and largely forgotten— the teacher as community leader, as someone who represented, in some meaningful way, the community's more noble aspirations and someone whose role and person were not subject to a continually negative barrage of government and media disapproval. Paradoxically, in late-industrial polities the changes in attitude towards teachers have their roots, at least partially in quite ancient anxieties about the liminal state of late childhood/early adolescence. But equally, these changes are also a consequence of the discursive closure about the purposes of education that has been transmuted into a technocratic view of the teacher (see Carr and Hartnett 1996). The opening section of this chapter attempts to understand the interplay between some of these forces and their consequences for our image of the teacher. In the middle sections I have attempted a brief archaeology of the trickster as an archetype metaphor that is simultaneously one of the most ancient in the world of human being and yet, refreshingly contemporary. The trickster is one who, in the patterns of myth, legend and folklore narrative, moves between symbolic categories of being and action, changing shape and identity in order to expose and redress various deep-seated human follies. He is related to the clown or fool and, like them, inhabits a borderland between different worlds or different conceptions of the world and its experiential content. He is frequently a religious or quasi-religious figure who serves a ritualised function in mocking and challenging the forces of the status quo. Of course, it was unlikely, particularly in small village life, that the teacher would have been seen as one who mocked and challenged in this way though, as I discuss briefly in the next section, she always incipiently carried some of these possibilities. The penultimate section attempts to explore the peculiarly Celtic inflections of the trickster, most especially in the person and works of the Irish novelist, Flann O'Brien, who sheds light on a neglected aspect of the moral role of the teacher in the educational systems of the British Isles and, I think, more widely.

The final section takes up this notion of the trickster as a metaphor that may be used to signpost a different, liminal way of making sense of the role and person of the teacher. In doing so, it attempts to uncover this particular, moral conception of the role of the teacher as one duty-bound to a certain discursive openness that runs counter to the prevailing impulses of government and corporation. Interestingly, the trickster's moral responsibility is primarily to the students and, through them, to society. This notion of accountability largely runs counter to the late-industrial view of the teacher as one who is, before everything else responsible, to society seen largely as an economic unit(y). The use of the trickster is also important as a vehicle that repairs that rupture with our own history that has impoverished the storehouse of our collective imagination with respect to the role of the teacher.

Who Is a Teacher?

Across late-industrial societies the notion of an expert has been subjected to profound challenge. From medicine to law, politics to economics the expert appears to be under increased scrutiny.[1] At least in recent times, teaching seems to have been particularly vulnerable to this trend, perhaps more so than other comparable occupations. There are a number of reasons for this vulnerability, some of them fairly prosaic, such as relative economic weakness of teaching as a white-collar occupation. However, there are yet more interesting reasons. These include the openness of its sphere of activity (for all, at some stage of their lives, see and experience the teacher *at work*), the focus of the work (children and adolescents), and the kinds of questions that arise about the exact nature of the expertise a teacher brings to her work. It is the last two of these that are of most interest here, especially given the concern to develop a liminal metaphor of the teacher.

Earlier we reflected on the discrete nature of the school child as one who is, *no longer*, but equally, *not quite yet*. Childhood is an in-between stage and those institutions devoted to this stage partake in that in-betweeness. The liminal status of schooling derives from the liminal condition of childhood and those who enter this world are, in some senses, occupationally separated from the adult world. There are, of course, other occupations where people work with children and adolescents, such as child law and paediatrics, but in such cases the qualifications are gained in the generic field prior to specialisation. Teachers, on the other hand, are expressly qualified (whatever might be meant by that) in teaching children, and even then, in teaching them at particular stages. This brings teachers into the world of the child in a manner quite different from that of a child lawyer or a paediatrician. Teachers occupationally live in the world *of* children, whereas lawyers and paediatricians, respectively, practice law and medicine with respect *to* children. A teacher doesn't practice teaching with respect to children. A teacher teaches children![2] One consequence of the very particular nature of teaching children is that teachers are themselves positioned in the liminal zone of childhood and adolescence in a way that is not the same for lawyer or paediatrician. This liminal location, in common with other liminal states, is suffused with ambiguity and, in turn, it attracts deeply ambiguous responses from adults. This ambiguity manifests itself in a variety of ways. First, on the one hand we may wish to qualify the kind of responsibility that may reasonably be assigned to children for their actions (see Schapiro 1999) while on the other, we have come to regard them as independently responsible consumers of goods and services in their own *sui generis* market. Second, as we have already seen, the period of schooling has been inexorably extended while the concerns and expectations of adult life have burrowed down to the earliest years of childhood. Third, there is a perception that childhood is a state that adults have grown out of, or gone beyond. It is a world they associate with immaturity as well as a certain unruliness. Yet simultaneously, an edifice of imagined innocence has been erected around it. Perhaps most importantly here, teachers themselves are seen to occupy this ambiguous space and appear to attract very mixed reactions from their fellow citizens. So it is that the populist criticism often heard of teachers is that, they do not live in the real world.

Teaching is prey to other significant ambiguities about its occupational status in the polity; indeed, teachers themselves are frequently implicated in the cultivation of some of this ambiguity. In his analysis of some of the ambiguities that surround the occupational identity of teachers, Carr (2003a) delineates a number of important sources of the cloudiness that envelops teaching as an occupation. I wish to refer to only two of these here. First, he points out in some detail that teaching appears to fall between a number of occupational definitions because, on the one hand, it is clearly not a skills-based trade. Yet, on the other, it is not immediately apparent that it is to be seen as a profession in the way that law and medicine are, given that it does not obviously and irrefutably demand a particular specialised study of some field of knowledge before the practice of teaching begins. The study of a variety of social and theoretical sciences notwithstanding, it is not obvious that I have to be a competent psychologist or philosopher in order to be an effective teacher. Indeed, as a student teacher I well remember a particular fellow student, let's call him Matthew, who was a very successful examinee across a range of theoretical considerations but who, on going out on his second-year practicum, was so practically incompetent that he called his supervisor to the school on the grounds that he had an emergency. When the unfortunate tutor arrived on the scene, she discovered that Matthew's anxieties were somewhat overblown. The teaching practice rubrics required that students complete specific parts of their teaching folder in red ink. Matthew didn't have a red pen and was in a state of high anxiety, not knowing what to do. On another occasion he threw a tape recorder out of a sixth-floor window because he couldn't get it to work. Clearly, Matthew's difficulties were more significant than the absence of the red pen, but they were not about his intellectual capacities. Even where a doctor or lawyer is bereft of all interpersonal skills we would still want to suggest that they may continue to practise their profession with the proviso that they retain the capacity to diagnose or analyse the situation appropriately and prescribe accordingly. But our attitude towards teachers in this respect might be somewhat different. Indeed, Matthew was required to pursue an alternative career that did not demand an awareness of the psychological, developmental and communicative needs of those with whom he was working. In some important ways teaching eludes a neat professional categorisation.

The second issue to which Carr draws our attention, which is germane to the discussion here, is the extent to which teachers can or should control their own occupational arrangements. Doctors and lawyers through their professional bodies have managed to control not only their professional practices but, more importantly, also the normative expectations and conditions under which they work. Teachers appear not to have similar oversight and control over their own practices and more importantly over the normative conditions under which they work. Nor, Carr argues, is it self-evident that they should have. "It may well be denied," he argues,

> "that teaching is a professional practice of the kind in which it is proper to involve practitioners in debates and decisions about the aims of education or the proper direction of educational policy. In a public arena in which such other social agencies as parents, politicians or employers are important stakeholders, and in which practitioners are (largely in consequence) required to operate in accordance with centrally or officially prescribed policy decisions about management, discipline, curriculum and pedagogy, it might be held that wider normative reflection upon policy is not the legitimate business of teachers, and that their role is more that of the efficient technical transmission of what is considered to be socially and economically useful by those to whom they are politically (albeit democratically) accountable." (Carr 2003a, 41f)

However, he does go on to argue that such a truncated conception of teaching, while popular in certain right-of-centre political views, may both be misconceived and possibly dangerous. Carr's view needs a little modification here. I take it that Carr does not intend to imply that professions like medicine and law are not subject to disciplinary practices and discursive permissibility, but that it is unlikely that lawyers and doctors would not have a significant input into these issues. He also, I think, wrongly assigns the phenomenon of professional discursive closure to the right-of-centre phenomenon.

Increasingly, governments of both the left and the right in a number of liberal democracies have legislated for central government scrutiny, articulation and control of the outcomes of teacher training programmes. This increase in the surveillance and control of programmes and courses for the preparation of teachers has come about for a number of reasons and certainly in Britain can be traced back to the "Great Education Debate" of the late 1970s, instituted by then British Prime Minster James Callaghan in his now famous "Ruskin College" speech (see Lawrence 1992, 80). At that time, and unwaveringly ever since, there was a perception in the corridors of power that the decline in the economic fortunes of Britain were at least partly attributable to failures in education, which were in turn laid at the door of teachers. There is the further reason, I think, that the many and deeply fissured ambiguities that surround and suffuse adult attitudes towards childhood/adolescence in general, and schools in particular, are apt to be also associated with teachers and teaching.

The note of ambiguity, which vibrates through school education, together with the increasing discursive collusion between government and corporation, has resulted in the evolution of increasingly doctrinaire perceptions of and policies towards teaching and teachers. Across liberal democracies a technicist model of the teacher has entered the mainstream. This model teacher is, above everything (putatively, at least), technically competent. In the course of her training[3] she has acquired a range of skills that can allegedly be assessed by some kind of objective criteria (see Blake et al. 1998). In Britain, the somewhat discredited notion of *competences* in teacher education has been replaced with *benchmarks* (Quality Assurance Agency for Higher Education 2000), but such a change "misses the point." It still retains the notion that being a good teacher is largely a matter of the acquisition of particular skills[4] together with the capacity to "hit the mark." The teacher then is to be regarded as part of a functional, putatively rational system that is intended to deliver certain kinds of measurable outcomes. As with education in general, the role of the teacher, at every level, has been subject to a range of strategies, the net result of which has been the deepening of the drive towards discursive closure. These strategies revolve around the increasing narrowing of not only the teachers' remit but also her practices and pedagogies. This tightening of the focus may be seen as contiguous with a growth in the apparatus of control and regulation focused on increased productivity (Merson 2000); the development of market and compliance models of Total Quality Management (Gewirtz 2000) and a central governmentally controlled framework and set of practices to train school principals and other potential leaders (Smith 2002).

Drawing on its frames of reference, each of these developments carries the genes of economic rationalism and, in yet one more way, demonstrates the lack of both the capacity and capability to nurture alternative linguistic forms for the development of what is a deeply human engagement. These hegemonising tendencies are crystallised in a British Government initiative to standardise leadership practices through the insistence that all university programmes on school leadership use national benchmarks and design their courses in accordance with those of the centrally controlled "College for School Leadership." In his analysis of this initiative, Smith (ibid) lays bare both the desire to cultivate a deeply centralised orthodoxy as to what is to count as good leadership. What counts as good leadership is the efficient enactment of government policies, irrespective of (1) their efficacy or (2) their morality. As a conduit for policy decisions made at another level, the headteacher is increasingly divorced from her colleagues. The discursive metaphors that shape her role and professional identity are increasingly drawn from the world of business, industry and the economy. She stands apart as a manager, whose success is determined by the achievement of targets established elsewhere. Until relatively recently, and despite the occasional minor despot, the notion of headteacher or principal was that they were teachers first and foremost. After all, the headteacher was deemed by colleagues to be "one of us." This situation is not without its ironies given that "behind the rhetoric of modern management lies the architecture of hierarchical management adopting processes that are redolent of very traditional, authoritarian and Taylorist regimes" (Merson 2000, 165).

The gradual but substantial shift in the language that bathes the role of the teacher in the tincture of an economic-managerial discourse is increasingly normalised. Those who do not see their role as some variant of the manager—school manager, curriculum manager, learning manager—are unlikely to experience much career progression. As I have suggested earlier, in late-industrial societies it would be entirely inappropriate to see education as having no connection with economic considerations.[5] Young men and women undoubtedly wish to work and to be successful. But, to reiterate a point made throughout this study, the question is one of priority. From the perspective of the liberal-democratic state, success in the workplace is to be measured against its contribution to the flourishing of the individual and community, not the other way around. On one version of this conception, teachers are good teachers to the extent that they nurture the flourishing of the individual and the school community, not to the extent that they process children in the service of a globalised economy. The role of nurturing the flourishing of the other is a complex one, not easily amenable to formulaic prescription. While the political centre may seek to secure particular kinds of teachers who can demonstrate that they have hit the mark, this is no guarantee that we will have teachers who get the point and are, consequently, effective in promoting the flourishing of individual or community.

It is here, once again, that the liminal metaphor may be of some assistance. It is interesting to note that our images of the efficacious teacher lie outside the categorisations of benchmarks or competences and are to do with the person of the teacher. Capacities and competences, skills and abilities, insight and understanding are all embodied in the particular. In literary and cinematic culture, the iconic teacher is not the efficient bureaucrat or the technically competent but the interesting, exciting and slightly dangerous inspirer of students. From *Dangerous Minds* to *Dead Poet's Society* to *Goodbye Mr. Chips*, the pattern of someone who, above all else, cares passionately about the students, and through them about the world is paramount. Despite significant differences in the narrative and even in the person of the hero they all share this passion for the world. It may well be argued these are not real-world teachers who have to live with the banality of the everyday in education but are mythological emanations of some sort of ideal state.[6] But, it is in harbouring precisely such ideals that we reflect some kind of desire for the state of affairs embodied by them. Moreover, as Day's (1999) researches show, it is precisely this kind of passionate care for student and world that is most likely to motivate students themselves. If students were asked to choose between Socrates and Plato, I suspect most would opt for Socrates.

The Trickster as a Liminal Metaphor

As we have seen, the model of the imagined teacher, articulated in and through the political centre, may be summarised as referring to a competent, technically proficient, fairly controlled purveyor of the dominant themes and motifs of policy that, in a closure of the circle, have their origins in the political and economic centre. As the discursive climate at the centre has closed down, so too has the imagined teacher. Imagination and creativity are desired traits to the extent that they contribute to the achievement of the centrally stipulated targets. But this model of human endeavour is rooted in a myth; one that is so deeply entrenched in our thought that it has become part of who and what we are and is barely accessible to investigation and analysis. It is the myth of the arithmetic, which Castoriadis (1997)[7] saw had come to be treated in our culture as ontologically originary, masquerading as the foundational principle upon which the existence of rational society and its institutions is predicated. But there may be other myths upon which we can draw to inform our conception of the teacher, which are less prone to the discursive closures of the centre.

   With some caution, I wish to propose a different and more ancient way of looking at the moral and social role of the teacher and the processes of education in which she is involved. This alternative perspective draws on older, more imaginative and complex sources of meaning than the latest Gallup poll or the latest adjusted performance indicator. It is the figure of the trickster, possibly the oldest and probably the most ubiquitous of all mythic figures. Before going on to say something about the trickster as a metaphor for the teacher, I wish to briefly outline some of the traits of the trickster to better understand how he might perform such a role.

As Leeming and Page (1996), among others, point out, it is very likely that the trickster is the most significant and the earliest mask of God. Rooted in the Palaeolithic era, his human-animal image is to be found in numerous places around the world, most famously in the caves at Lascaux. In different cultures he assumes quite different guises. In Northern Europe, he is Loki; in India, he is Krishna among the maidens; for the Greeks, he manifests himself as Hermes and Prometheus; for the Native Americans of the Pacific Northwest, he is Raven; for the Winnebago, Hopi and Navajo (among others), Coyote; for the Cherokee, the Bear-shaman; and for Polynesians, he is Maui. It is not my purpose here to provide an exhaustive list of his myriad epiphanies or indeed to recount the vast array of mythic stories attached to him. There are plenty of other sources for that (see Eliot 1990; Hynes and Doty 1993; Hyde 1999). Instead, I wish to draw some lessons from the trickster in order to develop the persona as an appropriate and sustainable metaphor for the teacher, as one who occupies a liminal (ambiguous) space in late-industrial culture. For sure, in many cultures the trickster is seen as an expression of darkness; one who plays wicked tricks on humans, drawing them into his confidence only to ensnare or abuse them. As Coyote he is often seen as a wily animal who, in being too smart for his own good, generally comes unstuck. He may still be found in this guise in the many extant popular stories for children.[8] As Iktome (the spider), or Maui, or Coyote himself, he is sexually promiscuous, prepared to have intercourse under any circumstances and pretty much with anyone. From a psychological perspective, Henderson argues that "The trickster cycle corresponds to the earliest and least developed period of life. Trickster is a figure whose physical appetites dominate his behaviour; he has the mentality of an infant. Lacking any purpose beyond the gratification of his primary needs, he is cruel, cynical and unfeeling" (Henderson 1964, 112). It is in this, his most rudimentary form, that Jung expressly sees "Trickster" as an archetypal psychic structure. He suggests that,

> In picaresque tales, in carnivals and revels, in magic rites of healing, in man's religious fears and exaltations, this phantom of the Trickster haunts the mythology of all ages, sometimes in quite unmistakable form, sometimes in strangely modulated guise. He is obviously a "psychologem," an archetypal psychic structure of extreme antiquity. In his clearest manifestations he is a faithful reflection of an

absolutely undifferentiated human consciousness, corresponding to a psyche that has
hardly left the animal level. (Jung 1972, 140)

Through history this reification of the dark, amoral self gradually gives way
to a more ordered, grown-up being. As Jung goes on to argue, "civilised man
has forgotten the Trickster" (ibid, 147), having buried him in his
unconscious. He has become a shadow figure who, just now and again, spills
over in late-industrial mass society. Jung goes on to claim that Trickster is
never very far way and may be glimpsed in all kinds of still-maintained
cultural and social rituals. Now, this may or may not be the case but there
certainly is a sense in which the trickster will not go away, representing, as
he does, a set of complex cultural relations that may well have their genesis
in perceptions of power and control.

Having regarded Jung's view as possibly too limiting, Campbell adopted
a slightly different approach to Trickster. He argued that Trickster is not only
the dark, demonic figure of Jung's analysis—one who has gradually been
overwritten to obscure or obliterate his anarchic and chaotic persona—but,
"in the Palaeolithic sphere out of which [he] originates, he was the archetype
of the hero, the giver of all great boons—the fire-bringer and the teacher of
mankind" (Campbell 1969, 274). This does not imply that he does not
subscribe to the idea that Trickster is a symptom of the unconscious; indeed,
in this and in much else he agrees with Jung (Campbell 1949 and 1993, 257).
However, he places more emphasis on the creative dimensions of the
trickster than Jung. This, however, doesn't result in the erasure of the
disruptive, contesting, slightly dangerous elements. These too have to be
retained, though Campbell does suggest that Christianity's concern with
good and evil has had some displacement effect on the creative energy
embodied in the trickster (see also Davidson, 1964). As much as he is a thief
and a clown, trickster is importantly also a creator and destroyer. In Greek
mythology, Russo (1997) argues, both Hermes and Prometheus are the
products of extensive rewriting that has erased the more disconcerting
elements of the trickster. In extant Greek mythological records, Prometheus
and Hermes, the two divine trickster-figures, lack the emphatically trouble-
making character seen in the caprice of Loki or Wakdjunkaga[9]. The Greek
attitude towards both is consistently positive. Prometheus "is a great founder
of culture, the bringer of fire and subsequent technologies, whose trickiness
is exercised at the expense of Zeus and on behalf of human kind" (ibid, 243).
It was he, whom Shelley thought to single out, over any other mythical
character, including Satan, because of "his courage and majesty, and firm
and patient opposition to omnipotent force" (Shelley 1967, 205). In
Prometheus Unbound, Shelley echoes Prometheus' own words (Aeschylus

1961, Lines 199–263). His contribution to humankind is summed up in the voice of the chorus of spirits who have lately,

> Come from the mind of human kind
> Which was late so dusk, and obscene, and blind
> [but] Now 'tis an ocean of clear emotion
> A heaven of serene and mighty motion

(Shelley 1967, 256)

Here, Shelley is recognising Prometheus' role as a historicised force of social transformation. While manifesting differences from Prometheus, Hermes too offers much to our self-understanding. He is, after all, not just the ferryman but also the god of the threshold or limen and, as Pelton observes, the trickster is above all a symbol of both the man and the liminal state itself, which is a "source of recreative power" (1980, 35). Whatever might be the truth of the trickster, in these Greek gods he has certainly been softened, but if so, particularly in the case of Prometheus, it is at the service of an increasingly expansive vision of human being. The trickster then represents myriad and powerful forces of creative energy and, with some facility. It is these refractions of Trickster identity that point to the possibility of seeing him as a metaphor, which is particularly helpful in developing a liminal conception of the teacher.

So far I have suggested that both schools and teachers are embodiments of contradictory and ambiguous attitudes in the polity more generally, and that the increasing attempts to define and tie down the practices and persona of the teacher reflect a deep-seated unease with the antinomian potential of schools and education. This anxiety, of course, comes increasingly to the fore as the discourse of corporation and state becomes ever more closely and carefully articulated. After all, as the financial pundits are forever telling us at the close of the evening news programme, the markets do not like uncertainty!

I have so far reflected briefly on the genealogy of the trickster as one who, while embodying the dark side of human nature, also offers a freshness, energy and, following Prometheus, the gift of hope to human beings. In the next section I should like to develop this theme a little further through a brief excurses into trickster emanations in Celtic literature. Emanations, where the trickster also embodies the Bakhtinian (Bakhtin 1968)[10] themes of laughter, absurdity, parody, comedy and social inversion as well as the festive, imaginative and adversarial powers of great antiquity (Cox 1969, 7–11; see also Welsford 1935). In this, tricksters are both progenitors and embodiments of the carnivalesque.[11] It is precisely these qualities that make the trickster eminently suitable as a liminal metaphor for the teacher. If our attitudes to education, schooling and the teacher are subject to the kinds of contradictions reflected upon at the opening of this chapter, then it is possible that the trickster may help to surface those ambiguities and use them creatively to energise the discursive potential (and arguably, end) of education.

The Celtic Trickster as Teacher

The trickster motif has remained both an enduring and resilient motif in Celtic culture and literature up to the present time. This may be because the Celts were more primitive than other Europeans. After all, Jung suggests, "outwardly people are more or less civilised, but inwardly they are still primitives. Something in man is profoundly disinclined to give up his beginnings, and something else believes it has long since got beyond that" (1972, 149). Given that until very recently, Celts, particularly the Irish, were more religious than other Europeans it might be suggested that the enduring interest and expressions of the liminal is a function of their primitive religiosity. However, such a connection is fairly unlikely given that; first, the inside-outside dichotomy is itself illusory; and second, there are long-established and complex literary and cultural traditions in the worlds of the Celts. Moreover, the complex history of the struggle between trickster motifs and emanations, and particular forms of Christianity going back through the rise of Jansenism to the counter-Reformation, and beyond would suggest quite different reasons for his durability. It is perhaps more reasonable to ascribe his resilience in Celtic culture and literature to a liminal response to the history of cultural subjection to England. Here the trickster motif may be seen as a source of power and resistance, facilitating the disengagement from those primary social signifiers seen to derive from English cultural supremacy. In both Scotland and Ireland this response was expressed in the persistence and the renewal of ancient, pre-Christian trickster traditions and stories with their extensive associations with liminality, borderlands and unexpected change (Muldoon 2000, Ch.1).[12] So it is that trickster lore continues to this day to exercise a powerful influence in the texts and the attitudes of the Celtic peoples of Scotland and Ireland; an influence that may be considered both seminal and standard in the production of regional and national identity, while simultaneously laying such potentially reified categories open to the voices of multicultural diversity and difference.

A virtual pantheon of Celtic writers, ancient and modern, stands as the embodiment of the trickster principle of opposition to discursive closure and its attendant practices. These include archaic culture heroes, such as Merlin,

Sweeney and Taliesin, through to key modernist and later writers, such as Flann O'Brien, Seamus Heaney, Paul Muldoon, Hugh MacDiarmid and Edwin Morgan. These modern writers embody that perennial ambiguity that exists between the centre and the periphery. In both their work and their own positions as literary figures they articulate the trickster myth within an overarching concern with the language of ambiguity. Thus are writers and texts woven together into a kind of tapestry of the trickster. In this sense, it is as meaningless to ask whether one is primarily interested in the texts or in the writer as a trickster, as it is to ask whether one is more interested in the person of Joyce than that of Bloom or Daedelus.

The roots of the specifically Celtic trickster figure, and the sources of his continuing influence, lie in the complex series of cultural and linguistic negotiations through which Celtic identity has been formed in Scotland and Ireland from ancient times down to the modern era. The transactions between the Celtic peoples, and their ambivalent relationship with their populous and dominant neighbour, England, have made the Atlantic archipelago a seemingly classic setting for the enactment of the centre-periphery model of national and ethnic self-definition (Hay 1968; Burke 1992). However, while the notion of a particular Celtic conscious may, on occasion, appear a little historically contrived, it is nevertheless clear that, even in an imagined form, it has given rise to alternative and culturally situated readings of history, power and identity. For the Celtic peoples of Scotland and Ireland, the continuing ambiguity of their relations with England has been felt most keenly at the level of language. The colonial impact of English imperialism is most immediately obvious in the fact that English is the main language of both Scotland and Ireland, pushing the aboriginal Gaelic tongues of each country into regional enclaves. In both Scotland and Ireland, nonetheless, separate and distinctive educational systems have flourished for centuries as vital compensating forces in the protection of national prestige and cultural difference. These systems have roots running deep into the medieval origins of each nation, and they are widely recognised as carrying within them cultural memories that antedate English influence and that have served as invaluable resources in the resistance to English hegemony. Education in Scotland and Ireland can therefore legitimately be said to face both ways: the withering of native languages in the face of the ubiquity of English language and culture is balanced by the deliberate and self-conscious preservation of a living literary heritage with atavistic sources in the indigenous folk and mythological traditions. The trickster has been an enduring presence in the desire to maintain a different sense of identity and self. Equally, those who would attempt to domesticate culture and identity have felt his presence as an eruptive and disquieting figure at the margins, constantly pressing them towards an imagined authenticity.

In the protomyth of the Celtic trickster, a doomed wild man or poet figure is driven mad by the catastrophic outcome of a huge battle to which he is witness. Overwhelmed by grief and loss, the poet flees to the woods, discarding the raiment and trappings of civilisation, abandoning rational discourse and classical utterance, and taking upon himself the mantle of the theriomorphic shaman (O'Riain 1972). From his forest habitat, the Wild Man assumes the status of an oracle or prophet, scorning the values of society and vilifying the deeds and the motives of the rich and powerful. In the legends that surround the British Saint Kentigern, or Mungo (Patron Saint and first Bishop of Glasgow), the Wild Man is Lailoken or Myrddin (a forerunner of the wizard Merlin of Arthurian romance). He rails against the hypocrisies and immorality of the kings and nobles whom Kentigern seeks to convert. He interrupts Kentigern's services by sitting on a nearby rock and uttering obscure prophecies. He repines bitterly at his own condition, yet pleads with the saint to receive the Blessed Sacrament. Moved by pity, Kentigern recognises the deep bond of brotherhood that exists between saint and seer, and finally consents to reconcile Lailoken to the Church (Jarman 1991).

In the Irish version of the story, the *Buile Suibhne* (*Frenzy of Sweeney*), the Wild Man suffers periodic recurrences of his battle-panic and at these moments can fly like a bird among the treetops. Seamus Heaney, in the preface to his own rendition of the tale, celebrates its trans-Celtic provenance and sees Sweeney in universal terms as "a figure of the artist, displaced, guilty, assuaging himself by his utterance...an aspect of the quarrel between free creative imagination and the constraints of religious, political and domestic obligation." (1983, 2)

> I am Sweeney, the whinger,
> the scuttler in the valley.
> But call me, instead,
> peak-pate, Stag-head
>
> Forever mendicant,
> my rags all frayed and scanty,
> high in the mountains
> like a crazed, frost-bitten sentry.
>
> (Heaney 1983, 2)

Heaney's account of the Sweeney myth makes explicit the identification of trickster and poet which is such a marked theme of the Celtic heritage. The

Wild Man's antisocial marginalisation has profound implications for the language of the poetic voice. In the conditions of Celtic self-understanding, the poet is institutionally alienated from, yet dependent on, his society. His status as prophet and oracle accords him a quasi-religious respect, but his scandalous behaviour and contumely induce embarrassment and discomfort in his listeners because they imply "the suggestion that any particular ordering of experience may be arbitrary and subjective" (Douglas 1968, 365).

This tradition of the literary figure as trickster in Irish culture surfaces again in the twentieth century, and its outworkings and implications emerge in the writings of James Joyce, Flann O'Brien, Seamus Heaney and Paul Muldoon. Flann O'Brien, the comic novelist and columnist with *The Irish Times* from the 1940s to the mid-1960s, embodies a singularly Celtic account of the notion of the literary trickster in both his own persona and in his writings. Constantly oscillating between his Gaelic and English identities,[13] O'Brien embodied the foundational principle of the trickster—as one who confounds the listener/reader, moving between different life-worlds and enabling them to be interwoven into new patterns so as to chastise as well as inform each other. He also switches between the language of the "oppressed" and that of the "oppressor." Sometimes a work will be penned in Gaelic, sometimes in English and sometimes the same text will draw on both, trafficking between the two. In a comic version of Joyce, O'Brien changes idiom and subject, moving seamlessly from the aphorisms of the vernacular to a comment on Keats or Goethe. So, in one of his columns in *The Irish Times* he opens with an extract from Keats' sonnet on the four seasons of man:

[H]e has his summer, when luxuriously
Spring's honeyed end of youthful thought he loves
To ruminate, and by such dreaming nigh
Is the nearest unto heaven; quiet coves
His soul has in its Autumn, when his wings
His furleth close.

(Keats *The Human Seasons*, 1998 232)

Having led his reader into the heart of English Romanticism, O'Brien immediately turns Keats' meditation on its head through the jibe that for Keats, "This is largely hearsay or guess work...[given that he] dies when he was a boy" (na Gopaleen 1968, 80). He then goes on to rework the central motifs of the poem, opining that,

> There is nothing I like better than an evening with a few quiet coves in the dimmer corner of a pub, murmuring together in friendship the judgements of our mature minds. As regards furling my wings close, that is also true enough. To spend a whole bob or a tanner in one go entails suffering. My little pension is woefully inelastic. A wing or two saved in ordering porter instead of stout is not to be despised. A borrowed match, a cadged filling of the pipe, all small things mount mightily in a year. (ibid)

His interlocutors in this, as in many other pieces, are "the plain people of Ireland," a description that embodies more than a hint of irony. Elsewhere, O'Brien's wit and parody serve to upbraid, in turn, the English, the intellectuals of Ireland, those who would deem themselves cultured, and in the case of the Irish, those who see themselves as morally, politically and culturally superior—the patriots.[14]

At the time of O'Brien's most productive work, Ireland was in the throes of shaking off its colonial past and emerging as a modern liberal democracy (albeit one that embraced a vestigial theocracy). In asserting its post-colonial identity it was busily establishing and reinforcing the iconographic status of all those patriots who traced and expressed their fealty to an image of Ireland that ran back through the rebellions and revolutionaries of 1916 and 1798, the Presbyterian Enlightenment figures of the late-eighteenth century, the heroic deeds of Brian Boru in the middle ages—to the mythic heroes of the Red Branch Knights and Cuchulainn himself. It was, by and large, not a good time to call into question Ireland's image of itself. The idea that there should, or even could be any ambiguity surrounding Celtic (in this case, Gaelic) identity would not only not have been much in evidence but would have been regarded with complete opprobrium in the public spaces. Attacks on the enemy across the Irish Sea were not in short supply and, while O'Brien was not shy about directing his withering gaze towards the English, they were not the objects of his scribing. The trickster's play is primarily directed at his own traditions and culture, and not at that of the outsider or enemy. O'Brien's tricksterishness was to prove no exception to the general trend. His liminal persona is worked out, and requires, to be understood in the context of specifically Irish notions of national identity and moral superiority, identity and superiority that arose out of that most passive of "virtues": being oppressed. Nowhere in O'Brien's work or biography is the transformative quality of the inside/outside more apparent than in *An Béal Bocht*[15], first penned in 1941. All the shibboleths of Irishness are here turned on their head: the innocent potato, the mainstay of the Irish (folkloric) diet is utterly transformed into the food of the gods, which, in this particular instance, happen to be the pigs who are regarded as more prized than the humans. The pigs inhabit not just the house but, more importantly, the spot in front of the fire! Even more tellingly, O'Brien—originally under the na Gopaleen *nom de plume*—parodies the great revivalists of the Irish language and culture; those who see themselves as "Gaels" on a moral crusade to restore Irishness and its language as the means by which they can overcome the oppression of being forced to speak in English. So at a Feis[16] in the west of Ireland, created by the eastern gentry, the self-appointed President delivers a stirring oration.

> Gaels! he said, it delights my Gaelic heart to be here today speaking Gaelic with you at this Gaelic feis in the centre of the Gaeltacht....We are all Gaelic Gaels of Gaelic lineage. He who is Gaelic will be Gaelic evermore. If we're truly Gaelic, we must constantly discuss the question of the Gaelic revival and the question of Gaelicism. There is no use in having Gaelic, if we converse in it on non-Gaelic topics...I don't think the Government is earnest about Gaelic, I don't think they are Gaelic at heart. (O'Brien 1973, 54)

O'Brien continues with this parody at some length, which, while amusing for the reader of the English translation, is much more potent in the original Gaelic. The verbose, self-appointed guardians of Gaelic heritage had, in truth, little enough in common with the residual native speakers. At, and immediately prior to the time O'Brien was writing, a virtual host of Gaelic biographies were being penned, the most famous of which was *An tOileánach*[17] by the Blasketman, Tomás Ó Criomhthain. O'Brien's *An Béal Bocht* is a deliberate parody of this genre, which tended to receive critical acclaim irrespective of its frequently limited literary merit. His scepticism was seen everywhere in this and a number of his other works, including *At Swim-Two-Birds*. It emerges again and again through his hijacking and distortion or repetition of a number of clichéd Irish proverbs and sayings, some of which are deployed by Ó Criomthain to reinforce the authentic provenance of his Islandman as the embodiment of the noble, rural, Gaelic and singular peasant Irishman. These included a quotation used on the title page of *An tOileánach*. *Ni beheidh ár leithéidi ann aŕis* (Our likes will never be again) (See Farnon, 1997) His choice of Gaelic as the medium of this particular novel is an integral feature of his tricksterish disposition. To use the internal modalities of cultural assertion as a way of critiquing the delinquent misappropriation of those very modalities is indeed a trick. This trick is even more pointed when it is realised that O'Brien thought Joyce wrong to have turned his back on his own Gaelic heritage in favour of classical sources as the mythological frame for *Ulysses* (Ó Hainle 1997).

It might be thought that O'Brien would be primarily interested in satirising the old enemy—the colonisers who had established and sustained the centre-periphery disequilibrium that had kept Irish-language custom and identity *beyond the pale*. But these were not his primary target. He was much more interested in resisting the hegemonising tendencies that can come in the wake of a cultural reassertion and political centring of myth so that myth itself, instead of offering a language of liberation can become an ensnarement. This somewhat provocative trope in his work finds resonances in recent indigenous historical scholarship in Scotland and Ireland that has cast doubt on the local applicability of the centre-periphery model by challenging accepted understandings of a shared, universalised Celtic consciousness (Pittock 1999). It has vigorously critiqued essentialist and historically continuous conceptions of the Celtic, drawing attention to a more contingent and constructed series of representations of the Celtic heritage, mediated by competing cultural and political ideologies.

Even in turning his eye inwards, O'Brien doesn't limit himself to the political and discursive closure that embraced the Irish language but extends his gaze to include attitudes to religion, sex and individuality. Irishness and Gaelic culture in the 1940s was largely synonymous with a particular rendering of Catholicism; to be authentically Irish was to be Catholic and, in consequence, to be dutiful and respectful of a Church that also claimed for itself a kind of originary status grounded in the pre-history myths of the *Fianna,* the Irish giant warriors and those other figures touched upon above. Given that Irish culture, language and history was mediated in the first half of the twentieth century by the Catholic clergy with their grip on the sexual politics of Ireland meant that O'Brien's gyrations were not held captive by his attention on the cultural revivalists but extended beyond to these other underlying, ecclesial influences. Even more, while his parody of Ó Criomthain's work (and that of other Irish cultural revivalists, such as Standish O'Grady) was relentless, he nevertheless admired him deeply (O'Hainle 1997, 36). It would be too easy to reduce O'Brien to a mere satirist who construed the Irish cultural revival as little more than cant.

The point at issue is not O'Brien's wit or satire, nor his literary or critical abilities, nor yet his inventive modernism, irrespective of the undoubted brilliance that he displayed in all of these. O'Brien falls truly into the Irish tradition of learned poet-fool and story teller: the *seanchaidhe,* or *shanachie* (Harrison 1989). The *seanchaidhe* is not just a storyteller, he is "an antiquary, historian or genealogist...one who traces relationships, [and is] versed in folklore" (Dinneen 1927, 1007). He draws upon the past to challenge the follies of the present. He stands as a foil to Rorty's (1999) claim that cultural heritage is no more than a bag of tricks. But, important as all this might be for pointing to him as a cultural critic, a voice on the margin, on its own it is insufficient. What distinguishes O'Brien is his existence, as Boston has it, as one who is "both outside the norms of society and at the same time somewhere very near the centre of human experience" (Boston 1974, 93). More than this even, he is one who loves his traditions but is prepared to turn them on their head to achieve the needed effect. He is capable of holding contrary opinions simultaneously. Those behind the Gaelic revival would never be able to castigate him as an outsider, nor would they be able to embrace him as one of us. Rather, O'Brien is in that long line of Irish poets, seers and teachers whose capacity to challenge and satirise the seats of power, whether they be king, priest or bureaucrat, is predicated upon their being deeply rooted in the exact same traditions upon which king, priest or bureaucrat build their own cathedra. He is unequivocally rooted in the anti-power stories of Ireland that go back to the pre-middle ages figure, Anier MacConglinne, and beyond. Both O'Brien and the narrators of his tales fall within the trickster tradition—that is, as "beneficent culture hero, ...clever deceiver, or the numskull" (Welsford 1935, 88–93). Indeed, both he and his tellers constantly weave in and out of these roles.

The Trickster as a Liminal Representation of the Teacher

At the opening of this chapter, I argued that the role and identity of teacher as both pedagogue and administrator has been increasingly subjected to the discursive closure that has absorbed education in particular, and conceptions of human flourishing in general. I have also sketched some of the ambiguous attitudes towards teachers in the wider polity; attitudes that are themselves, in part, refractions of adult anxieties about the potential unruliness of large numbers of adolescents and in part, a by-product of the discursive closure. Standing against this has been the articulation of the trickster as an oppositional metaphor to such closure. His force derives from a complex network of related dispositions that have both evolved in and been captured by the trickster over time and geography. Even those primitive palaeolithic incarnations have something to offer our understanding of the teacher as one who is charged with entering into and accompanying students in the transitional space of the school. Because of the peculiarly modern concerns with resisting ideological closure and willingness, nay desire, to live the life of ambiguity, the modern Celtic trickster is particularly useful in this regard. In this final section I wish to weave the trickster into a liminal conception of the teacher and her role. Admittedly, this is not a straightforward task since it may not be argued that the teacher, much less the head-teacher, can ignore the cultural expectations of the wider polity. Additionally, the teacher is not a poet or shaman but an educator. Against this, it should be remembered that what is being advocated is the cultivation of the liminal as a trope in education. There is no expectation that the teacher has to be a trickster all the time, or indeed that every teacher has to be a full-blown trickster. But the trickster, as a liminal expression of the educative possibilities of a discursively open liberal democracy, may offer a pathway that circumvents the closure of the markets while remaining faithful to broader considerations about human flourishing.

The trickster performs this task because, as Prometheus, he is prepared to stand against powerful elites. He embodies the human desire to have a way of accessing knowledge, wisdom and insight. He is an advocate for human advancement and flourishing in the face of Zeus' desire to keep humanity in a diminished state. Every now and then we should expect our teachers to stand for their students as human subjects and not as objects to be tested and prepared for a particular, monoglot expression of flourishing. As Hermes, the teacher-trickster is one who stands at the limen, at the doorway between the world of the politically and economically powerful and the world of the student in all her incarnations. He is, as I hope to demonstrate a little more in the next chapter, the one who can help and guide the student in her growth towards wisdom. Moreover, as Hermes is the patron and teacher of all the arts (including the sciences), so too is the schoolteacher. The teacher must share something of the Hermes-trickster's reverence for mystery (see Campbell 1949 and 1993, 73). In a culture that, despite the alleged religious fervour of many political leaders, has eschewed the desirability, or even existence of mystery, the liminality of the trickster is an important potential corrective.

As I suggested in the opening section, the role of the teacher is hedged with ambiguity. From a variety of quite disparate perspectives this ambiguity is not something to be resolved but lived with and once again, our metaphor may be seen as hermeneutically helpful. As a shape-shifter the teacher may move back and forth across the terrain of education, now supporting the status quo, now challenging it. As the student resolves one difficulty the teacher should excite her imagination with a new one. The teacher is a foil, playing with ideas as she journeys with her students. The teacher-trickster is constantly open to the new, while at the same time maintaining roots in her cultural history and traditions. Laughter may be deemed an important feature of the intellectually and personally robust classroom. The dual bequest of the Celtic trickster to modern Irish and Scottish literature is communicated most sharply in the traditions of comedy, underlining William Hynes' insight that "the Trickster's humour melds entertainment and education" (1993, 20). The teacher has to draw on this insight, most especially in a culture where entertainment itself has often been reduced to a cipher for consumption. To be a trickster-teacher is to embody a way of being a teacher where texts are opened to the unsettling influences and counter-readings of pleasure, joy, sexuality, ethnicity, embodiment and laughter; where new readings and innovative methodologies are sought at the edges of texts, where readers connect with cultural expressions in unexpected ways. Inhabiting the role of the trickster, the teacher harnesses the energies of childhood and adolescence not to deface established texts but to reanimate them pedagogically, attending to those areas of meaning and language choice that mainstream readings overlook or actively repress. The teacher opens zones of learning to the unorthodox, the prohibited interpretation, and the manipulation and recasting of texts into new and unprecedented forms. Clearly, the image fits best when applied to the teacher of personal and social education and the humanities, such as religious education, literature and the arts, but it is not their exclusive prerogative. Equally, the maths and science teacher may be expected to don the cloak of the trickster, to play with number, to imagine the absence of number, to open up different understandings of the way in which number shapes, and is used to shape, the way we look at ourselves. The connections between number, harmonics and the vibrations of the universe may, with the perspective of the trickster, open up new possibilities for play.

In following O'Brien, the trickster in the classroom is never merely an outcast figure, a high-minded maverick condemned to institutional incomprehension and intellectual martyrdom. Such a figure would fail to communicate with his audience while the authentic trickster revels in a surfeit of communication with his interlocutors. One has only to think of O'Brien's deep attachment to the very culture he is compelled to critique to see this at play. The teacher-trickster also has to have the capacity to connect the interior world of the student with the world of shared experience. In other words she stands in an in-between space. As one who inhabits such a liminal position the teacher must, for example, help students to subject the mainstays of democracy to constant scrutiny precisely in order to sustain and protect themselves and the world. In a world where the value systems of students appear to be different from those of their parents (but not as different as might often be claimed), the teacher has to be in touch with both, moving from one to the other and back again; shifting shape and offering a challenge to both worlds.

A Few Queries

There are a number of reasons why the trickster might be regarded as an unsuitable metaphor for the teacher in late-industrial society. First, it might be suggested that the teacher is not a poet and that it is a mistake to confuse her role with that of the mythic or poetic or trickster voice. Second, the discursive, somewhat unpredictable and at times downright mischievous character of the trickster makes it difficult to see how he could be a metaphor in the structured environment of the classroom. Third, some might see this metaphor as no distinctively different from that of the discursive contests as advocated by postmoderns or critical pedagogues. Finally, it may be argued that teaching is a professional (or similar) practice that is funded out of a public purse for public ends determined, according to liberal-democratic principles, by government. Rather than spend energy on re-imagining themselves as Trickster, teachers would be more usefully employed improving their skills base in order to enhance students' literary or arithmetic capabilities.

Let me briefly take each one of these in turn. It is true that the teacher is not the poet, nor should she be regarded as performing the same function, but she does have a poetic role in as much as poetry is concerned with the disclosure of the world. The teacher, through her craft no doubt, but more importantly through her person and disposition, facilitates this disclosure by giving voice to the myriad ways that human beings come to construe and make sense of the world. She facilitates her students in their naming of the world. Her voice may carry different inflections from those of the poet but they share overlapping intentions. To suggest anything less is to confuse education with training, and while training may be a perfectly noble activity it is not education. With regard to the second point, it may be argued that there are particular representations of and elements within the trickster myth that might seem inappropriate in the context of the classroom. Surely, one might say, we do not wish for teachers who are licentious and rapacious, we do not wish for teachers who are liars and cheats, even where they manage to make everything turn out okay. Clearly there are trickster figures, particularly in early cultures, who might not be seen as suitable "role models" or metaphors. The answer is both straightforward and complicated. Just as the metaphor of the liminal has an openness that can, on occasion, be somewhat disturbing and carry a "down side," so too with that of the trickster. But in both instances what we are concerned with is the development of open metaphors and that requires us to flirt a little with some of these difficulties.

As we have seen already there is always a liminal dimension to education, precisely because the school sits at the interstices of the privacy of the home and the world of public appearance. The interstitial always carries an element of the unpredictable. In any event, given that children in liberal democracies regularly encounter the shadow side of human being (in film, narrative, news, divorce, bereavement), then it would be tantamount to naivety to suggest that whatever metaphors we use for the teachers' role must draw only on those images and models untainted by the experience of living. Moreover, there is no suggestion that the teacher becomes the trickster per se. (After all, assiduously pursuing Flann O'Brien's path of "dying from the drink" is hardly to be recommended as a course of action for the average teacher!) In the way in which it has been used here metaphor is not syntagmatic—we are not replacing the term teacher with trickster, we are learning from the polyvalence of the trickster to inform our liminal conception of the teacher. It is more that the discursive closure around the role and identity of the teacher is in danger of squeezing out the excitement and perennial freshness of teaching as a naming of the world. The teacher-Trickster is a liminal metaphor and as such will always be at the threshold but, as with laughter and play, indeed with the liminal itself, it throws light on the teacher's role and engagements. Like the trickster, the teacher inhabits a borderland—in this instance between the world of adults and the world of children and adolescents; between the education of the self and preparation for public activity; between the ethically desirable and the reprehensible; between educating for a critical stance and education for social cohesion; and between world and school.

Finally, the image of the teacher-Trickster is a liminal one, and in its liminality there is no expectation that the classroom or school is likely to be turned into bedlam. It is rather that the teacher's disposition towards the openness of possibility is being nurtured through the application and embrasure of the metaphor. Here, O'Brien's relationship to the centre is instructive. Not only does he know and use the traditions of his culture—this would always be necessary if one wishes to turn such things on their head—he *loves* them. It is this passion for the world that gives him permission to upbraid those who would hijack and close it down. By simultaneously revering and reconfiguring both the dominant language and the other tongues and cultures with which it coexists, his work is a response to the pervasive presence of an historically conflicted linguistic culture, etched with a history of displacement and oppression. At a time when schooling is subjected to a similarly conflicted culture, the teacher has to move back and forth between the imperatives of government and corporations on the one hand and the claims of students on the other to access a suitably complex education. In having to meet the marks set by government, the teacher partakes in the hegemony of schooling. In inverting, challenging and, here and there, displaying a scurrilous distaste for conformity, she partakes in the heteronomy of the world. To see the teacher as a permanent trickster would not only be self-defeating, it would be to miss the point.

Conclusion

This chapter has offered a discursively enhanced and rather more complex understanding of the teacher's role and occupational persona. Such an understanding mirrors the increasingly complex and diffuse engagements and experiences of late-industrial society. Of course, it can be argued that the trickster is predestined by his own nature to sit uncomfortably at the edges of educational acceptance in even the most utopian of contexts. For him to be comfortably recuperated by such a mainstream institution of cultural authority would represent an abrogation of everything we have come to see him embody. To find ways of inhabiting the zone of ambiguity is one of the central challenges for the teacher of literature or religion, moral or personal development, art or science. But it would be a mistake to think that many teachers, even headteachers and principals, do not already endorse tricksterish elements in their own engagements. Many spend much energy on finding ways of ameliorating the effects of discursive closure and government fiat in so far as they think these harmful. Many others develop pedagogies that soften the arithmetic imperatives of the technicist, competence-driven culture within which teachers' role, identity and occupational practices are increasingly framed. In any event, as I suggested at the beginning of this chapter, discussions of the status and occupational nature of the teacher already locates her in zones of ambiguity. Indeed, in her exploration of Lévi-Strauss' work with the Tsimshian people of the northernmost part of the Pacific Northwest, Mary Douglas offers a telling insight into the world of the trickster myth that could hardly be more apposite for the teacher.

> On the assumption that it is of the nature of myth to mediate contradictions, the method of analysis must proceed by distinguishing the oppositions and the mediating elements. And it follows too that the function of myth is to portray the contradictions in the basic premises of the culture. The same goes for the relation of myth to social reality. The myth is a contemplation of the unsatisfactory which after all composes social life. (1967, 52)

In education, the trickster myth may be seen in precisely this light, as a myth-metaphor that portrays the basic contradictions in our social attitudes to teachers and, at the same time, enables us to both contemplate and live with such contradiction.

Notes

1. In Britain this scrutiny has been manifest not only in performance-related target setting but also in the accelerating predilection for suing doctors, lawyers, social workers and teachers. In those instances where someone dies, or fails to get what they wanted, or feels that they have been subject to abuse. Even for those who have never heard of Foucault, expertise is increasingly subject to certain scepticism.

2. In using teacher here I am aware that there are other kinds of teacher in higher/further education, but these constitute a quite different category.

3. For after all, in England and Wales a Teacher Training Authority controls access to and control of the approval and inspection of courses for teaching.

4. For further testament to the ubiquity of the notion of skills, targets and competences together with the almost complete absence of any reference to theoretical foundations, it is worth perusing the Teacher Training Agency's website: www.canteach.gov.uk.

5. See earlier comments on Winch's discussion on the moral desirability of education for work.

6. The rather prosaic and mundane motivations of teachers are revealed in the extensive Mori survey commissioned by the General Teaching Council of England and Wales, concerning teacher attitudes carried out in November 2002. Asked to list three factors that led them into a career in teaching, 62 percent said that they "just fell into it," and 48 percent, that they failed to achieve the grades they wanted for the course they wanted. In response to the request that they list three reasons why they remain in the profession, only 3 percent said it was because it afforded them professional autonomy. It would be interesting to compare such responses to other occupations, such as medicine, pharmacy, law, financial services and so on.

7. For Castoriadis the arithmetic is myth because it fundamentally shapes the way in which human societies look at themselves, their goals and their existence. "There is," he says, "no society without arithmetic. There is no society without myth. In today's society, arithmetic is, of course one of the main myths. There is not and cannot be a 'rational' basis for the domination of quantification in society. Quantification is merely the expression of one of its dominant imaginary significations" (1977, 11). For a more extensive discussion of Castoriadis' views and a different perspective on some of these ideas, see Conroy and Davis 2002.

8. For entertaining and apposite examples of the enduring popularity of the trickster as protagonist in children's stories, see Gerald McDermott's series of trickster tales, published by Voyager/Harcourt Inc.

9. The Winnebago Trickster.

10. In Rabelais and his World, Mikhail Bakhtin has carefully developed the themes of the carnivalesque and humour as central motifs in medieval culture and polity. These he believed represented sites of legitimated resistance to the hegemonising tendencies of the ruling classes.

11. There are of course a variety of positions on the socio-psychological and religious functions of the carnivalesque (of which the trickster, as we have

intimated here, is one manifestation). Bahktin promotes the existence of the carnivalesque as an intimation of the deeply rooted need for subversion and inversion. Others such as Terry Eagleton maintain that these figures, plays and performances serve only to reinforce the ethico-religious and socio-political status quo. In her study, "Parody in the Middle Ages," Bayless (1996) suggests that recent anthropological studies point to the legitimacy of both conclusions and that the important determinative factors are time and place.

12.   In his fascinating set of lectures, Paul Muldoon discloses the transformative and liminal qualities of Irish mythico-literary figures going back to the reputedly first Irish poet, Amergin. In his discussion of a poem by William Allingham that tells the story of an eviction (an everyday event in Ireland and Scotland throughout the nineteenth century), he sees in the figure of the old man being evicted "the image of a critically positioned figure, a figure who is neither here nor there, at some notional interface [who] may be traced back beyond the mid-nineteenth-century Ireland…to some deep-seated sense of liminality that was, and is, central to the Irish psyche" (Muldoon 2000, 8). In his own poetic works such as *Hay*, (1998) Muldoon is himself the embodiment of the Trickster, playing with, inverting and changing traditional forms and the relation of himself as author to these forms.

13.   Flann O'Brien is one of two pseudonyms of the Northern Irish modernist writer and columnist, Brian O'Nolan. His other is Myles Na Gopaleen.

14.   Interestingly, a term given a new valence in the light of Martin Scorsese's film, Gangs of New York.

15.   "The Poor Mouth."

16.   The Islandman.

17.   Again, further detail about the complexity of the centre-periphery relations in Great Britain and Ireland is to be found in Conroy and Davis (2002).

Chapter 5

Poetry, Liminality and the Education of the Imagination

The Star Tribes

Look, among the boughs. Those stars are men.
There's Ngintu, with his dogs,
who guards the skins of Everlasting Water in the sky.
And there's the Crow-man, carrying on his back
the wounded Hawk-man. There's the Serpent, Thurroo,
glistening in the leaves. There's Kapeetah,
The Moon-man, sitting in his mia-mia.

And there's those Seven sisters, travelling
Across the sky. They make the real cold frost.
You hear them when you're camped out on the plains.

Aboriginal Oral Tradition (Related by Fred Biggs in Murray 1986)

Introduction

The previous chapter focused on the trickster as a metaphorical expression of the liminal possibilities of the persona of teacher. Here, attention turns to the pedagogies and practices of education as a primary site for the instantiation of the metaphor. Liminal approaches to teaching and learning provide an important site for the maintenance of discursive openness. Clearly, some parts of the curriculum are more hospitable than others to the discursive cadences of the liminal. Those areas of human experience and reflection that engage with the ambiguity of our relationship with our selves, with other selves and with the world tend to be most amenable to the possibilities of liminality. As I have already suggested, aesthetics, religion, and personal, moral and social development have the potential to be fertile ground for the approach developed in this volume. However, this does not mean that other areas of the curriculum that appear to engage with the facts of the material world are not susceptible to the modification brought about by the liminal metaphor. Clearly, in a single chapter it is not possible to deal with the whole curriculum, or even a very small part of it. In such a case it makes sense to focus on one or two areas while demonstrating the possible lines of connection between these and other areas of inquiry. In this instance I wish to concentrate on the generic field of the aesthetic, and within this, more particularly on the poetic. I choose this for a number of reasons connected with the relationship between its liminal status, both in the public spaces of a liberal democracy and in the school curriculum. Perhaps more obviously than any other part of the aesthetic curriculum (though all have fared badly in late-industrial liberal democracies), the poetic has been truly marginalised. By this, I do not mean to suggest that poetry is not used in the classroom for purposes of such things as language development and cultural solidarity. Indeed, the difficulty is that it is used but not, as C. S. Lewis put it, "received" (1961, 19). Educational policy and planning in Scotland mirrors trends elsewhere in being increasingly driven by the instrumental and economic priorities of the global market that require even the arts and language domains of the curriculum to align themselves with the aims of competitive capitalism (Scottish Consultative Council on the Curriculum 1999). While this marginalisation may be regarded as deplorable, the appropriate response may not be to attempt to establish or re-establish it at the heart of the late-industrial curriculum. This merely smacks of nostalgia or naïveté. And, in any event, placed in the centre it is likely to loose its power for evoking dissenus. Nevertheless, we can hardly ignore a form of human thought and expression that Carr (2003b) argues is, at the very least, amenable to normative appraisal in terms of its possible contribution to practical wisdom of an Aristotelian kind. Despite the temptation to argue for a rehabilitation of poetry in the centre of educational provision this may not be the most propitious approach, since it exposes the poetic to the hegemonising stratagems of domestication and debilitation. Better to see it as a liminal aspect of the curriculum. Such a claim underpins the discussion in this chapter which, in turn, surfaces a number of the features of the poetic that both establish its interstitial status and mark it out as a possible site of resistance against the impulses of discursive closure. To do this I intend to follow a number of contiguous lines of enquiry. First, I explore how the poetic stands at the threshold of the political and the personal, the self and the world and subjectivity and objectivity. Second, I reflect on how its subject matter and mode of entering into the world militates against closure. Meaningful to the extent that it can frame and be framed by metaphor, poetry lends itself to the ambiguity that attends all human exchange. Finally, I look at how the poetic imagination keeps the possibilities of openness and wonder, when other, more centrist discourses in and around the curriculum, are supplicant to the closure of the senses.

Discursive Closure and the Marginality of Poetry

It is difficult to imagine discursive closure arising in those contexts where there is ready access to a range of competing claims to and expressions of human purpose and value. In other words, a doorway to a language that is, in some sense, worthy of the complexity of the world. Our belief in the importance of access to such a language is given voice in the anxieties of liberal philosophers about the deficiencies and/or dangers of (liminal) religious schooling in liberal democracy. Such apprehension generally focuses on a perception that a truncated or singular narrative of meaning and value is available to students, with the concomitant absence of alternative perspectives on such value. The overriding desire is to have alternative narratives available to the students. They may then, it is argued, draw upon these to make sense of a particular feature of their own being or being in the world. These narratives and perspectives are accompanied by certain heuristic strategies for determining the meaningfulness, helpfulness, worthwhileness or even truthfulness of the narratives in question. These may be seen as going beyond the spoken and written word to include other cultural signs, such as liturgies, iconography and cinema.

In this context, what liberal philosophers seek is an assurance that children, in whatever community, have the possibility to access a rich and complex language, often one at variance with that which their own community may wish to allow or even acknowledge. Alternatively, it might be suggested that what they wish to secure is the conditions whereby children, who live in liminal (or outside) communities, should be so prepared or educated so as to act independently in the world. This, I venture, amounts to the same thing. We can see this in looking at what is certainly one of the most discussed communities among liberal philosophers of education: that of the Amish (for example, see Spinner-Halev 2000; Audi 2000). Here there is no suggestion that the education of Amish children within their own community is likely to be injurious to the safety or well-being of the polity more generally. It is, after all, difficult to imagine that the Amish are on the point of undermining the democratic principles that ostensibly underpin the United States Constitution, or even that they are likely to occasion much civil disobedience! Therefore, the liberal concern cannot be about the actual behaviour of the Amish. It must be about something else, say the freedom to choose. But again, while particular forms of education may ultimately give rise to particular kinds of behaviour or action, it may not be confused with such behaviour or action itself. The precursor of choice is capacity and such capacity to choose is a function of having been exposed to possibilities. This exposure derives from access to communication and reflection; that is, to a sufficiently complex language.

This position of liminal (or in this case, possibly outsider) communities requires further exploration and will be dealt with more fully in the next chapter. For the moment it is important only to make a couple of further observations. In the context of a liberal democracy, it is difficult to do other than at least partially sympathise with the anxieties of the liberal philosopher. But the point here is that if access to a rich and complex language is deemed important for a liminal community, which may not, in any event, care to underwrite liberal democracy, it must perforce be substantially more so for the liberal democratic polity itself. Unlike the closed religious community, the liberal democratic polity has no authentic choice available other than the provision of a rich and complex vocabulary in its schools and one, moreover, however inadequately, reaches out towards the actual complexities of human experience, desire and hope. That is, a language that fits our being in the world (Arendt 1968b).[1] This is a basic need in liberal democracies that have as their central goal the flourishing of their citizens. It surfaces time and again in the somewhat prosaic goings-on of schools, and is readily identified by teachers dealing with students in their very early teens who, struggling to find their voice, are prey to drug abuse, sexual exploitation and violence. The resolution of conflict between students in a great many schools, especially those that face the greatest social challenges, is violence. This violence is itself a kind of closure since, for the students, no alternative appears to be available. An oft expressed desire of the teachers working in such situations is that the students be offered the linguistic and discursive capacity to shape rather than be shaped by the daily contingencies of their living (Conroy 1999b; Conroy, Boland and Davis 1999).

Set against the lives of individual students, the antithesis of linguistic poverty is linguistic richness. In the life of the liberal democratic polity, poverty is manifest as discursive closure, richness as an awareness and admission of complexity in the polity at large. Such poverty, it should be understood, is not confined to spoken and written language but embraces other cultural signs, such as advertising, film and television. Indeed, nowhere is this linguistic poverty more evident than in the emergence of globally franchised quiz and reality television programmes. These programmes purvey a global view of how people think, feel and behave. From Argentina to Australia, Britain to Bombay, their format and content are uniform with simulacra of the local provided by the host and contestants. Of course, it is possible to pursue Baudrillard's line of thought and imagine that there is a kind of creative paradox evident in the entanglement of the masses and the media. "Is it," he asks, "the media that neutralise meaning and that produce the 'formless' (or informed) mass; or is it the mass which victoriously resists the media by diverting or by absorbing without reply all the messages which they produce?" (2001, 220). Baudrillard believes that the latter is the case, But if he is right, and the masses resist by refusing to speak, so much the worse for the maintenance and development of liberal democracy. More significantly, there is no evidence that he is right. If we attend to the advent of a new breed of apparently interactive programmes we see that they do indeed draw representatives of the masses into participation. This participation is not, however, based on dialogue but in the relatively passive acceptance of the linguistic signifiers as signifying a reality with which the participants themselves increasingly identify. These signifiers have also been globalised in the service of maintaining the financially lucrative dialectic between the use and value of objects to be consumed, including entertainment itself. In any event, passivity may not be mistaken for action, even action borne out of negation or absence. Here indeed is the actualisation of discursive closure made manifest—As I am drawn into the world of the media the media itself comes to represent the world!

Clearly, if the claim made throughout this essay is true, that discursive closure represents a significant danger for liberal democracies in late-industrial society, then it is important that educationalists and teachers have some sense of what might count as appropriate curricular and pedagogical responses. Rather than argue that this should entail either the playful irony of linguistic detachment that Baudrillard appears to favour, or some kind of belligerent response, neither of which is likely to do much to promote and sustain liberal democracy, it may be better to look at how the liminal curriculum can offer students an alternative language (poetic, artistic, cultural and so on) from that which dominates the centre. But, it might be immediately countered that poetry, history and art form part of the mainstream curriculum. In Britain at least, they are ensconced in the National Curriculum, which all students must study. How then, can they possibly be liminal? One response to this charge is to point to current trends in educational policy, which construes the arts generally as important to the extent that they dispose and prepare students for jobs in the entertainment industry. On this account, art is just another consumer item and aesthetic education is no more than a preparation for consumption. Thus, so much of the teaching of poetry is a victim of consumer society (Jasper 1999, 24). Second, despite the odd rhetorical flourish, the place of the arts has consistently been on the periphery of resource and time allocation and, in England and Wales at least, is under increasing pressure in the face of the push to concentrate on the "basics" and ensure that education is relevant. Relevance here is a byword for "related to one's capacity to find appropriate employment." If the engagement with poetry has some relevance, then it is to be restricted to a certain kind of student and not the "hewers of wood" and "drawers of water." In an article in *The Times Educational Supplement* (Scotland), Neil Munro (1997) rightly observes that the denial of such possibilities to the vast majority of students constantly runs the risk of teaching the next generation to despise their culture. Of course, it might be argued that such a denial serves precisely the ambitions of the globalisers.

Finally, in this connection, where art and literature do appear in the curriculum there is a profound confusion as to their purposes. It is too often imagined that they serve as a cultural ballast to maintain a certain kind of identity. Seen this way it is intended that they provide a solid foundation upon which particular loyalties and allegiances may be predicated. In performing such a function it has to be predictable, steadfast and resolute in its determinations about meaning and identity. On the surface such a use of art may appear to run counter to the claim that liberal democratic governments are deeply entangled in the hegemonic economic discourse of the global corporations; after all, the curriculum is local. This misses the point that it is often in the interests of the globalisers to maintain a certain illusion of the local in order to perpetuate an appearance of stability and suppress expectations of the local population, while simultaneously conducting quite another agenda (Woodiwiss 1997, 89f). In any event, there is something of an irony in all this. From Shakespeare to Shaw, Milton to Muldoon, the poet has, with few exceptions, spent much of his or her time as a transitive figure between confirmation and contest.

So then the claim so far has been that discursive closure may be challenged by the availability of a rich and complex language together with the cultivation of the capacity to draw upon it. Because of its peculiarly liminal status, poetry may well offer one possible strategy for sustaining and cultivating openness. And, while it is true that there is always a temptation by government and corporation to hijack or otherwise corrupt the poet and her art, this is not an insuperable obstacle to engaging the poetic in the service of maintaining openness. This is due, in part, to the way in which poetry itself operates "betwixt and between."

Poetry in the Liminal Space between Self and the World

If the only claim in favour of the importance of poetry were that it languishes at the margins of the curriculum then the case for its inclusion as a paradigm of liminality in the curriculum would be a little weak. However, poetry's liminal status and contribution run much deeper than this. Poetry stands at the interstices of the world and the word, the personal and the public, and the local and the universal, and in doing so has a crucial role to play in maintaining discursive openness. This capability of the poetic makes it ideally suited to perform the liminal function of discursive engagement while, at the same time, not placing the individual student or group in a position of outsider. In this section I wish to develop this idea a little further.

On September 9th, 2002, while travelling by road along the border of Queensland and New South Wales, near Mount Warning, I saw for the first time, certainly in my conscious memory, the Milky Way. The sky was crystal clear with no more than the merest sliver of a new moon and, as I came over the top of one of the ridges, a deep, midnight-velvet sky with more stars than the imagination can comprehend opened up before me. It is not necessary to be a romantic, much less indulge in theological, or even teleological speculation to be aware of the immensity of the universe and garner some sense of one's individual place under such skies. The encounter with such an opulent night sky opens up the possibility of reflection on the relationship between the self and being in general. The Aboriginal verse, with which this chapter opens, unveils not only the experience but also the reflection on the experience of seeing the stars in such a light. For the aboriginal, the stories and myths of her culture are etched in this midnight raiment. It is not just that she observes or even encounters something like Otto's (1959) *mysterium, tremendum et fascinans*; it is that she reflects upon the encounter, and out of such reflection emerge her symbols. Here, similarities to the ontological origins of the trickster become evident, in that both represent the move from the immediate apprehension of the world to the reflective attempt to distance the self from the world. The moment of apprehension represents the passivity of receipt—that is, the world presses itself on me and can only be felt emotionally. Yet, almost simultaneously, a reflection arises that distances me from, and makes an object of, the world. To merely feel the world is to be its slave; to reflect on it is to stand back and no longer be merely its subject

(Schiller 1967).[2] It is in the act of standing back that the world is shaped into its symbolic representations. Caprice becomes Trickster.

In their own turn these symbols are given shape and form in the myths and stories that both become the shared property of the tribe and help shape its communal identity. What might be regarded as a private experience and reflection is or becomes a shared signifier. Subsequently, when any member of the tribe looks at the night sky they are as likely to see *Ngintu* or *Thurroo* or *Kapeetah*. The poem is, or becomes, available to the community. This is perhaps more clearly seen in those instances where no authorship is claimed or acknowledged, as in this case, than in cultures with an established literary tradition. A poem that arises out of the individual apprehension, once uttered in the public space, is no longer a private creation. Yet, neither is it entirely public property. Being in the public space does not turn it into an artefact that, once created and placed in the public domain, acquires an assigned use and value. Rather, each time the poem surfaces in the public space it is read anew. This is no less true in the classroom than the Australian Bush. While the poem is created, wrested from its natural surroundings by its creator, he or she no longer controls its reception and interpretation once it enters the public space. Of course, while not any or every interpretation will do, there is a certain indeterminacy attached to any work of art once it enters the public spaces. The purpose here is not to offer any new reflections on structuralism or, for that matter, post-structuralism,[3] but to recognise that control of the word moves out of the private, into the public and returns, in the one who reads the words, back to the private. However, this second sense of the private appears to me to be somewhat overplayed. For sure I bring my own being and history to bear on the encounter with the spoken or written poem and while this undoubtedly colours the interpretation it does not thereby mean that any interpretation, compatible or not, will do. Scruton, with whom I disagree on many other issues, usefully summarises this in-between position as follows.

> [We] should be able to draw the distinction between meaning and association—between what is in the work and what is not. (The sadness is in the music; my melancholy in hearing it is not.) It is surely not implausible to suggest that part of what enables us to make this distinction lies in a "sense of intention" with which every work of art is imbued. We do not, of course, say that a work of art means whatever the artist intended it to mean. But nor do we feel we can impose any interpretation which is incompatible with anything that might have been intended. (Scruton 1983, 30)

So then, poetry lies at the threshold—between the world and the poet, between the thing signified and the language that signifies it, between the signifiers and the reader and between individual and community. Despite the admission that not any interpretation will do, more than any other art form, the very *isness* of poetry depends upon the open possibilities of language that arise in these spaces.

I now wish to turn to the related question about the way that poetry mediates between the local and the universal and, in doing so, make some important distinctions between these and the notions of the particular and global with which they may be confused. Poetry is always local in the sense that it is both the poet's response to and emerges from the present, proximate experience of its author. Yet, at the same time it gives rise to the possibility of the universal. As a European, my knowledge, much less experience of the southern night skies, would be reasonably described as limited, and my metaphysical and epistemological frames of reference have little enough in common with the Aboriginal mythic corpus. Nevertheless, I can both understand and see the point of the poem; its deep local condition carries the seed of its universality. This universality gets its existence from the possibilities of the imagination, which are limited by neither time nor location. The imagination can go beyond the limits of the possible, the observed and the taken-for-granted. In the sense in which it is used here, the local is to be distinguished from the particular. Northrop Frye (1963) argues that art is universal precisely to the extent that it is not particular. This is an important observation given that the slip from the local to the particular appears an easy move. But easy as it might appear it would be deeply mistaken. The importance of the distinction between the two may be seen if we digress for a moment to reflect on a Donne love poem such as the elegy, *Change*. Like much of Donne's poetry—both love and religious—it is haunted with the shadows of inconstancy, infidelity and treachery. Thus,

> Women are made for men, not him, nor me.
> Foxes and goats,[4] all beasts change when they please,
> Shall women more hot, more wily, wild than these,
> Be bound to one man, and did Nature then
> Idly make them apter to endure than me?
>
> *(Donne 1971, 97: Lines 10–14)*

It is no accident that Donne's work vibrates to the rhythm of his questioning anxiety since it is firmly lodged in his local history. His work, fed by the taproot of his apostasy from his Catholic background in which his family was so deeply immersed, reverberates with unresolved tensions and paradoxes. The experience and sense of treachery, which he both endured and partook of, is transferred from religion to love. The indispensability of personal continuity is matched only by its seeming impossibility (see Carey 1981). From this we may reasonably claim that Donne's poetry is embedded in the local: local time, place and metaphysics. Indeed, without these elements his poetry, as we meet it, would not exist. Yet it is never refrigerated by his own particularity. Escaping the ensnarement of the events and moments of Donne's life it meets, and is met by, the reader in an entirely different time and place, who comes to it with different preoccupations but apprehends something in it, to which she can relate. Knowledge of the particular circumstances that gave rise to the words on the page is not necessary to an encounter with the poem. Donne's work, rooted in the local, transcends the particular to embody the universal.

"Because of its concern with the universal rather than the particular, poetry, Aristotle says, is more philosophical than history.... We may think then of literature as an area of verbal imitation between events and ideas or, as Sir Philip Sidney calls them, examples and precepts" (Frye 1963, 55). While Frye's account is clearly at odds with contemporary post-structural accounts of the relationship between language and the world his point remains important, highlighting, as it does, the nature of the poem as a kind of interstitial or liminal space between the local and the universal, and one into which students should be invited. For the Australian Aboriginal peoples their stories are deeply rooted in place. This need for the local is not reserved to the poetry of those cultures that have not been enveloped in the disruption and dislocation of the history of the twentieth century. Even a poet like Muldoon (1994), so thoroughly at home amidst the postmodern, and whose work delights in the possibilities of complexity, intertextuality, speed and playfulness afforded the poet and reader in late-industrial polities, constantly returns to the local to locate his poetry.

The universality of the poetic stands as a reprimand to the late-industrial conception of the global because, in its own terms, the global represents sameness and a lack of attachment to the specifics of being. The claim of the global is that everything is, or can be, the *same* and that all is caught up in the ubiquity of the monoglot discourse of the markets. Since an economic conception of the global manifests itself, as we have already seen, as co-extensive with the material world (since only from the material world can it wrest the resources that feed its ambition), it is everywhere. And, of course, being everywhere it is nowhere. The language of the global has no home in the world. The distinction between global and local is not primarily a question of size, power and influence, though all of these might be relevant. To the extent that it may be about power, it is so only because the global negates both place and the stories that attach to it. Moreover, whereas the universal mirrors a sense of the other and, at least potentially, consideration for their well-being, no such values are or can be embodied in the global. Of course, my use of global here might appear unnecessarily circumscribed. After all, it may well be claimed, there are apparently perfectly benign, even constructive uses of the term. Hence, in education, there has been a recent fashion for "education for global citizenship." I can understand what might constitute citizenship: membership of a given geopolitical space; allegiance to a given form of governance; the capacity and the possibility of exercising and having vouchsafed certain kinds of rights. But what any of these might mean when qualified by the adjective global is a mystery, unless of course it is intended to imply that the same political and social possibilities may be exercised anywhere in the globe. Clearly there is no empirical evidence to substantiate any such claim. Alternatively, it might be intended to denote the fact that as we all inhabit a single planet and consequently have, at least potentially, congruent interests. But again this is not unproblematic and its use is apt to lead to confusion. This confusion is likely to arise when we ask what such congruence might entail and discover that many of my interests within a globalised world are not congruent but oppositional with respect to, say people in Central America or southern Africa. It is a misunderstanding that becomes particularly apparent when we return to the earlier discussion on globalisation, a term that has become a cognate of global capitalism; an energy configured by the self-referencing and circular mastery of utility and consumption.

In his discussion of Castoriadis' views on the loss of value, Luc Ferry summarises them thus: "capitalist society is the very example of one that 'believes in nothing [and] does not truly value anything unconditionally,' since, mastery over the natural world refers to nothing but itself" (Heidegger called it "will to will")" (1990, 243).[5] However, Castoriadis' gloomy prognosis is not entirely shared by Ferry. Rather than rant at the gathering storm in a Lear-like fashion, we must understand the relationship between the unique individual and the universal. A person is not to be seen solely as an independent consumer nor as exclusively autonomous but as a "synthesis of concrete particularity[6] with the universal. For the individual to be an individual, he has to be rich with a discrete, specific content that is all the same generalizable" (ibid, 261). This is an important point for the teacher. Through poetry and the other arts, we can offer something of a challenge to the discursive closure that appears to be the handmaiden of the evolution of the global corporation. We may do this precisely because poetry stands between the local and the universal in such a way that I can come to it out of my own particularity. As one poet aptly puts it,

Between the writer and the reader
Somewhere the meaning floats
And, waiting on the sidelines,
The poem holds the coats.

(McGough 1999, 33)

Seamus Heaney's (1999) translation of *Beowulf*, the litmus test for and doorway into Anglo-Saxon, lends certain substance to such a claim. In his introduction to the text, Heaney observes that in the poem, "we are dealing with a work of the greatest imaginative vitality, a masterpiece where the structuring of the tale is as elaborate as the beautiful contrivances of its language. Its narrative elements may belong to a previous age but as a work of art it lives in its own continuous present, equal to our knowledge of reality in the present time" (ibid, ix). Neither the advent of the postmodern and its shadow self, neo-liberalism, nor indeed changes in literary or poetic fashions, can occlude the deepest connection between the modern self and its ancient forbearers. In *Beowulf*, the constancy of gold as an element in the narrative is instructive here. Seen as a "trustworthy substance" of constancy, beauty, affirmation, wealth, power, friendship it nevertheless begins to look tarnished "and its status as the ore of all value has been put in doubt" (ibid, xviii), so not much change there. The connection remains in our attachments to the hero myth, already touched on, and its echoes continue to sound within our embrace of those popular cultural forms, which surface heroes and anti-heroes, good and evil, integrity and dishonesty.

Heaney invites us into a further expression of the liminal space occupied by the poet; that is at the threshold of remembering. The pillars of history, that proved amazingly robust up to the French Revolution and the European Enlightenment, have since then collapsed. Subsequently, they have been constantly re-erected only to quiver and "collapse anew" (Arendt 1968b, 11). And so it is difficult to secure much more than the most fleeting glimpses of those traditions that we vestigially retain as odd dislocated and discontinuous echoes of something we only vaguely recall. In such a condition it is understandable that the public seek nothing more than the securing of some immediate gratifications and present stability. While root causes are notoriously difficult to establish in such cases, it is clear that the unravelling of the threads of connection between the present and the past has had some part to play here. Neither knowing, nor understanding the eighteenth-century struggle for representation in the public space, the public has withdrawn into the private, leaving the public spaces to the global corporates, politicians and a few isolated and marginal pressure groups. Standing against this is the poet whose narration of this past may not be silenced. Through her art, the poet recalls us to our origins, retells on our behalf the stories that shape us. In her advocacy for the past, the poet makes it present to each succeeding generation while not leaving it prey to our temporising. Dante's "truths" do not rest in his own time but in ours. We may be able to erase traditional conceptions of hell from public conversations but we cannot ignore Dante. We cannot turn our back on him because his poetry is for *us*, not just about *them*. Through his writing, Dante stands at the threshold between his and our lives. In this context the poetic act is particularly important for students because it assists them in connecting with something that stands outside the immediacy of the present with its allurements of consumption.

It would be naïve to think that these themes, retained for us by the poet, may not be (indeed are not) exploited for commercial advantage and relegated to pastiche and cliché. It is precisely for this reason that the educational imperative is to engage students in the apprehension of the original poetic form upon which populist literary and cinematic products are so often parasitic. While the populist re-workings of these ancient tropes of human being may well occupy centre stage, both politically and economically, the liminal power of the poetic originals must perforce intrude into the classroom precisely because it continues to elude the grasp of the globalisers while retaining its universality. Poetry's capacity to maintain its independence in the face of such powerful forces resides in its liminal status. This liminality is nurtured by three interrelated features of the poetic that always, and inevitably, escape all centrist impulses and attempts to control. They are its metaphorical nature, its relationship to the imagination, and its inherent ambiguity. In the final part of this chapter I will briefly discuss each of these and show why they are important for challenging discursive closure.

The Metaphorical Status of Poetry and the Impossibility of Closure

The elusive nature of poetry and its capacity to defy all attempts to close it down lies, at least partly as we have seen, in its capacity to draw on the local without being tied to the particular and at the same time address the universal. This capacity is at least partly tied to the way in which metaphor operates in the poetic. Poetry, after all, is metaphor. But what does this mean and how does it impact on the maintenance of discursive openness? Despite their deep structural dependence on metaphor (a point to which I shall return), corporations and government alike are quick to consign the metaphoric trope in public language to the periphery. Like emotion it has apparently no significant place in public discourse about such matters as the management of education, the conduct of the curriculum or the flourishing of

students. Such matters should be dealt with in straightforward terms;
describing a particular state of affairs and establishing a set of processes and
procedures for dealing with it. On this account metaphor adds little to our
understanding of the existing corpus of knowledge. And, in so far as it does
anything at all, metaphor is merely the substitution of one sign for another.
Thus, instead of saying something new, metaphorical words merely replace
one word for another by a straightforward replacement or paraphrase. It is, in
this respect, merely an emotionally charged description of a particular state
of affairs that might just as easily, and less confusingly, be rendered by a
"straight-forward" non-metaphorical description. If you can establish a series
of descriptions of education as merely substituting for other descriptions, it is
possible to change a language and yet maintain that there is no claim to some
underlying reality. But metaphor does much more than this. While it may
indeed perform a semiotic function (and here I wish to avoid much of the
structuralist and post-structuralist debate), it also plays a semantic role in that
it offers us a new way of relating to its object; it enables us to generate new
images, new sensations and changes in emotional states. In his essay,
Metaphor and Symbol, Ricoeur (1976) suggests that poetry as metaphor
offers itself to us by bringing into existence new cultural descriptions that are
not, as has been commonly held, mere substitutions for other terms or
descriptions. Following I.A. Richards, Ricoeur argues that a metaphor
represents new information about the world wherein non-equitable terms are
juxtaposed in combinations that offer new ways of seeing, understanding and
interpreting. Way goes further still in suggesting that psychological evidence
has been adduced that demonstrates that the interpretation of and engagement
with metaphor involves not "just the terms of the expression but, rather, the
entire semantic domain of these terms" (Way 1994, 52). In other words,
engagement with metaphor is an engagement with a wider world within
which metaphor operates.

Again, it must be stressed that "poetic language is no less about reality
than any other use of language but refers to it by means of a complex strategy
which implies, as an essential component, a suspension and seemingly an
abolitions of the ordinary reference attached to descriptive language"
(Ricoeur 1977, 153). This complex strategy entails the dislocation and
relocation of words and phrases in such a way that we suspend our normal
understanding of how they work with respect to the things or states to which
they refer. So it is that metaphor is not solely concerned with our feelings but
embraces and takes into itself our comprehension. While a poem may well
demand an emotional response it also requires a cognitive one, for as Redfern
(1986, 55) has it, the appreciation of poetry cannot rest on its sensory impact
alone but is, at least in part, dependent upon the particular literal predicative

meanings of words and their normal or characteristic order and organisation. What is interesting for us here is that poetic metaphor—and after all, without metaphor there is no poetry—requires that we suspend our thoughts about how particular words are normally used and come back to them afresh to look at what they now tell us about some thing in the world. We cannot escape this suspension and its ubiquitous presence in the poetic constantly demands that we attend to the hidden meanings of words and our own emotional and cognitive relationship to them. It is as Heaney remarks about Norman MacCaig, that he "had the poet's gift for 'flying crooked,' down the paths of irony and surprise" (2002, 400).

The metaphor in which poetry consists is perennially straining at the edges of meaning in its attempt to exact a little more truth. By this I mean that in *Wuthering Heights,* when Kathy declares that her "love for Heathcliff resembles the eternal rocks beneath – a source of little visible delight, but necessary," (Brontë 1965, 122) the use of "eternal rocks" presses any sense we might have of love to its very outer edge. In giving voice to the hardness, the coldness, the sheer immovability of the earth's substratum against its permanence, endurance, expansiveness and sheer *isness*, Brontë unearths a new, more dangerous understanding of love. Moving beyond any convention we might attach to love, she takes us to its elemental edge while simultaneously inviting us to stare into the heart's core. Here, the image of the "eternal rocks" at one and the same time hides and discloses. In the act of displacing more usual predicates of love it hides them from view. Yet when we attend to the metaphor we must know that these others lie covered by the new image since it would be otherwise impossible for us to understand what it is that Brontë drives us towards unless we had these prior understandings of love. We are both called to see love afresh, from a new, more perilous (we might say liminal) perspective and yet, having been brought to the edge of what love might mean, we are allowed to return to our more conventional understandings. As Heaney reminds us, "poetry is more a threshold than a path, one constantly approached and constantly departed from, at which reader and writer undergo in their different ways the experience of being at the same time summoned and released" (2002, 190).

The continual interplay between closure and disclosure, the known and the unknown, the old and the new, the hackneyed and fresh is in the very nature of the poetic act. It is in this act where students may be offered the possibility of understanding the deeply complex nature of language and the ways in which it can be used to close down options or open up possibilities. Students need to have some sense of how many of the metaphors that are used in the public spaces are actually about closure. They also need to understand the extent to which metaphor shapes their understanding of how things appear. This is a point not lost on the global corporations who sell their wares through the manipulation of metaphor. From Benetton to Volkswagen, advertisers have hijacked metaphors from myth, religion, politics, development aid and so on to manipulate taste, choice, aspiration and meaning. In redeploying metaphors from fields of human being and experience that are quite different from the products being placed, they both open up new ways of seeing while obscuring or hiding the original relationship between the signifier and the signified—between say Islamic prayer beads and the desire for transcendence.

Of course, metaphor is not owned by poetry; all language is to some extent implicated in the metaphoric—in approaching the world we continually struggle to find new means of given expression, to access what Hopkins called "the deep down freshness" of things. We are surrounded by metaphor but, like air, we are usually unconscious to it. When we approach its poetic instantiation it is akin to breathing pure oxygen. Awareness of it comes to the fore and in doing so is apt to make us a little light-headed.

It would be a mistake, albeit an understandable one, to think that while metaphor may give us some new information or insight it doesn't materially affect the way we act and/or behave. As we have seen, metaphors are not only interesting ways of saying something, they offer particular ways of understanding how things are. There is a significant body of evidence to suggest that the metaphors used in describing both identity and working realities do indeed carry significant formative energies. In education, analysis and review of studies in this area (Thomas and McRobbie 1999) make a strong empirical case for seeing and understanding the power of metaphor to change and shape teachers' and students' practices. Metaphor appears to carry the potential to determine action, behaviour and attitudes. The result of constantly deploying a metaphor such as "classroom as workplace" appears to be that it exerts a constraining influence on the teacher. These constraints include the kinds of interactions that teachers permitted, or saw as permissible, between themselves and their students as well as between student and student. Moreover, the use of particular metaphors was likewise seen to alter students' views of learning.

As we have already seen, metaphor depends on a degree of ambiguity. Where this ambiguity is squeezed out metaphor is no longer operative. In the everyday exchanges of the public spaces and the classroom there is a temptation to kill the metaphor, and in so doing make it appear as if they were unequivocal descriptions of reality. This has been the pattern of economic globalisation. The term "classroom as work place" is intended to convey a particular, enduring, and stable image of the proper conduct of the classroom. Yet we also know that the power of metaphor to unfurl the newness in the old is a function of its referential instability and ambiguity. In a language-shaped world, ambiguity is important in both reflecting the complexity of being human and in maintaining openness. Poetry reflects the ambiguity of our living but, in the teaching of poetry, we are also concerned to assist our students in "rowing through" ambiguity with an eye on what constitutes human flourishing. From a moral perspective, perhaps the teaching of poetry is the single most important pedagogical activity in the school. In the next section I would like to explore this a little more.

The Richness of Ambiguity

To reiterate the point already made, the poet embraces ambiguity because she sees that words themselves are ambiguously related to the world and that to attempt to establish a world of correspondences is likely to lead to a lesser rather than a greater access to how things are. Discursive closure represents the attempt to reduce the range of possible hermeneutical positions available to individual and group alike. This ambiguity of poetry is important in obliquely helping students deal with a world where words and their associated meanings are constantly in danger of being suborned by those in control (Jung 1954). It is important to recognise that while postmodern philosophy regards ambiguity as a badge of office it neither started with it nor is it its preserve. One only need glance at Hopkins' (Hopkins 1972) early poetry to catch the glimpses of a struggle that finds full expression in his later work. Hopkins, holding these early struggles in common with a number of late-Victorian poets faced with the fallout from Darwinian evolutionary theory, evokes and re-works the contest between the "Glory of God" in nature and human progress. These germinal intimations of conflict find full voice in the deeply personal, sometimes bitter and ultimately unresolved struggle with the ambiguity of living itself. Later works such as "Thou art indeed Just, Lord" (ibid, 75)—a poem that attempts to address the poet's attitude to his own incompleteness and sense of failure—give clear voice to the paradox, lack of resolution and inherent contradictions that mark Hopkins' life. The original "platonic" vision that precipitated his joining the Catholic Church for "aesthetic" reasons ultimately gives way to a greater sense of disorder and disunity in the world of his actual experience. He has been neither as creative nor as ascetically successful as he had hoped for. The existence of constant paradox in human endeavour is attested to in both the narrative and structure of this and other works. The narrative is a story of disappointment and incomprehension at the appearing indifference of the creative, fecund God to the poet's overwhelming sense of barrenness. The poetic/linguistic structure supports the narrative claims; thus, the opening line provides a pattern, repeated throughout the poem, where opposites are laid down side by side. Consequently, the use of "Lord" in the phrase, "Thou art indeed just, Lord, if I contend/With thee," is marked out as a pivotal point with affirmation on one side and contestation on the other. This is done by placing the addressee inside the commas so that it might be read either as "Thou art indeed just Lord!" or "Lord if I contend with thee." As Finn (1992, 48) points out, the very act of successfully creating a poem that denounces oneself as a creative "eunuch" provides a potent example of the powerful contradictions at work not only in the poetic structure but in being.

In another of his poems, "That Nature is a Heraclitean Fire and of the Comfort of the Resurrection," there is a grand attempt to resolve all difference in Christ wherein all the ambiguities that mark (his own) life are to be regarded as part of a unified whole.[7] At the point of recognition, the poet simultaneously confronts the "truth" that the Heraclitean fire is indeed beyond resolution. He can do no more than choose, in the certain knowledge that the choice must always be condemned to its own provisionality. His time spent in Liverpool, Glasgow and Dublin brings new and disturbing experiences to the poet that forces the growth and change to recognition that steady states are illusory. Here we are confronted with not only a complex and moral vocabulary, but one that echoes Jung's (1961, 178) claim that poetry brings into our consciousness that which we ordinarily evade or feel only dully, as both acting persons and as pedagogues, that all our attempts at morally rooted education leave us with a sense of incompleteness and ambiguity.

For educators, the sense of incompleteness and ambiguity is compounded by the loss of rootedness, the collapse of our traditions or something stable to which we might anchor our thoughts and purposes. This sense is eloquently captured by Arendt's thought, commented on above, that "The 'pillars of the best-known truths'...which at the time [of the Enlightenment] were shaken, today lie shattered; we need neither criticism nor wise men to shake them any more. We need only look to see that we are standing in the midst of a veritable rubble heap of such pillars" (Arendt 1968b, 10). Once again, attention to imaginative literature can provide a language for dealing with these deep-seated complexities. Christina Rossetti offers something of an entrée here, to the extent that her pre-Raphaelite impulses—seen most evocatively in "Goblin Market" (Rossetti 1984, 80–97)—constantly draw her poetry back to the lyrical language of an earlier era, while at the same time the themes of her work represent attempts to wrestle with modernity as conceived in her own time. A rustic, mediaeval world of colour, vibrancy and danger are juxtaposed with mid-nineteenth-century allusions to human sensuality and sexuality. Thus, in the opening stanza the laughing goblins (fruit sellers in the marketplace) offer a host of delights:

> Maids heard the goblins cry
> "Come buy our orchard fruits,
> Come buy, come buy:
> ...
> Plump unpecked cherries
> ...
> Wild free-born cranberries...
>
> Figs to fill your mouth,
> Citrons from the South,
> Sweet to tongue and sound to eye;
> Come buy, come buy.
>
> (Rosetti 1984, "Goblin Market," 80f, Lines 2-4; 7; 11; 28-31)

The undertones of sensual pleasure are worked out later when Laura, one of the two sisters at the centre of the narrative, falls for the seduction of the goblin men and the other, Lizzie, effects a rescue. Here, the earlier enticements to pleasure with references to "The Tree of Life" become sexually menacing as the goblin men coax, bully, scratch, kick and maul in their attempts to tempt her to eat the fruit that has seduced Laura only to rob her of her vitality. Yet, even in her denial the language is unmistakably sexual:

> Lizzie uttered not a word; Would not open lip from lip
> Lest they should cram a mouthful in:
> But laughed in heart to feel the drip
> Of juice that syruped all her face,
> And lodged in dimples of her chin,
> And streaked her neck which quaked like curd.
>
> Rosetti ibid, 93, Lines 430-436)

Approaching Rossetti's poetry with this notion of moral ambiguity in mind is to recognise that while the world of middle-class nineteenth-century England is very different from the globalised hi-tech late-twentieth/early-twenty-first century, the traditions that allow her to interrogate some of the allures of her world may also be deployed in our own: the goblin men (global sales corporations) of our time sell us wondrous appearing fruit that we need to feed on regularly if we are not to become unfashionable, disappointed, wasted and angry. Are the temptations of the goblin men and Nike so very different from each other? Once our students have tasted Nike trainers, K-Mart won't do! To explore the richness of Rossetti's language is to explore simultaneously paradoxical meanings. As Gadamer (1975) would suggest, it is here that we may offer our students approximations to the moral truth of ambiguity by being partakers in a shared tradition rather than despisers of it.

As I have suggested earlier, students themselves live in the midst of ambiguity. This is frequently manifest in the conflict between the inside and the outside. It is a conflict that fixes them between anxiety and bravado, and the attendant ambiguity leaves them particularly vulnerable to the rhetorical excesses of the market. Consequently, education in a liberal democratic polity concerned to promote human flourishing should have as a key concern the cultivation of pedagogies that help them confront their own ambiguity, while ensuring that they do not spend their education in an overly self-conscious state of anxiety. Ironically, since her own life was marred by anxiety, among modern poets, Sylvia Plath (1967; 1971) enables us to recreate that sense of inner and outer reality that is so much a part of adolescence. In the short poem, "Small Hours" (1971, 46), she explores her own outward appearance of hauteur with her inner state of insecurity and sense of barrenness by using the language and images of a museum full of ornate architectural splendour, but ultimately empty. As she says (of herself):

In my courtyard a fountain leaps and sinks back into itself,
Nun-hearted and blind to the world. Marble lilies
Exhale their pallor like scent.

(Plath, 1971, "Small Hours," Lines 3-5)

Here, the transposition of one sense into another (visual into taste/smell) is part of the important play on the texture of language that offers some possibility of engagement for contemporary students. The creativity leaps for a moment only to fall back: the lilies are at one and the same time part of the externally created grandeur and simultaneously a symbol of death. In the second stanza, she imagines herself the "Mother of a white Nike and several bald-eyed Apollos." Here too, the particular choice of gods whom she would like to have fashioned or created is not accidental—Nike, the God of success and Apollo, who makes humans aware of their own guilt, stand as a reproach to her own perception of failure. Of course, Nike in particular carries different symbolic value for many of our students, if only by extension, and can thus serve to extend their hermeneutical horizons. Through an exploration of what the language has meant in different contexts, the ways in which words and phrases carry contrary meanings and questions raised about value and purpose, we offer the possibility of perspective-taking and linguistic understanding as conditions of moral understanding. "Small Hours" supplies parallel linguistic and narratival structures to a student through which they may interpret their own situations—situations frequently figured with anxieties about their own personal power and position. In that major sense of the shared tradition, Plath's voice is not just personal and private.

One of the most significant contemporary poets of ambiguity is Seamus Heaney. His work is particularly apposite in this context because he himself claims "poetry is value." By this, he does not wish to imply that all poetry is valuable, but that the idea of it as a place and space for possibility is there. In a radio interview on BBC Radio 4's *Kaleidoscope* programme on May 4th, 1996, with Kate Kellaway, he quotes Joseph Brodski, suggesting that poetry "is not an art; it's an anthropological necessity through which language projects us towards the future." In one of his early works, he offers the multilayered "digging" (Heaney 1966, 13) as an image of moral as well as literary complexity. As his corpus developed, Heaney has built on early images of ambiguity, juxtaposing and playing with contrary images. In "Field Work" (Heaney 1979, 42), he explores the painful incompleteness love. In "every day tales of romance," love is perceived as that which may provide wholeness and healing, but in one of the *Glanmore* sonnets, we come face to face with its ultimate and perennial incompleteness. Thus,

> When you came with your deliberate kiss
> To raise us towards the lovely and painful
> Covenants of flesh; our separateness;
> The respite in our dewy dreaming faces.

> (Heaney 1979, "Glanmore Sonnets X" Lines 11-14)

In locating the poem in the dream and in the references to classical partnerships, Heaney brings us back to the centrality of Jung's belief in the universalising voice of the poet. In the poem "Keeping Going" (Heaney 1996), he exposes, with increasing intensity, the moral ambiguity of place and time, of history and event. The listener is invited into a world of complex utterance that draws its power from the overlapping discourses of the historical moment—religious, political, social and economic. A whitewashed wall is the backdrop to children's laughter, to the silent contemplation of the women of the house and to the spewing out of brains when a young reserve policeman is shot. All the history of a small Northern Irish town is drawn into this moment; a history that embraces innocence and guilt, goodness and evil, life and death. And, of the central figure (Heaney's own brother and a man of heroic ordinariness) the poet can say:

My dear brother, you have good stamina,
You stay on where it happens…
…you keep
Old roads open by driving on the new ones.
But you cannot make the dead walk or right wrong.
                    (Heaney 1996, "Keeping Going," Lines, 67f; 70f; 74)

The "good stamina" is, for Heaney, the ultimate moral accolade because it is characterised, in his own phrase, by "keeping going." These poems, from different phases of Heaney's work, represent a deepening, increasingly penetrating exploration of existential ambiguity. For him, it is ultimately in the act of "keeping going" that we make our moral response to the vagaries of our being in the world. The poet properly valorises the moral courage and worth of everyday existence; in doing so, he offers the listener a kind of redemption in her or his own existence. The redemption comes not out of resolution but acceptance and choosing. Heaney's poetry is particularly helpful to the teacher because he comes back time and again to revisit earlier themes in the effort to constantly refine the understanding of primal human activities and choices, as well as to face their complexity with increased candour. In an environment that focuses increasingly on the utility value of schooling and education, the ambiguity that suffuses the lives of students (in this case, adolescents), is increasingly itself a matter of the margins. But this should not deter us from cultivating pedagogies that turn to the poetic for inspiration and insight. The key to both unlocking the poetic and using the poetic to unlock the closed-in discourse of the public spaces is the imagination. I now wish to turn to this briefly.

The Life of the Imagination

Here I do not intend to make any comprehensive pronouncements on the imagination; others (Scruton 1974; Warnock 1980), much better qualified to do so, have already covered this ground extensively. I do wish, nevertheless, to make some observations about the distinctive place of the poetic imagination and its relationship to nurturing an understanding of the "in-between." It would be a mistake to think that it is only in the poetic or the aesthetic as a whole that we are offered the possibilities of the imagination. However, given that it has a freedom from a certain view of progress, the poetic imagination is particularly important. The curriculum has been increasingly dominated by a conception of human being and exchange that draws on the images and metaphors of science. There are two aspects of this that are of concern here. First, there is the idea that, properly conceived, education is itself based on a scientific world view and that adherence to scientific principles of cognition and neuropsychology will axiomatically deliver better-educated students. This may or may not be true but the evidence (which is actually more generally of a social science variety) has certainly to establish anything of the sort. Despite the lack of—or dubious provenance of—much of this evidence, we are busy developing technologies of teaching and learning that are rooted in such science. Second, there is the idea, touched on earlier, that progress and process are somehow axiomatically good things. As I have already suggested much of public life, particularly education, has been subjected to the limitations imposed by the appearance of an inexorable march of progress transformed into process. The result of this scientism is that education has been subject to significant imbalances, to the extent that even the teaching of literature has been increasingly subordinated to the technology of language teaching and the poetic, and other arts largely marginalised. Northrop Frye distinguishes the arts from the sciences as follows:

> The sciences begin with sense, and work toward a mental structure founded on it. The arts begin with vision, and work toward a complementary mental structure, and as science continually evolves and improves, what sense declares to be impossible in one age, such as aeroplanes, may become possible in the next. The arts do not evolve or improve, partly because vision, being pure wish, can reach its conceivable limits at once. The aeroplane is a recent invention, but the vision that produced it was already ancient in the arts when Daedalus flew out of the labyrinth and Jehovah rode the sky on the wings of a seraph. (Frye 1963, 153)

Clearly, Frye conceives the arts and sciences as complementary streams of the activity of human consciousness and not as countervalent forces. As ways of being in the world they offer something like a coherent picture of how things are, a kind of harmonic accord. This is fine as long as we ensure that both perspectives are vouchsafed in our public spaces. But, where this doesn't happen, or where one perspective becomes overly dominant, the resultant imbalance is likely to have substantially deleterious effects on the polity. Where we truncate vision (which here may reasonably be taken as a metonym for imagination) we are left with activity evacuated of purpose and possibility. It is precisely because we can envision some as-yet-unrealised possibilities that we can direct our other rational activities to their accomplishment.

The ensuing domination of vision—or what I prefer to see as the life of the imagination—by the senses has had a profound impact on the school curriculum. Schooling is increasingly absolved from responsibility to attend to the life of the imagination. Of course, this does not mean that imagination is never mentioned in curriculum documents. Quite the reverse—it is indeed mentioned, as a subordinate and contributory category to and within the process. A reasonably attentive exegesis of curriculum documents illustrates the way in which imagination is perceived as a tool to equip or skill the student for maintaining the momentum within the processes of late-industrial living.

In any such culture, denial of the importance of such a use of the imagination is likely to be poorly received by educationalists and policy-makers alike; indeed, its cultivation is probably deemed as an indispensable feature of education for progress. The danger is that, contrary to the rhetoric, such a utilitarian view of the imagination is likely to do exactly the opposite of that which is claimed for it. This claim is intimately connected with Jasper's (1999, 24f), though in another context, that the reading of texts and associated teaching has become both a victim of the consumer society and a deeply corrupt activity in our education system. This corruption occurs where the reading of texts, of poetry in particular, serves purposes that are directly or indirectly about closure. Such closure happens where it is imagined that the function of poetry is to bolster and confirm the extant order or to manufacture particular closed conceptions of civic loyalty and identity (Harrison 1994). Of course, it would be naïve to imagine that this corruption is a feature only of late-industrial polities. Schiller's view of the artist and of art is that the one must always strive to be free of corruption and the other can never be contained by it. "The artist is indeed," he observes, "the child of his age; but woe to him if he is at the same time its ward, or worse still, its minion! Let some beneficent deity snatch the suckling betimes from his mother's breast, nourish him with the milk of a better age, and suffer him to come to maturity under a distant Grecian sky" (1967, 55 and 57). [8]

In truth, authentic poetry cannot play such a role, because, as we have already seen, it is perennially open-ended, whereas science (in its physical, economic or social sense) can easily fall prey to closure with the phrase "that's how things are" easily falling off the tongue. In contradistinction, vision is much less susceptible to limitations.

Some, like Castoriadis, abandoned the arts as a means of redressing the imbalances that have resulted in closure, believing that they couldn't cope in the face of so powerful a culture rooted in the liberal individualism that has become a cognate of consumptive excess. Such an option is not available to the teacher, who retains some attachment to the vocation of education. Rather, she is charged with fostering the imagination of children so that they can keep alive not-yet-dreamed-of possibilities for and beyond themselves. Indeed, the point about Frye's understanding of the imagination is that it is bounded by no limitations, not even those that might conceive of the inevitability of viewing life as a particular kind of process. In any event, the freed imagination is always open-ended and offers the capacity to simultaneously look within and without.

Practising the Poetic in the Classroom

To this point, I have made the case for conceiving of poetry as a truly liminal expression of our capacity to communicate without the imposed categories that might issue out of any attempt at discursive closure. In this final section, I wish to reflect on how we might approach poetry in the classroom. As with laughter, so with poetry, *habitus* is important. The kind of climate cultivated in the classroom—primary or secondary—is important to the kinds of dispositions our students are likely to acquire. But, in pedagogical terms these dispositions have to be intentionally nurtured. Where students are generally not persuaded that poetry is useful or interesting it is not because they do not understand the words or that they are incapable of feeling. It is, rather, that they have not been able to "see." In an interesting discussion on this subject, Colin Lyas (1999) points out that the requirement for a social services worker to develop a relationship of friendship with her clients, but not forget that her first duty is to her agency, represents a debasement of language. Such a proposition would entail some kind of moral evaluation— How for example are we to measure the terms friendship and duty? Yet some may not be able to "see" that there is a moral question here. In this sense, and for Lyas, however, *seeing* is all. It may be that we can be told that there is a difference in the notion of friendship, but in this and in other cases, we may not be able to see. This lack of sight is not necessarily remediable by telling you again and again that there is a confusion of the notion of friendship, though you may believe it because I (an authority) have told you that it is so. Such believing frequently takes the place of seeing. But, as Lyas observes, "For when we do not see we become shadows cast in a place by the opinion of others, and that sits ill with the wish to be autonomous from which, presumably, all education gets its point" (ibid, 374). This can become the case with the arts, and poetry in particular. The purpose of teaching poetry is not to make people behave or enhance their functional literacy, it is to introduce them to something of value either, in its own right or with respect to what it unfolds for us. Such an education has as its focus the desire that students will be able to see what it is that the poem tells them about human being. Consequently, they will be able to personally reflect on it the better to understand their own place in the world as subject and the relationship of their own subjectivity to universals.

Lyas proceeds to argue that the study of the poet's context, her mastery of form and technique, her cultural and personal influences are all parasitic on a prior decision, that what she has penned is, in the first instance, worthy of study—we study great poets because they are great, and, in doing so, we may learn more about what it is that makes them great in the first place. As he puts it, "I operate, then, with the assumption that a genuine debate goes on between those who claim, in literary, ethical and religious contexts, to see something and those who claim not to be able to do so. I operate with the further assumption that a literary, religious and ethical education seeks to produce insight. In the literary case this will be a matter of helping people to a capacity to see what is in literary works for themselves" (ibid, 377). He goes on to suggest that trying to offer some kinds of proof as to why a particular work is great is to misunderstand the nature of artistic creation as well as the nature of the kind of thing that would count as an appropriate judgement. The proofs that are looked for in establishing the claim to greatness of a particular poem lie outside the realm of the poetic. The result of the imbalance discussed in the previous section is that the kinds of proofs that we look to in establishing such judgements are inevitably coloured by the scientific and arithmetic, and equally inevitably likely to lead us up a cul-de-sac. I cannot deduce that because a poet uses a particular metre, which has proved successful in the past for other poets, that this particular poem will be "great" or even "good." The failure to establish some sort of deductive, or, for that matter, inductive proofs by which a particular work may be evaluated has no doubt contributed to the diminution and marginalisation of the arts and poetry.

Again, I may be able to get students to believe that Tom Paulin or Paul Muldoon or Seamus Heaney are great poets because they have received public accolades, occupy or have occupied prestigious positions in the academy at Oxford, Harvard and Princeton; but that is an entirely different matter from getting them to see that this is so. This is no less true for ethics or religion, and it might be argued that the reason religion, where it is taught in both public and religious schools, is taught so badly and has so little effect (cf Francis 2001; Francis, Astley and Robbins 2001), is because it is too little concerned with seeing (insight) and overly preoccupied with telling and proving. Lyas argues that we should be training students to "see." This is a somewhat unfortunate use of training, since training implies the mastery of technique. I prefer to think of these engagements slightly differently. If I wish to discriminate the mediocre poet from the great poet, I must be immersed in poetry. This can be seen in nearly every walk of life. As a young man, travelling around cattle auctions with my cattle-dealer father, I was particularly struck by another dealer called Crawford Scott. Scott was a man in his sixties when I first knew him, had virtually no schooling, couldn't sign his own cheques: a man, in every sense, functionally illiterate. Yet, without the benefit of scales he could tell to the nearest kilo what a milk cow would weigh after slaughter, long before it was killed. On the back of his knowledge of the weight and meat conformation of cows, Scott had become a very successful businessman. The point at stake is not that Scott could be a successful businessman yet functionally illiterate, it is that he could make judgements about livestock precisely because he had been immersed in the trade all his life. In other words, he could see what others could not. Now, coming to be able to discriminate between great poetry and the merely ordinary may require quite different perceptions, but the principles are not dissimilar.

This seeing entails understanding, not primarily of the structure, form and metre of the poem, but the application of the hermeneutical principles of *Verstehen* (Conroy 1999b). Such an approach requires that we place the free personal response of the student alongside the disciplined application of hermeneutical reflection when we look at a work. This is likely to bring about a creative dialogic tension focused on the web of meanings encoded in and around the notions of creation and reception. To create the conditions which enable this to happen is to assist the student in locating herself in the "midst of given complex of expressions" (Truzzi 1974, 11). In other words, it is the teacher's task to bring the student in her marginal state together with the poetic in its marginality and to help the students to see in the encounter that the merger of personal horizons may be merged with those of the historico-cultural situatedness of the work (Gooderham 1983, 62; see also Gadamer 1975). What is on offer in an approach through poetry is, in fact, the possibility of more authentic and complex formulations that may help students deal in a morally constructive and positive manner with the oversimplifications of market and political rhetoric.

It is not the object of these reflections, however, to recuperate the marginalised poetic voice any more than that of the trickster. Such a recuperation would merely serve to place the poetic at the mercy of the centre, turning it into a popinjay—all form and no substance. There is already too much of this in education in late-industrial liberal democracies. In those places where, for example, religious education is taught its mythopoeic substance is substituted by the banal and trite excurses into others' worlds in a vain attempt to draw parallels and spread sameness. The disruptive and liminal energies of many of religions founding figures are reduced to dubious moral exemplars, which, as Bayless (1996) points out, is to miss the point entirely. Indeed, the contesting and challenging spirit manifest in the founders of many of the world's religions is, in turn, subverted and inverted by curriculum documents and their enactment in the classroom. Founding figures are used in religion and in religious education as its concomitant, as forces of conservatism and not as exemplification of the importance of liminality to communities and their conversations. Better that, like the trickster, poetry continues to inhabit the liminal space. To do so is to reject the impulse to domesticate and anaesthetise its power; it is also to recognise that it will continue, by its very nature, to sit uncomfortably at the threshold of educational acceptance in even the most utopian of contexts.

Conclusion

In this chapter I have attempted to reflect and reflect on the liminal, interstitial quality of the poetic. It is, I would contend, an under-utilised resource in maintaining and nurturing discursive openness. But, it retains much power and many possibilities for challenging, opening up, connecting, breaking down and re-establishing a relationship with the world of ideas that refuse to be contained. It does this by occupying the spaces between the world and the self—other worlds (historical, cultural, interpretative); by evoking the liminal status of childhood and adolescence; by being metaphor; by embodying ambiguity; by facilitating the imagination; and by being a vehicle that draws into conversation the personal and private engagement with text and its public, social and cultural meanings. But, perhaps most of all, it is because it is irrepressibly political without succumbing to or being dominated by the political domain. Heaney eloquently summarises the position of poetry in discussing the role of Northern Irish poets during the peak of what is euphemistically called "The Troubles." He does so by insisting that,

> [T]he idea of poetry as a symbolic resolution of opposing truths, the idea of the poem as having its existence in a realm separate from the discourse of politics, does not absolve it or the poet from political responsibility. Nobody is going to advocate an ivory tower address for the poet nor a holier-than-thou attitude. Yet "pure" poetry is perfectly justifiable in earshot of the car bomb and it can imply a politics, depending on the nature of the poetry. A poetry of hermetic wit, of riddles and slips and self-mocking ironies may appear culpably miniaturist or fastidious to the activist with his microphone at the street corner, and yet such poetry may be exercising in its inaudible way a fierce disdain of the activist's message, or a distressed sympathy with it. But the reading of those political implications is in itself a political activity... The poet is stretched between politics and transcendence, and is often displaced from a confidence in a single position by his disposition to be affected by all positions, negatively rather than positively capable.

> (Heaney 2002, 118f)

Notes

1. See especially Arendt's essay, "Thoughts about Lessing."
2. See especially the "Twenty-Fifth" letter. Admittedly Schiller's conception of humanity's relationship with the universe is coloured by his romantic inclinations. This does not, however, nullify the observation that the world is first felt in an uncontrolled manner and through subsequent reflection brought under control. In Schiller's essay we also see intimations of Freud and Jung.
3. Gould (1981) offers an interesting summary of some of these issues of interpretation.
4. It is hardly by accident that Donne uses animals, such as the fox and the goat, to draw his analogy.
5. Here, Ferry is quoting from and discussing Castoriadis' denunciation of the corruption of the notion of liberal in liberal democracy in *Carrefours du Labyrinthe ll.*
6. Ferry's use of the particular here is not at odds with my earlier discussion of the local since here he is concerned with the person, whereas in the earlier discussion my concern was the poetic impulse.
7. Heraclitus: While all is appearing flux, it is resolvable. Fire turns to water to earth to water to fire; everything is ultimately one.
8. Blackmore is paradigmatic of those towards whom Schiller's ire is directed. Under his pen, as for that of many other poets, poetry was indeed an apologist's tool designed to maintain a particular religious and political view. But then again, following Frye's line, it is his inability to escape the particularity of his political and cultural circumstances that has ensured his absence from and serious literary canon.

Chapter 6

The Liminal Possibilities of the Liminal School

It is better to listen to the quiet words of a wise man than to the shouts of a ruler at a council of fools.

(Ecclesiastes 9:17)

Introduction

Randall Curren distinguishes the argument for public schooling from that for common schooling, seeing the former as rooted in the requirements of justice but the latter arising because of the identification of "important public goods which there is some reason to think we can effectively promote through educating children of disparate backgrounds together" (2000, 215). Despite his clear preference for common schools, he acknowledges the possibility that separate schools may also deliver the educational and social goods required in liberal democracy (see also Callan 1997, 178–182), though it has to be said that this acknowledgement is somewhat grudging. Such liberal philosophers inevitably carry out their discussions about extra-state schooling in permissive terms—the state has to ensure what ever it is that it regards as flourishing is effectively promoted. This is its public agenda and it must in consequence ensure that schools deliver on this agenda. Schools may be afforded limited permission to operate slightly differently providing the state retains control of the overall agenda. This is, at least in part, because public education must reflect the particular readings and understandings of particular cultural, political and social happenings and circumstances Consequently, where a culture and its political leaders/administration make it clear, explicitly as well as implicitly, that consumption, democracy and education are intimately linked in a strategy to acquire an ever-increasing share of the earth's resources, we can expect the dominant operational and curriculum practices in schools to reflect this. But, we might wish to argue, there are other conceptions of flourishing which should be given a voice. Now if the central etatist doctrine about flourishing is so dominant that other conceptions cannot be recognised then we are apt to be concerned about the general flourishing.

Indeed, throughout this essay it has been argued that this philosophy of closure and its concomitant practices are evident in the drive by certain liberal democratic governments to align their notions of flourishing with those of the globalised corporations. And again, as we have noted, this alignment is fuelled by a substantial attachment to consumption. After all, without ubiquitous consumption global corporations would cease to exist in anything like their present form. This is, of course, both an empirical and a logical point. Moreover, given that the interests of the global corporation are to be regarded as more or less coterminous with those of the liberal state, then ever-expanding consumption is a *sine qua non* of the philosophy of public institutions like schools. How then can it be possible for these institutions of the centre truly to challenge, where challenge is needed, their own bedrock assumptions? Can the challenge be responded to be effectively by teachers working in state schools as state servants on their own? Up to this point I have argued for the cultivation of various kinds of liminal metaphors as they obtain for both teaching and the teacher. But there are limits to the efficacy of these approaches and, I would wish to suggest, they need to be supplemented by a further instantiation of the liminal metaphor—the liminal institution.

As I have argued earlier, it is logically dubious and empirically unlikely that students should or can be in the frontline of agonistic politics. But, it does not follow from this that institutions may not offer a backdrop to the engagement of students with the world which would assist them in growing up with the capacity to see the world somewhat differently from the political centre. While reiterating my earlier claim that the individual student cannot be expected to operate in the political domain we can nevertheless assert that liminal educational institutions may be able to offer a variety of perspectives on human flourishing and that there may be legitimate choices that parents and others have to make on behalf of and /or with their offspring. Such choices may embrace the decision to send one's children to a non-mainstream state school precisely because one wishes them to grow up with a different view from that promulgated at and by the centre. Liminal institutions may legitimately and robustly represent a view from the threshold that challenges those taken-for-granted assumptions of the centre.

Such offerings may be inconvenient for certain kinds of libertines but should present no threat to liberals.

In this final chapter, I would like to explore in some detail this third expression of liminality: the liminal institution. While there is some overlap with the question of voice and complexity raised in the previous chapter, in some ways this is the most difficult of the three areas with which to deal, since liminal experiences/pedagogies and dispositions can be reasonably identified as interstitial practices and conditions, and would appear to lend themselves more readily to the cultivation of communitas. Moreover, the qualities of unpredictability and eruption are more easily seen in, and as pertinent to, the small, the local and the individual. In liberal democracies, it is more difficult to identify institutions in this way since they tend to be subject to the kinds of structural arrangements—government regulation; institutional, fiscal and other forms of accountability; employment and other forms of legislation—that both constrain them and constantly press to determine much of their character. Such anxieties, while not unfounded, nevertheless can be reasonably addressed by returning to Turner's analysis.

In his (1969 and 1995) discussion of liminal communitas, normative communitas frequently evolves out of existential or spontaneous communitas, giving shape and form to the original impulses of the *liminar*.[1] The example used by Turner is that of the Franciscan Friars of the Catholic Church who, under the influence of St. Francis, eschewed all material attachments and turned to a life of the utmost simplicity and poverty. As the community attracted increasing numbers of followers and alternative doctrines about possessions and property evolved in the Catholic Church, however, the community had to evolve structures in order to sustain the original vision. This pattern is seen in other religious groups such as Quakers and Shakers, Buddhist monasticism and Vaisnavite movements of Northern India. The important point here is that something of the liminal state is preserved, not in aspic but in the motive spirit or charism that informs choices, decisions and practices of the liminal group. Certainly, Francis wished to see his friars as occupying a permanently liminal space, albeit it one that had to modify the manner of its engagement with the wider structured world. Of course, teachers also have many constraints—practical, legal and moral—on their actions but may still be open to and facilitate liminal possibilities. In any event, it is perfectly possible to operate institutionally, say as a registered charity, and still manifest the eruptive and unpredictable character of the liminal. In the polity, more generally, such organisations as Greenpeace appear to exemplify precisely this condition, although there may be an argument as to whether or not Greenpeace is more marginal than liminal.

Of course, Greenpeace may perform such a task in the liberal democratic polity because it operates as an institution governed by adults having the express intention of communicating with other adults about how we should conduct ourselves, and about what is an appropriate and worthwhile way to live. When we ask whether or not liminal institutions should play a significant role in the education of the young within a liberal democracy, we may be faced with quite a different set of issues. It is hardly an exaggeration to say that, in liberal democracies, most of the non-state institutions that wish to be involved or retain their involvement in education are, in some sense or other, religious. Clearly, this is partly a result of the historic role of Christianity. It is also a consequence of the desire of émigré (frequently Islamic) communities to sustain their traditions, coupled with their uneasy relationship to some of the behaviours manifest in their host cultures. Most discussions of the role of separate schooling (generally on religious grounds) centre on the extent of the liberal democratic state's responsibilities to facilitate parental rights with respect to their children's upbringing (McLaughlin 1984; Callan 1985; Hand 2002) or group rights (Kymlica 1989, 1995; Spinner-Halev 2000). For many liberal philosophers, these rights need to be weighed in the balance when set against the claims for common education in the service of a common liberal culture. While the liberal arguments about parental and group rights play some part in the reflections here, the focus on the obligations of the centre towards the liminal or marginal is but one side of the coin. From the perspective of discursive freedom, it is equally important to understand what the liminal has to offer the centre in virtue of its liminality.

The central questions for this chapter focus on whether or not it is desirable for religious communities, through their institutional arrangements, to seek to play a liminal role in education; and, if it is, how this is to be manifest. To do this, it is necessary to initially clarify the complex nature of religious institutions within a liberal democracy, especially as they pertain to education. This must take account of a range of possible arguments against viewing religious institutions as having some kind of privileged position with respect to liberal democracy. Second, there is a need to establish the liminal credentials of religious institutions and, moreover, argue that these credentials can only be taken seriously to the extent that (to use McLaughlin's 1999 phrase) they avoid the temptations of commonality. Finally, I hope to demonstrate how the liberal democratic state, far from eschewing the values of liminal religious institutions, should embrace their potential as politico-economic correctives. Most of the discussion will revolve around the Christian Church for two reasons. First, in liberal democracies Christian denominations have been and continue to be, collectively, the most significant religious group(s) involved in education and, more prosaically, it is about these that I know most. However, any principled positions that emerge from these reflections should have a much more general application. This is particularly important with respect to non-European and non-Anglophone cultures that are in the process of developing their own democratic structures in both politics and mass culture.

The Ambiguous Status of Religion

Central to the argument of this volume has been the claim that, in Turner's sense, liminality can play an important and constructive role in, and in favour of discursive openness in a liberal democracy. At this stage, I wish to explore whether or not religiously denominated education can be construed as a liminal site in this sense. Clearly, there are many who believe that this is not the case, variously arguing that there are simply too many sociological and epistemological objections. In Scotland, for example, there have been sustained and virulent attacks on the continued existence of Catholic schools from academics, politicians, media pundits and union representatives alike (see Conroy 1999a; 2001). It is therefore necessary to see what these objections look like, and whether or not they decisively tell against the claims that it is in the interests of liberal democracy itself to support the liminal possibilities that may inhere in such institutions. Many of the arguments against seeing religion as having any kind of role in education and schooling in a late-industrial liberal democracy have been well rehearsed in the philosophical and educational literature as well as in the popular media. Among the reasons advanced for regarding religiously denominated education as being unable to serve this function in a liberal democracy, is the claim that religious institutions have not, obviously or decisively, been on the side of discursive freedom in and for liberal democracies. Many of these arguments are tied to the notion that religious institutions are de facto, if not inherently, irrational, obscurantist, undemocratic or indeed, corrupt. Moreover, at best religions have a deeply ambiguous relationship with secular or liberal states. Second, religious institutions have hardly distinguished themselves as offering the polity unique wisdom and insight. Third, it is not obvious that there is a single discernible line of argument or moral position on liberal democracy, global capitalism and discursive freedom even within a particular denomination. Finally, religiously denominated schooling is culturally, politically and socially divisive and as such has a tendency to undermine democratic harmony. Of course, a number of these objections are rooted in the key issue of epistemological authority:

If religion is non-rational then why should a political system rooted in rational deliberations about justice treat it seriously?

While there are, no doubt, many other objections that might be voiced against seeing religious institutions as playing this liminal role, there is not space to deal with each of them here. Possibly the most significant is that the processes of secularisation have rendered religion obsolete and a late-industrial liberal democracy (Martin 2001; Bruce 2002) cannot take seriously the claims of a worldview to which virtually no one subscribes. Related but different, is the view that religion is a purely private and largely aesthetic (interior) matter of no importance to politics beyond (Rorty 1999, 148–167). I will only observe here that these issues can largely be dealt with under the discussion of the relationship between state and religion, since it is precisely the shift in or loss of religious allegiance within liberal democracies that opens up the possibility of quite traditional (even conservative) religions occupying a liminal space.

Religion: Master or Servant of Liberal Democracy

The first objections, which revolve around the claim that religions are not on the side of freedom and liberty, is summed up in a characteristically robust polemic by the philosopher Anthony Grayling. He is quoted in Dean as opposing church schools because, "given the great harm that religions do… in the way of conflict, war, persecution and oppression and preventing the growth of science and freedom of thought I object to my taxes being used to this end" (Dean 2001a, 3; see also Wheatcroft 2001). Grayling's views have precedents in other philosophers of what might be termed a republican or secular rationalist bent. Indeed, it is a major theme in Enlightenment social theory. In his seminal essay, "Religion and the Legitimation of the American Republic," Robert Bellah asks if "there has not been a historical antipathy between republican government and Christianity. Most Christian political theorists down through the ages have considered monarchy the best form of government (Christian religious symbolism would seem to be much more monarchical than republicanism), and the great republican theorists…have wondered whether Christianity can ever create good citizens" (1992, 165f). Certainly, Rousseau was of this opinion, arguing that allegiance to Catholic Christianity was dangerous to the good functioning of the state, because it is divisive and antisocial (1968, 181). This antisocial trope, Rousseau believed, could be found in the Church's unwillingness to see the general will of the people as paramount in civil society because of its claimed allegiance to sources of authority that lay beyond civil society. The question, it appears, is whether or not one can have twin loyalties. It seems to me that it would be a fairly unexceptional to claim that one might have allegiances to two quite different entities. It might be argued that there is a point where one has to choose between two extremes. While this does happen, it is as likely to be occasioned within a social or political entity as between two different entities. But even here, one may choose parts of a particular agenda and reject others. For example, I might be in favour of controlling world terrorism but I may be against deploying similar methods to those of the terrorist in bringing about their defeat. In any event, it doesn't seem that this is really Rousseau's concern, since his remarks are particularly directed against Catholicism. It must be that his distrust of Catholicism is really about its having been identified with the European seats of power and about its strong centralist governance, which sometimes stands over and against that of the state and its frequently asserted claims to moral authority over the state. Of course, Catholicism no longer exerts such a strong influence over public life in liberal democracies (though that may be disputed by some). Nevertheless, it is certainly true that there are particular features of institutional Catholicism that are not easily relegated to the annals of history; there is too much controversy surrounding the role of the hierarchy within the Catholic Church, in relation to sexual abuse, to believe that institutional corruption and wrongdoing are historical anachronisms. Where the Church is revealed as having been implicated in wrongdoing, the response has not always been as forthcoming, honest and open as circumstances demanded. Moreover, it has, at times, and during the modern era, been seen as allying itself to particular forms of discursive closure, most especially in matters of personal morality or the ordination of women. Some might suggest that the drive for closure around such issues is symptomatic of an organisation that is essentially and constitutionally undemocratic and that this makes it incapable of seeing itself as fully accountable for the actions of its "servants."

It is true that the Catholic Church in particular has, time and again, demonstrated that sexual morality and gender issues have been, and continue to be, its Achilles heel. Further, it might be suggested that the substantial problem with paedophilia in the Catholic Church is a direct consequence of the particular kind of culture that arises out of its structural and foundational problems. Before proceeding, it should be pointed out that the charges of misogyny and abuse are not possessed of the same logic. There is a rhetorical tendency to confuse two quite different things, lumping them together under the heading of "reactionary, hierarchical authoritarianism." The first case is quite simply one of wrongdoing, arising, I suspect, from confused and corrupted loyalties. Those who threw a blanket of secrecy over the abuse of children did so in a mistaken allegiance to the institution. The stated aims and intentions of the institution are pretty much antithetical to such practices. It might then be reasonably asserted that the malpractice of some members may damage the institution in the eyes of both members and outsiders, but this does not *ipso facto* make the institution antipathetic to human flourishing any more than the principle of democracy should be called into question because there are many examples of political corruption, subterfuge and dishonesty in European or American political culture. Certainly, some in authority are not always seen to have practised well the virtue of discursive openness, though, as I have argued at the beginning of this study, attempts at discursive closure on these matters have been largely unsuccessful. Moreover, while an institution such as the Catholic Church may not be democratically accountable to its members, it cannot shirk its responsibilities to have integrity, be manifestly truthful and visibly act in accordance with its claims about human flourishing. The corruptibility of officials in a church, however, is logically no different from the corruptibility of officials in a liberal democracy and we are not likely to suggest that the corruptibility of, for example, the Belgian officials who engaged in a substantial cover up of sexual abuse in the 1990s, provides any kind of reason for doubting the principles of a liberal democracy or the values for which it stands. So it is with churches.

The case with respect to gender is quite different. It may be argued that the treatment of women in many traditions is—seen from a late-industrial liberal perspective—discriminatory and inappropriate, since it fails to treat persons as equals. But, there are different possible interpretations of the Catholic Church's refusal to treat men and women alike, which might include the claim that it is not always self-evident that treating people of different sexes is the same as treating them justly. Now, from certain perspectives within a liberal polity, this treatment may be deemed wrong or inadequate. However, there is at least here some argument to be had.

A further dimension of the charge that religions are not obviously on the side of liberty, is the claim that some institutionalised religions have had a tendency to align themselves with political forms and regimes that are antithetical to liberal democracy. It is certainly true that there are a number of countries that continue to be effectively theocracies. And indeed, some liberal democracies, like post-independence Ireland, have at times looked too much like one of these. On the other hand, as we noted in the discussion of the trickster, the influence of the Catholic Church emerged out of its history as both object and agent of resistance to perceived oppression. Certainly, matters are rarely as clear-cut as Grayling either sees or wishes them to be. In opposition to his view, it might be argued that if there is a real danger in late-industrial liberal democracies in the relationship between church and state, it is more likely to be manifest in Erastianism than in theocracy. The temptation for government to draw religion under its ambit and use it for purposes of propagation and dissemination of particular ideologies, or even policies, is not particularly new. It is not necessary to posit a Soviet totalitarian kind of abuse of religious institutions to see this in action. In 2001, the British government decided to expand the number of religiously denominated schools. It did this in the face of some quite virulent opposition (Dean 2001b; Dawkins 2001), which I shall deal with shortly. Why does a government seek to expand religiously denominated schools when the religious demography consistently and inexorably appears to point away from such a move (Bruce 2002)? Moreover, we might ask if it is appropriate for a government, in an increasingly pluralised and post-religious liberal democracy, to wish to increase the number of such schools. Part of the answer to such a question may lie in the public league tables on school performance so beloved of successive British governments, and in the growing body of research that appears to indicate that church schools in general, and Catholic schools in particular, appear to be more successful, across a range of academic and social indices, than their public school counterparts. More importantly this appears to be most especially the case when demographic particulars are factored into the studies (Bryk, Lee and Holland 1995; Morris 1998). It is in such circumstances that the Government may be seen as wishing to use church schools to enhance performance, and because of their perceived values-based perspective that requires the state to pass no judgement on their expressly religious claims.

Church groups may be flattered by the state, turning to them for assistance in the education of children, but there are significant dangers. In liberal democracies, religion is rightly independent of the state and vice versa. While it may be appropriate and just that religious groups have their voice heard in the public spaces, it is equally right for the state to seek to control organisations and groups, including religious groups that might be considered inimical to human flourishing as defined by the tenets of liberal democracy itself. But such control must be established in conformity to some publicly accessible principles. Let us suppose that the government aims to use church schools as a tool to enhance economic performance in order to increase the nation's share of global resources. Let us also suppose that the acquisition of such resources means that other human beings starve. Should a religious organisation—which claims as its guiding principle universal love with its imperative to go beyond the demands of justice—allow itself to be such a tool? The relationship of religious group and state should be based on what Audi (2000) describes as theo-ethical equilibrium.[2] Thus, while it may be appropriate for religious schools to exist in a liberal democratic state, it is not appropriate that they should simply become instruments of government policy. Such an arrangement is good for neither party, nor their cognate and diverse principles. Wogaman sums this up in suggesting that, "when the state itself is treated as the highest good—as is usually the case with Erastianism—the integrity of religious organisations and institutions is fatally undermined. They can no longer be taken seriously in their own terms, that is, on the basis of the faith they profess. Now they are important only for their political utility" (Wogaman 2000, 255). The charge that religions are likely to carry disproportionate and inappropriate influence in the state is more likely to be reversed. Religion can only serve the liberal democratic polity in freedom. If it is too closely allied to the state, it cannot perform its critical functions. Equally, if it is entirely without the liberal state—as we have already noted with regard to the Amish—it also has some difficulty, since liminality requires some kind of communicative relationship. The liberal state may be enjoined to uphold the right to maintain separate educational provision, but that of itself does not necessarily bring about a liminal relationship between centre and periphery.

On Whether or Not Religions Bring Unique Wisdom

Clearly, arguments against giving religions a significant place and role in the public spaces are partly rooted in principle, but equally, partly in distrust. Some of this distrust emanates from a sense that religions certainly have no monopoly of wisdom and that, in every generation, some church leaders have behaved in a foolish fashion. It is no part of the argument here that religious leaders have categorical access to the unmediated truth about how we should live. On the contrary, it is certainly the case that the fools of Ecclesiastes are in little danger of being mistaken for Ben Jonson's fool; that is, as one so "worthy of men's envy and admiration!" Rather, the fools of Ecclesiastes are those popinjays who would rule the earth out of ignorance, vanity, greed, self-aggrandisement, and all with only a modicum of hubris! Yet, both are called "fool" because of their behaviour.

It is both a delight and a puzzle of language, no less of religious language, that we may use exactly the same word to mean entirely opposing things. (Again, language may be simultaneously reveal and hide.) Jonson's fool discloses the vanity of the other, while the fools of Ecclesiastes try to mask the ruler's vanity. This apparent contradiction arises because we know what it is to behave foolishly, but equally, we can interpret both context and motivation. The one *acts* as a fool so as to disclose stupidity; the other, thinking he is nothing of the sort, *behaves* stupidly. The subtlety with which we perform the art of discrimination is certainly one key to understanding the kind of liminal role that religion may play in the sustenance of discursive openness in liberal democracy. It has so far been admitted that over many years institutional religion has had no shortage of fools of the Ecclesiastes variety; men (notably, though not exclusively, in the Catholic Christian tradition) whose very name has been a byword for corruption and mendacity (see de Rosa 1988). Indeed, it is this wonderful play of the dual meaning of fool that offered Erasmus such scope in his *Praise of Folly* (Erasmus of Rotterdam 1971). [3]

However, in religion—as in politics, education, and in our everyday existence—we live in a zone of ambiguity and conflicted perceptions. Since ambiguity and conflict are etched into the fabric of our actual lives and experiences, we can no more ignore or sideline them than we can choose not to breathe. Nor may we easily suggest that these ambiguities and conflicts are merely appearances and that somewhere in a kind of logical substratum they are resolved into a singular, coherent account of how things really are. But, as I have suggested in the previous chapter, ambiguity is there to be "rowed through." We cannot prescind from making choices, judgements and decisions. Indeed, it may be argued that the quality of decision making is a significant consequence of liminality

Corruption and foolishness is but one side of institutional religion, and hardly represents an exhaustive characterisation. May it not be reasonably claimed that there have been many occasions when religion has played an important liberating role in circumstances where particular individuals or communities have been oppressed? Religion has thrown up quite as many fools of the Jonson kind as those subject to the scorn of the author of Ecclesiastes; women and men of integrity and vision who could invert the dominant categories of their time in order to display some important truth, or, perhaps more frequently, expose some falsehood at the heart of the polity. [4] But, we might ask, would it be possible for him to launch such a critique as is to be found, not only in Ecclesiastes, but also in Isaiah, Jeremiah and Amos, from outside the tradition? Just as the "Asses Masses" and "Spaghetti Processions" occupy a liminal space within the tradition, so too does the prophet. He is neither of the centre nor excluded from the polity, but erupts here and there in the midst of betwixt and between. The prophetic protest of the religious fool is only made possible by the institutionally enshrined claims to human flourishing to which he calls, or calls back, his co-religionists. And so, in parts of Central and South America and South Africa, the institution has given rise to such as Helder Camera and Oscar Romero who, with thousands of unnamed women and men, have worked tirelessly for the liberation and well-being of the poor and oppressed and against the anti-democratic impulses that have so bedevilled Latin American politics. In a similar vein, under Denis Hurley, Archbishop of Durban, and in the face of enormous government hostility, Catholic schools unexpectedly took the lead in school desegregation in South Africa at the height of the apartheid era. In these and many other cases, institutional Christianity may readily be regarded as creative, constructive and in support of those discursive freedoms necessary for a sustainable and robust liberal democracy.

What we see here is that institutions have not always played an unequivocal role in the support of democracy, but they have played a substantial one. In one way, this complexity and ambiguity simply serves to reinforce the relative and surprising nature of the liminal. It erupts into institutions, and in the process of doing so, can occasion an institutional eruption into the wider polity that can serve to challenge the dominant centre. Just as the trickster makes manifest the social and cultural reality that not all things appear as unequivocally "this" or "that," so it is for religious institutions. What one must do is make a balanced judgement about the whole, albeit that all such judgements are themselves provisional. Part of that judgement will be based on the capacity of the institution to generate both positions of principle, and the individuals and groups who can enact these principles, even in the face of the institution's own negenthropic energies.

One Church, Many Voices

The apparent resolution of the previous issue, however, appears to open up a new front against religiously denominated schooling as an important site of liminality in liberal democracy. Since it appears that not even one denomination, never mind one church, speaks with a single voice, which version of Catholicism or Presbyterianism, or Islam or Mahayana Buddhism is to govern the role of the religious school in a liberal democracy? Is every version of a particular religious tradition to be treated equally seriously? After all, even in the same tradition, differences may not necessarily be relegated to peripheral or arcane details of doctrine or practice. For example, on the one hand, Catholicism appears to embrace those like Michael Novak (1982; 1993), who regard capitalism and democracy as inextricably and positively linked and, to that extent, he appears to reinforce those views ascribed earlier to British Prime Minster Tony Blair. On the other hand, there are a host of left-wing Christian theologians and intellectuals (Sobrino and Wilfred 2001; Gutiérrez 1999) who, in drawing their inspiration from the seventh-century Israelite prophetic tradition, regard capitalism as inimical to what they would see as true democracy rooted in a notion of redistributive justice. When we venture beyond a single denominational tradition, matters get yet more complicated. And if we go further, as between religions, we arrive at a point of interminable claim and counter-claim as to how society should conduct itself. Moreover, there are many religious people who variously regard their religious beliefs as private, distinguishing between their personal preferences and their political position. There are yet others who retain a religious affection from romantic attachment, but do not expect that their religion should play any part in their public life. The question then arises, which version(s) of religion are permissible or properly seen as liminal? Or again, should some religious groups be permitted to operate separate schools under official sanction and others refused? Or yet still, would the support (tacit or substantive) of such schools not lead to a certain kind of anarchy that would undermine a key liberal democratic aim of common flourishing?

We need not delay too much on the first two questions, but the third might provide a few more complexities. Liminality embodies a degree of unpredictability as well as discordant possibilities and challenges to the dominant discourse of the centre, most especially about relationships. And it is precisely these qualities that make it so important for education in a liberal democracy. Therefore, we should be careful about sanctioning only those alternatives to the centre that we deem orthodox and safe. Before an institution, be it church or other organisation, is forbidden from the establishment and maintenance of schools, there should be evidence that it is inimical to the flourishing of both the individual and, more widely, the liberal democratic polity. Moreover, the burden of proof should lie with the state, precisely because of its asymmetrical hold on power.

The reason that religious groups, among others, wish to establish their own schools is because of an attachment to the principle of searching for some notion of truth and meaning. Admittedly, some think that they have found it and therefore wish to fight to retain it for themselves and their children. But, in either event, the desire to search for or defend particular conceptions of truth is not of itself immoral or undesirable. Indeed, we should welcome those who still think that truth is something to be searched for and defended. They stand in a long tradition of human thought that has been almost expunged in late-industrial democracies (and throughout this essay, I have intimated my belief that while we may well have to reconfigure and recast our traditions, they continue to be important for human flourishing), concerned with the search for fundamental questions of truth and meaning. Of course, in the light of the pragmatic scepticism of contemporary philosophers like Rorty (1999), such a search has itself been deemed meaningless. Equally, "postmodernism, wedded as it is to the particular, would be reluctant to accept that there are propositions which are true of all times and places, yet which are not simply vacuous or trivial" (Eagleton 1996, 112). A generation earlier, Eagleton's anxieties were shared by Berlin, who argued that there have been "sceptics in every generation who suggested that there were, perhaps no final answers, that solutions hitherto provided depended on highly variable factors such as the climate in which the theorist's life was lived, or his social or economic or political condition, or that of his fellows, or his or their emotional disposition, or the kinds of interests which absorbed him or them" (1969, 22). With extraordinary percipience, given that this essay was first penned in 1950, Berlin goes on to argue that it is only in the twentieth century that human societies have taken the next step, the eradication of the question. Those recurrent questions that once "perplexed and often tormented original and honest minds in every generation" (ibid, 23), could now be expunged from the public spaces, not by rational means or the demonstration of the false premises upon which a particular claim might be based, but by altering the outlook that gave rise to them in the first place.

> Thus if a man is haunted by the suspicion that, for example, full individual liberty is not compatible with coercion by the majority in a democratic state, and yet continues to hanker after both democracy and individual liberty, it may be possible by appropriate treatment to rid him of this idée fixe, so that it will disappear, to return no more. The worried questioner of political institutions is thereby relieved of his burden and freed to pursue socially useful tasks, unhampered by disturbing and distracting reflections which have been eliminated by the eradication of their cause. (ibid)

For both Eagleton and Berlin, along with a host of other thinkers, difficult questions about truth need not be consigned to the waste bins of superfluity of either the postmodern philosopher, who rarely if ever lives according to her own nostrums, or the globalised consumer culture. If different religious traditions, or even different traditions within a religion, promote and uphold very different conceptions of how human flourishing is best secured, so much the better. Liberal democracies continue to lay claim to a truly agonistic public space. The fragility of liberal democracy lies not in the discursive potential of different schools, offering children varying conceptions of truth and meaning, but precisely in the closure around the chimerical notion that liberal values and associated human meaning are located in conspicuous consumption. Even where a particular school or community appears to challenge some of the most cherished values of liberal democracy, such a democracy should exercise great care in its role as censor. Again, I would reiterate, the burden of proof should always lie with the liberal democratic state.

It is, nevertheless, important to introduce a cautionary note here. Just as the state has certain obligations to secure group as well as individual rights, groups have responsibilities. For a school community or system to realise its liminal potential with respect to the wider polity, three things must be in place. First, it needs to see itself as engaged in more than the protection of its own historic territory. Liminality can no more express itself hidden away in a cellar bolted on the inside, than it can if it were to be bolted on the outside. Second, the institution must have some sense of the freedom of possibility. Alongside its rules and regulations, doctrines and dogmas, the liminal community must allow for the creative possibilities of the moment. Third, it must give expression to some conception of human flourishing.

Church Education: A Breeding Ground for Discrimination

The condition of human flourishing would certainly be compromised if the charge that religious schooling promoted discrimination and sectarianism were to be sustained. This is possibly the most rhetorically potent charge to be made against the active presence of religious institutions in education, most especially where they are funded from the public purse. If it were to be upheld, then this indeed might be a telling objection to the claims being made for the role of the liminal institution in education, so it may be as well to examine it reasonably carefully. From time to time, and across a range of liberal-democratic polities, such a charge is made (see de Jong and Snik 2002; Judge 2001; and Short 2002) and is manifest in both the philosophical literature and in the discourse of the public spaces. In Britain, the resurgence of government interest in supporting religious schooling has evoked something of a backlash that has, despite its reliance on academics, ignored more traditional forms of academic argument in favour of conducting a high profile, coordinated news-media campaign. Thus, Atkins argues that because religions are intolerant of each other, "schools set up on the shoulders of religions inevitably propagate that intolerance into future generations" (2001, 7). This is, of course, not a new charge. Ball and Troyna (1987), a little more circumspectly, argued that Catholic schools are incipiently more intolerant than their state counterparts because they were less likely to adopt the local authority's guidelines on multicultural policy. In a separate but not, I think, unrelated move in Scotland, Catholic schools have been subjected to a prolonged and concerted media attack on precisely these grounds. In recent years, there have been a plethora of calls for the withdrawal of state funding and their closure from a broad spectrum of voices in the public spaces.[5] The justification for these calls is grounded in the claim that Catholic schools are, by virtue of their very existence, either unjust or sectarian. Bruce, for example, argues that, "irrespective of *any virtues*[6] that Catholic education may have, and irrespective of the rights of any group of parents to raise their children as they wish, a segregated school system is divisive [because] the dual system separates young people" (1998, 5).

Whether or not religious schools are likely to promote divisiveness is largely an empirical question and, so far, the evidence is somewhat less than conclusive (see Callan 1997, 179). Indeed, as Short (2002) argues, most of the empirical evidence in Britain and elsewhere points in the opposite direction. Moreover, he observes that the key determinant of divisive education is not context but the nature of what is taught. So it has been that the anti-Semitic education prevalent throughout Europe until the middle of the twentieth century took place in a wide variety of institutional settings. To this end, Short approvingly quotes from the reflections of the British Chief Rabbi, Jonathan Sacks, who opines,

> [F]aith schools must teach and exemplify tolerance to those of other faiths. The way to do this is not to insist that they may be compelled to take pupils of other faiths or no faith. It is rather, to require that they demonstrate through teaching and practical programmes, a willingness to engage with society, beyond the boundaries of their community.
>
> (Sacks, quoted in Short op cit, 565)

There is a further, logical point to be made about Bruce's claim. He falls into the common error of seeing the existence of distinctive modes of being, institutions and so on, as interchangeable with the pejorative notion of divisiveness. Educationally and socially, children (who are or may be friends and neighbours) are separated from their peers for all kinds of reasons, sometimes for nothing less arbitrary than children on one side of a street are in one education authority and children on the other are in a different education authority. They are also divided according to their particular propensities and abilities, arguably for both good and bad reasons; some take ballet lessons, others join a football club. But then, it might be argued, these divisions are both reasonable and rational and reflect children's interests and are no business of the state. So it is, in Bruce's world, that parents may make trivial choices with respect to their children, but not serious ones. The serious choices must be left to the state.

Bruce's claims are all made with respect to Scotland—though it might be supposed that his comments are made with respect to any polity. If this were not so then his arguments may be dismissed as arbitrary. Challenging his claims, Finn rightly maintains that "social-group differences cannot be disallowed, unless one wishes to advocate moving towards suppression...Scotland must move towards becoming an open and proudly pluralist society, with a diversity of ways of being Scots" (2000, 79). He recognises, however, that, "most societies and most people do have undoubted problems in working through what a pluralist society does really mean" (ibid). If Bruce and others want a common education system because they wish Scotland to develop as a polity with a shared sense of purpose, can this be compatible with the claims of plurality? The problems of identity and affinity, which attend public discussions of plurality in Scotland, partake in quite general considerations about the relationship between the political centre and the liminal and/or marginal in a liberal democracy. Those who criticise the continuation of state-funded Catholic education, implicitly at least, ground their objections in some general considerations about the importance of strong public and common educational provision. This they do in the belief that a cohesive polity requires common provision so that the polity can develop a common identity.

As we have already noted, one of the most articulate and thoughtful proponents of this view is Randall Curren (2000), who argues that the demands of justice and the claim of any community to a set of common goods with respect to human flourishing require that there is a public education available for all, and further, that there is a requirement on those within a community that they should attend those institutions that provide a public education. Grounding his claim in an Aristotelian metaphysic, he maintains that (1) the individual should be afforded the opportunity to achieve her natural end, which is goodness; (2) since they promote a citizen's *eudaimonia*, an education in virtues is essential for all; (3) the natural end of the city is the promotion of the happy life, since the good of all is to be preferred to the good of one; and (4) since the city has as its natural end the promotion of the good life for all, and since this can be achieved through the practice of the virtues, then education in the virtues is a responsibility of the state so as to ensure the fulfilment of its own ends. In Curren's words it may be summarised thus: "Taken together, then, the ability and inclination of each citizen to not only participate in the best life himself, but also assist his fellow citizens in doing so, would seem to be just what is meant by the citizens of a city sharing or being partners in the common end of living the best life" (ibid, 128). For Curren, education is one means by which a city can become a polity; an organised and unified social unit that has at its centre the aim of eudaemonia for all its members. Without such unification, the eudaemonic aims striven for are unlikely to be realised. In any event, for him, it is a matter of justice that a public education system is established that "provides an adequate moral, political, and disciplinary education and an education preparatory to respected work for all children"(ibid, 212). He further claims that what underpins Aristotle's (and his own) attachment to regulated public education for all, is an attachment to justice for all. On the back of this, he maintains that separate schools are unlikely to promote the kind of collective eudaemonic aims necessary for the realisation of justice, since it is not clear that those parents who chose to educate their children privately have the broad conception of justice and the common good that he wishes to promote. Indeed, as he, no doubt correctly, points out, many parents who send their children to private schools do so to promote their individual success, flying in the face of any claims to a preeminent ethical stance in support of the common eudaemonia.

Callan (2000) also makes the presumptive case in favour of common schooling. He does, however, put forward quite a nuanced case for the possibility of separate schools in very limited circumstances, on the grounds of developmental association; for example, that children gradually need to increase the circle of those they trust and can engage with, and so they may have their early education in the culture that is most contiguous with that of the home, but as they make the transition towards citizenship they should enter a more dialogically robust environment.

Both Curren and Callan offer persuasive arguments in favour of common schooling, but both partake in the anxieties of a number of North American scholars that religious fundamentalist schools are the alternative to common public schooling. Their case is therefore established with respect to the exercise of parental rights as somehow oppositional to the eudaemonic aims of the whole polity. I wish to make one brief point in relation to the exercise of such rights and then go on to make some further observations about the claim that the polity is necessarily better served by having a single, common system of schooling, which is, after all, the claim made by Bruce and others.

Philosophers have a tendency to predicate their arguments on worst-case scenarios and Scotland may be quite unlike North America, but there is some, albeit anecdotal, evidence that those who wish to exercise their parental rights with respect to their children's education are doing so precisely because they believe that the education offered in the common public school is antithetical to human flourishing—as a concern for the distribution of justice, as a search for authenticity, and as the exploration of truth. Rather, they perceive the common public school as prey to the vagaries of a discourse, which confuses economic success with virtue and conflates democracy with the middle classes, and in doing so, subverts what may be understood by human flourishing. It is not self-evident that parents should sacrifice their attachment to the very virtues Curren wishes to uphold on the grounds that the state should do it when, de facto, it appears on many occasions to do nothing of the sort. As Curren admits, Aristotle does suggest that where the state fails to provide an education in goodness, then the parent should supply it (op cit, 81ff).[7] He does, however, argue that this does nothing to undermine the regulatory role of the state.[8] Whatever virtues there might be in creating a polity with a common public education in Aristotle's Greece, it is not self-evident that these are easily translatable into obligations in late-modern plural democracies. Maybe this is exactly the point, though. The claims to plurality in the governance of late-democratic polities may be somewhat overplayed in Curren's analysis and it may be that such polities are not quite as plural as might be thought. In fact, plurality may have come to mean in practice secularity.

Let me take an example of what this might mean in practice. Suppose there were a public education authority that decided that sexually transmitted diseases were on the increase among teenagers and, consequently, there was a need for the development of a "common" sex education programme, which, among other things, provided information on gay and lesbian sexual relations. This might include advice on where to get further information, screenings of educational and related media materials, how to have safe sex, and so on. Suppose the curriculum materials provided for the students are of a very explicit and graphic nature and assumes that underage sex is normative among teenagers. Let us further suppose that, while not explicitly encouraging it, the materials lack any meaningful or substantial alternatives (such as sexual continence) to the assumption that such behaviour is normal, and, as such, normative. Of course, it is possible to have mention of alternatives, but that is a different matter from having them substantially represented in the discourse. Just as poetry may be mentioned in school but be given no substantial place in the life of the school or classroom, so the more conservative positions on teenage sexual relations may be treated similarly. Suppose that the curriculum materials include a range of URL addresses that direct students to information sites on STD clinics and sex advice centres, but none on issues of continence. Are parents who think that such centres may not in fact promote the flourishing of their child not entitled to at least demur from the received orthodoxy? Further, suppose that a group of parents do decide that what they perceive to be the "implicit" support of current sexual relations is antithetical to the common good; would they not be justified in claiming a different kind of education for their children? After all, they might wish to claim that the kind of education on offer is not plural but secular—there is, within its frames of reference, no place for a serious articulation of a view of the common good that draws upon the range of voices available to the public sphere. Justice demands that the public sphere is a space where all groups feel that their voice is listened to and taken seriously, yet the common school in this scenario is unlikely to deliver a voice to those who view the sex education programme on offer as detrimental to the common good.

If the public sphere, in Taylor's (1995) terms, is to be truly a place where the worlds of politics and economics[9] do not form a particular hegemonic coalition but are subject to a range of voices, then it has to be sufficiently robust to withstand the dominant centrist force or forces. The separate school, because it can be subject to a different values system than the dominant secular one, offers one possible site of resistance. Of course, it may be deemed as politically awkward given its unwillingness to wholly and uncritically embrace the political/civic centre, but in terms of the preservation of democracy this may, paradoxically, be its strength. To remain at, or return to the threshold, is not a weakness of such schools, but a strength. Where they are state funded, schools are subject to certain constraints about that which promotes the common good, but their very existence helps the polity discriminate what is actually in the common good from what just happens, at any moment in time, to be the dominant discourse. At the same time, they are institutionally strong enough to offer different insights from the edge as to what might constitute human flourishing. The demands of justice, which are Callan's and Curren's major concern, are not necessarily well-served by having one account of the "common good." Checks and balances in a polity only work where the institutions embodying different, sometimes liminal, perspectives are sufficiently robust to withstand the domination of the centre. Once again it is worth reiterating the claim that liberal democratic values are more likely to be subverted by the discursive domination of the market than religious schooling. In any event, the health of a liberal society depends on the toleration of difference and the accommodation of the liminal if we are to successfully construct something like a workable plural polity.

Religious Schooling as Signs of Contradiction

To date, I have outlined some of the main arguments against seeing religiously sponsored education as a liminal site in education. I have also suggested in each case that these objections are not insuperable. But this merely secures a platform upon which to build the more substantive claim, that religious institutions can play a liminal role in liberal democracy. So far I have suggested that religion can embody an ontology and anthropology which is quite different from that which reflects the dominant political centre in a liberal democracy. This may be seen where we look at the notion of the self: in particular, how the embodied self is constructed as a site of consumptive exploitation by what might be called the wraiths of liberal democracy. In the Christian tradition, for example, with its notions of natality and incarnation, the individual embodied person is herself sacred. Value is determined not with reference to position or possession, nor even rights and justice, but love. It is not that a liberal democracy must necessarily embrace the values of position and possession. Rather it is that religious (or at least some religious) ontologies cannot by definition do so.

Let me pursue this a little further through a particular reading of the threat to discursive freedom within a liberal democracy, posed by late-industrial patterns of consumption. It is hardly novel to suggest that something is awry in the patterns of consumption manifest in late-industrial democracies (Korten 2001). What happens when the government, ostensibly the regulator of public goods, not only opens up schools to the predatory practices of these corporations, but also positively encourages schools to embrace them?[10] What tools of critique do public schools have at their disposal that they can offer their students when, increasingly, curriculum materials are supplied by corporations, where programmes are sponsored by corporations, where food is supplied by corporations, and where media access is the gift of corporations? To ask these questions is not to minimise the work of teachers in the public school systems, but to point out both the practical and logical difficulties they face. If the government or the education authority wishes to apply particular commercial policies to and in them, schools generally are obliged, or are subject to intense pressure, to behave accordingly. More importantly, if the authority wish for schools to comply with a curriculum philosophy that instantiates consumerist ideals, they largely have to do so because they have no official epistemological or ontological alternative. Public education must reflect the particular readings and understandings of particular cultural, political and social happenings and circumstances. I do not wish to claim that schools and teachers are entirely powerless here, only that they are faced with an uphill struggle to define themselves and their pedagogies over and against the dominant, monoglot culture that they are perceived to serve.

It is here that separate schools may have something to offer that asserts itself, interstitially, into the schooling of a liberal democracy. Religious readings of the nature and effects of consumption can legitimately inform a different curriculum philosophy. And the readings of consumption that emerge out of many religious traditions are very different from those available at the political centre. Moreover, a religious reading must, of logical necessity, underpin the outlook and practices of the church school. If religious schools, consciously and reflexively, operate according to the imperatives that emanate from such readings, they can do nothing other than contribute to the general critical reflection of schooling in the public spaces. This may only happen where there is some relationship between the religious school and the centre—where a religious community withdraws entirely from engagement with a wider polity, this task inevitably becomes much more difficult.[11] So what might a religious reading of the dangers of consumption look like and how might this enhance a more general understanding of its corrupting influence? Given that their political instincts were rooted in their religious beliefs, it may be useful to begin with some of the Founding Fathers of American democracy.

In his seminal work on civil religion in the American republic, Robert Bellah explores how the Republic has become corrupted, a condition that Benjamin Franklin thought incipient in its very foundations. This foundational corruption, Franklin believed, lay in the corruption of the people. Bellah quotes his rather hesitant assent to the new Constitution, on the grounds that, while it may be well administered for a while, it would almost certainly end in, "[d]espotism, as other forms have done before it, when the people shall have become so corrupted as to need despotic Government, being incapable of any other" (quoted in Bellah 1992, 184; see Ketcham 1965).

Corruption, in this eighteenth-century sense, carries quite different connotations from modern usage, which generally focuses on dishonesty, mendacity and so on. For Bellah, as for Franklin, it is more likely to be "found in luxury, dependence, and ignorance. Luxury [being] that pursuit of material things that diverts us from concern for the public good, that leads us to exclusive concern for our own good, or what we would call today consumerism" (Bellah 1992, 185). He then goes on to argue that "Dependence naturally follows from luxury, for it consists in accepting the dominance of whatever person or group, or, we might say today, governmental or private corporate structure, that promises it will take care of our material desires" (ibid). Bellah's interpretation gets support from others among the Founding Fathers of American democracy. In his correspondence with Thomas Jefferson, James Maddison observes that one of the most intractable constitutional problems of political economy is the distribution of property. He ultimately comes down on the side of those who favour redistribution, asserting that "from a more equal partition of property must result a greater simplicity of manners, *consequently a less consumption of manufactured superfluities*"[12] (Morton Smith 1995, 424). Or again, on writing to Jefferson with some observations on Jefferson's draft of the Constitution for Virginia, he raises the question of the relationship between property and voting. In doing so, he suggests that the "time to guard against the danger of putting too much emphasis on property is now, at the first framing of the constitution and in the present state of population when the bulk of the people have a sufficient interest in possession or in prospect to be attached to the rights of property without being insufficiently attached to the rights of persons" (ibid, 557; see also Jefferson 1943). These meditations of the threat to democracy may be read as issuing from the eighteenth-century concern for human rights and individual advancement, but this would be to underplay the religious tropes that weave back and forth through the deliberations of even men as lukewarm to traditional Christian religion as Franklin (Bellah et al. 1985, 28–33). Thus, it can reasonably be asserted that their anxiety about corruption was at least partially informed by a religious understanding.

Similar religious notions about corruption emerged in Aung San Sui Kyi's Buddhist-inspired analysis of corruption, discussed earlier. That is, the fear of *not having* as the root of all other forms of corruption. This, in turn, echoes Augustine's notions of earthly love (*cupiditas*) and craving or covetousness (*appetitus*)—the constant desire for some thing or object or state of affairs that one already knows. (If I crave chocolate, it is because I have experienced chocolate. In this sense, I know chocolate.) For Augustine, the core of the individual's will is love—this love is manifest as cupiditas, where it desires or craves possession of the object, thing, idea or person. But, in the very moment of getting, craving gives way to fear (*metus*)—the fear of losing. In this way, the present is perennially compromised by the future. In her study of Augustine, Arendt puts it thus: "Constantly bound by craving and fear to a future full of uncertainties, we strip each present moment of its calm, its intrinsic import, which we are unable to enjoy. And so, the future destroys the present" (1996, 10). The craving for more and more of the world simultaneously gives rise to the fear of losing it. In Arendt's reading of Augustine, this craving itself arises out of habit *(consuetude)*—not to be confused with Bordieu's use of *habitus*, which is more correctly seen as disposition—as habit that drags the mind along, even against its own will. Thus, "insofar as the man is of the world, habit has already delivered him to the world" (ibid, 82); habit consolidates covetousness. As long as one lives in the world of things, this cycle is inescapable because the will is enchained to the world and its contents. Of course, Augustine's notion of attachment to the things of the world is not exclusively concerned with objects, but includes attachment to position and power. Fear of loss of such *cogitationes* is just as real and just as damaging for the conduct of liberal democracy. It is only where the will turns away from the world, as the creation to the creator, that any possibility of escape may be effected, but this, of course, would be to eschew consumption as any kind of goal.

From an Augustinian perspective, we may say that education is driven by the fear of failure in the competition for the earth's intellectual, aesthetic and physical resources. As we have seen, schools are increasingly subjected to the rhetoric of the globalised markets with their explicit and implicit messages of consumption. Indeed, schools are being turned into sites for the cultivation of consumption. Advertising, an industry that barely existed at the turn of the nineteenth century, is today possibly the largest business in the world. Its *raison d'etre* is consumption and its practices function as devices for habituation, precisely because they establish and sustain the dialectic between appetite and fear. It is not for nothing that corporations increasingly seek an advertising/sponsorship role in education (Klein 2001). This desire is no longer even thinly disguised as altruism. Korten quotes a Coca-Cola spokesman who, in 1994, were lobbying to retain access to schools as saying, "Our strategy is ubiquity. We want to put soft drinks within arms' reach of desire. We strive to make soft drinks widely available, and schools are one channel we want to make them available in" (2001, 157). Additionally, the behavioural habits of consumption occlude the very thing that Franklin and his colleagues were seeking—a public space for the exercise of opinions and a preparedness to act. And such patterns of consumption could not, so to speak, be purchased without habituated covetousness (Conroy 2003). This constant dialectic between fear and appetite clouds our judgement and corruption is its issue.

It might be reasonably asserted that a reading of the deleterious effects of overweening consumption need not necessarily be religious. After all, quite a number of philosophers and commentators, including Arendt herself and others discussed earlier (such as Giroux, McLaren and Baudrillard), have referred our attention to precisely the same issues. However, the incommensurability of the secular perspective, which dominates the liberal democratic centre, and religious perspectives is more than an eschatological or teleological disagreement. It is a fundamental disagreement about human nature. In its deep indebtedness to the philosophies of utilitarianism and pragmatism, the secular perspective harbours some notion of the perfectibility of desire in its, at least, notional realisation. So, for those who look to a secular philosophy, there is no doubt an optimum balance of redistributed consumption that equates to something like justice. Augustine, however, regards such desire as a tantalusian illusion given that the redistribution of desire doesn't turn it into something else other than desire. For him, this is simply a category mistake. The relationship between person and person, person and the world, is not justice but love. The foundation of this love is not, however, cupiditas, since such love would clearly fall prey to the accusation that it was simply a different manifestation of desire. Rather, love of the other begins with the self-denial that issues from a rejection of the attachments to the world, as a species of object to be used. This denial enables the will to free itself so as to turn from the created to the creator, as source of all. The denial also includes turning one's back on the other as one more object to be used or possessed in this or that manner in the world. And, since there is nothing to be gained in the world of materiality from love of God (*amor Dei*), this love is its own end. It is this unequivocal loving of God (that which is to be loved only in and for itself and not for what it can or might deliver for me) that allows one to turn back to the world and configure one's relationship with it anew. Clearly, this has implications for one's relationship with the other (my neighbour). Since the Gospel injunction is to love one's neighbour as oneself and one has denied oneself, then one must also deny one's neighbour. At the heart of this contradiction lies the search for the self, which exists beyond the desire for possession. Arendt's summary of his position is that, "I deny the other person so as to break through to his real being, just as in searching for myself I deny myself" (Arendt op cit, 96; see Augustine 1953, IV, 4, 7–9, 14).

However, Augustine also recognised that one had to live along with others, so how is the Christian to relate to the normal, everyday transactions of the social? Social life is configured by interdependence, what we might regard as an instrumental relationship. For the Christian, redemption is for the whole world and not for some sections of it to which I happen to be geopolitically related. As Paul says, "There is neither Greek nor Jew, free nor slave" (Galatians 3:28). In being the object of God's salvation all are radically the same. Thus, when the Christian comes to look at community it is configured, not instrumentally, but by a radical equality borne out of natality, sinfulness and redemption. This is usefully summarised by Arendt:

> The explicitness of equality is contained in the commandment of neighbourly love. The reason one should love one's neighbor is that the neighbor is fundamentally one's equal and both share the same sinful past. This is another way of saying that it takes the past to turn mere sameness of belief into the common faith (*communis fides*). Moreover, one should love one's neighbor not on account of his sin, which was indeed the source of equality, but on account of the grace that has revealed itself in him as well as in oneself (*tamquam te ipsum*)." (1996, 106)

In the light of this radical equality, the Christian returns to the world and lives in it in a quite distinctive manner; one configured not by a utility of means but by a community of ends. But then, it might be argued that what is being called for, by Augustine and by implication, the Christian, is a denial of the world and therefore it can have no contribution to make to the education of students to live in the world. There is some truth in this charge, given Augustine's desire to show even the materially enslaved how they might be free. "Historically," Arendt suggests, "it is interesting to note that the appearance of the problem of freedom in Augustine's philosophy was...preceded by the conscious attempt to divorce the notion of freedom from politics, to arrive at a formulation through which one may be a slave in the world and still be free" (1968a, 147). Of course, it is a moot point as to whether or not the inner freedom of which Augustine speaks has much to offer a world where the self is dissolved into its patterns of material consumption, but I shall return to this.

Now, it is certainly true that Augustine, and Christian philosopers more generally, see withdrawal from the world as desirable, but only because it presages a return to it in the light of that love that has its source in the creator. Indeed, as Arendt shows, Augustine's philosophy informs a different conception of being (*existenz*) in the world. It is no part of the argument here that Augustine's thought is not replete with contradiction. Indeed, as Jaspers points out, nothing is easier to find. "No philosophy is free from contradictions—and no thinker can aim at contradictions. But Augustine is one of the thinkers who venture into contradictions, who draw their life from the tension of enormous contradictions.... He makes us aware of the provocative question: Is there a point, a limit, where we are bound to encounter contradiction?" (Jaspers 1962, 111). However, since this essay plays with the notions of contradiction this is hardly inappropriate. It would be naïve to imply that Augustine's notions of desire, appetites and love represent the totality of Christian thinking on these matters. But, given the huge influence his thought has had on subsequent generations of Christians across many denominations, and for the purposes of the argument here, we may say at least that his is not an unrepresentative view. Moreover, from within a Christian perspective, he deals with precisely those issues that underpin the particular discursive closure with which we are concerned.

To the late-industrial mind, much of Augustine's thought can appear, at the very least, odd. This is most especially the case when it is applied to schooling, a space primarily concerned with preparing students to live in the world. But, it is precisely the specific form of living in the world that has been normalised and promoted in late-industrial consumer society that Augustine's, and Christian ontology more generally, challenge. As I have argued, education in late-modern liberal democracy has been increasingly subjected to the discursive control of markets. Under this umbrella, schools are increasingly places predicated on assisting students in the acquisition and deployment of resources.[13] From a liberal-democratic perspective, the main questions then centre on justice—that is, the just distribution of these resources. But, even those schools that prepare students to perfect the redistribution of the earth's resources, through an appeal to justice, are locked into the view that somehow human being and its concomitant relationships are primarily configured with respect to these resources. It might be argued, then, that the critical capacity of state schools, even in a liberal democracy, is limited, since late-industrial capital globalisation is just a particularly virulent form of the power of the "secularist" doctrine it embraces. Given the growth of this doctrine, we can see that it increasingly represents the dominant centrist position and that schools are ever more subject to its rhetoric and practices.

Public schools are not immune from, and arguably should not be immunised against, the climate of opinion outside their gates. Yet, this provides a deep contradiction—and not one of Augustine's making. In a quite fundamental way, public schooling is concerned to generate cupiditas—an attachment to the world. However, public schools are also spaces that should generate at least the future possibilities of critique of the prevailing politico-cultural climate. But what could they replace cupiditas with? Certainly justice and equity, but these, unfortunately, bring us back to the problem of consumption and the redistribution of goods and services. Additionally, and from a secular, late-industrial perspective, this seems to be a not entirely unreasonable position. But, it does mean that enterprises like moral education can play little more than a kind of regulatory function, ensuring that the attachments of desire are not so overwhelming as to leave the attachments of others completely unfulfilled.

We can immediately see that in some fairly fundamental way, schools predicated on something like Augustine's view of *caritas* are bound to be at odds with the dominant view of secular schooling so favoured by many Americans and Europeans. Christian schools, at least formally, have to operate out of a quite different ontological paradigm. The relationship to the world is configured not by *cupiditas* but by *caritas*. Moreover, the school community is not a place of mutual security predicated on the preservation and regulation of particular kinds of attachments and desires, but on the love of the other in and for themselves. This love can have no utility value. The academic, cultural and personal development of a student cannot be predicated on their being a better plumber, teacher or accountant, but on their becoming more whole human beings who, in turn, will love their neighbour in the light of their loving God, since God is unequivocal love.

None of this implies that such schools are less likely to attend to students' educational potential than their public school counterparts. However, it should point to something different about the discourse of the school and the operational and pedagogical practices it embodies. This might be reflected in very subtle and in not so subtle ways. For example, during the late 1980s and early 1990s, the bishops of England and Wales fought a robust, if only partially successful, campaign against the then Government's avowed intention to strongly encourage schools to become self-governing, opting out of their local authority and/or denominational framework. In this, the government's desire was to instantiate the neo-liberal principles of Hayek, Friedman and others. The bishops' Conference stood against this on the grounds that competition configured in this way was not in the interests of communal or individual flourishing. Whether or not they were right is, in one sense, beyond the point. What is important is that this independent voice, configured by a different relationship to the material world, is heard in the public spaces. Again, Gerald Grace's (2002) study of Catholic schools throws up some very interesting manifestations of the different ontology that can underpin the denominational school. His discussion of the partnership arrangements of a group of schools in the south of the Birmingham Archdiocese in England is quite instructive. In the face of the relentless push to create independently competing schools, these Catholic schools decided to form a mutually supportive partnership where the group would support any of the schools or principals or students who were struggling for whatever reason. Here, there were no obvious advantages measured against *cupiditas*, but seen as *caritas* this mutually supportive environment offered a clear statement of both philosophical and practical difference.

Conclusion

The argument here is not that religiously denominated schools should, or are ever likely to, supplant the common public school. In a plural, secular culture this is neither realistic nor desirable. Nor is it that common schools are somehow de jure immoral places; to allege this would be grotesque. What I am arguing, however, is that such schools can, do and should perform a liminal function in and for the liberal-democratic state. Where the state has shaped the general educational provision within a particular framework, alternatives are important. But, these alternatives should mirror something more substantial than mere whimsy. They have to be able to offer the liberal polity different perspectives on the key object of liberal democracy that is human flourishing. To the extent that they succeed, such schools (institutions) may serve the function of potential correctives to the dangers of an excessive preoccupation with a particular understanding of human flourishing. As liminal institutions, they exist geopolitically in the midst of the polity, opening up the possibility of eruptive engagement in the midst of that polity. The system of schooling in liberal democracies is unlikely to be conducted according to principles derived from Augustinian caritas or some cognate notion, but it is possible that it may be influenced by its particular discourse of human flourishing where the student is not a resource for a nation, or one who is to be cultivated within a consumer teleology. Nor should the argument here be seen to necessarily support the view put forward by educational privateers who wish to promote tax incentives, charter schools and student vouchers as a way of freeing schools from central government control. Arguably, their intentions (Pollard 2001) are part of a particular view of the liberal state that sees it as acting only as a regulator of the market. Such a view is more likely to promote the discursive closure between state and market. The liminal, as I have attempted to elucidate it throughout this essay, is a constructive position that challenges the apparently ineluctability of that structured differentiation that entrenches discursive closure around the tropes of the market. It promotes a consideration of the other that transcends their consumptive possibilities and offers back to the state a language and practices that have more in common with the aspirations of Jefferson, Adams, Franklin and company. It is difficult not to conclude that the alternative offered by Pollard and others is a world ever more deeply embedded in cupiditas, allowing little possibility of a genuine critique of current pedagogies, practice and structures.

Notes

1. A liminar may be regarded as the one who stands in a liminal space within a broader structured social situation.
2. It is no part of Audi's argument, nor indeed my own, that such theo-ethical equilibrium should preclude disequilibrium. Rather, disequilibrium may be seen as a necessary and constructive part of the political processes of change, development and decision. This "disequilibrium is not mere confusion or perplexity" (Audi 2000, 138), but is bound to the search for equilibrium. "Wisdom here consists in part in knowing how much, and in what ways, to reflect on one's commitments" (ibid, 139).
3. For further discussion of this, see Conroy 1999a.
4. Religious or secular.
5. These voices have included academics such as Bruce (1998, 5); senior politicians Lord MacKay and John Maxton (see Conroy 2001; 1999a; also Starrs 1998, 4); senior Trades Union officials; Fred Forrester, recently retired Depute General Secretary of the Educational Institute of Scotland (EIS) (Forrester 2000); and leading broadsheet newspapers (Glasgow Herald 1998, 15). It is commonplace among these figures that Catholic schools are seen as a source of and cause of discrimination by virtue of their existence.
6. Italics added.
7. See *Nichomachean Ethics* 10:1180a.
8. The strength of Curren's claim is based on the translation of taxin as arrangement. Alternative translations such as Ross' render it as "care" and

Thompson's as "supervision," which would seem to suggest a slightly less emphatic allegiance to the superordinate role of the state.

9. After all, pornography may be seen as just as much a matter of economics as it is of ethics.

10. For an interesting discussion, see Korten 2001, 157–159. Recent evidence of government moves in this direction are to be seen in a suggestion by the First Minister (Labour party) of the Scottish Executive, that a national strategy for getting children to eat more healthy meals should revolve around the introduction of commercial satellite television in every lunch room and dining hall so that children would be attracted to stay in school for lunch. This exemplifies twin difficulties. First, it is a luminous example of the incapacity of adults to assume their responsibility for looking after children by providing them with appropriate food and prohibiting their leaving school during the day except to go home for lunch. Second, it demonstrates the powerful hold that the global media has over the public political imagination.

11. Though as Spinner-Halev (2000) points out, even here it is important that the liberal state take care in expunging or overriding the rights of groups to be different and to deploy a range of strategies to sustain and protect that difference.

12. Italics added.

13. The very term "human resources," which now dominates human relations in education as in industry, demonstrates above all the functional utility of human engagement.

References

Aeschylus (1961). *Prometheus and Other Plays*. (P. Vellacott, trans.). London: Penguin.

Allen, J.L. (2001). Cardinal Ratzinger: The Vatican's Enforcer of the Faith. New York: Continuum.

Arendt, H. (1951 and 1973). *The Origins of Totalitarianism*. New York: Harcourt, Brace Jovanovich.

———— (1958). *The Human Condition*. Chicago: University of Chicago Press.

———— (1963). *On Revolution*. New York: Penguin.

———— (1968a). *Between Past and Future*. London: Penguin.

———— (1968b). *Men in Dark Times*. San Diego, CA: Harcourt, Brace and Company.

———— (1973). *The Origins of Totalitarianism*. San Diego, CA: Harcourt, Brace and Company.

———— (1977). *Between Past and Future*. New York: Penguin.

———— (1996). *Love and St. Augustine*. (J. Vecchiarelli Scott and J. Chelius Stark, eds.). Chicago: Chicago University Press.

Aristophanes (1961). *The Acharnians*. (D. Parker, trans.). New York: Mentor.

Aristotle (1952a). "Nichomachean Ethics" in *The Works of Aristotle, Vol ll*. (W. D. Ross, trans.). Chicago: Encyclopedia Britannica.

———— (1952b). "On Poetics" in *The Works of Aristotle, Vol ll*. (I. Bywater, trans.). Chicago: Encyclopedia Britannica.

———— (1976). *The Nichomachean Ethics*. (J.A.K. Thomson, trans.). Harmondsworth, UK: Penguin.

Atkins, P. (2001). The Church School—Good or Evil: Against. *The Independent* (education supplement), March 1.

Audi, R. (2000). *Religious commitment and Secular Reason*. Cambridge, UK: Cambridge University Press.

Augustine, St. (1953). *The Fathers of the Church. St. Augustine: Confessions*. (V.J. Bourke, trans.). Washington, DC: Catholic University of America Press.

Aung San, S.K. (1991). *Freedom from Fear and Other Writings*. (M. Aris, ed.). London: Penguin.

Averintsev, S. (2001). "Bakhtin, Laughter and Christian Culture" in S.M. Felch and P.J. Contino (eds.), *Bakhtin and Religion: A Feeling for Faith.* Evanston, IL: Northwestern University Press.

Bakhtin, M. (1968). *Rabelais and His World.* Cambridge, MA: Harvard University Press.

Ball, N. and B. Troyna (1987). Resistance, Rights and Rituals: Denominational Schools and Multicultural Education. *Journal of Educational Policy* 2 (1): 15–26.

Baudrillard, J. (2001). *Selected Writings.* (M. Poster, ed.). Cambridge and Oxford, UK: Polity and Blackwell.

Bauman, Z. (2001) *The Individualized Society.* Cambridge, UK: Polity.

Bayless, M. (1996). *Parody in the Middle Ages: The Latin Tradition.* Ann Arbor: University of Michigan Press.

Beattie, J. (1779). "An Essay on Laughter and Ludicrous Composition" in *Essays*, 3rd edition corrected. London: E and C Dilly.

Bellah, R. (1992). *The Broken Covenant: American Civil Religion in Times of Trial.* Chicago: Chicago University Press.

Bellah, R., R. Madsen, W.M. Sullivan, A. Swidler, and S. Tipton (1985). *Habits of the Heart: Individualism and Commitment in American Life.* Berkeley and Los Angeles: University of California Press.

Berger, P. (1997). *Redeeming Laughter: The Comic Dimension of Human Experience.* Berlin: Walter de Gruyter.

Bergson, H. (1913). *Laughter.* (C. Brereton and F. Rothwell, trans.). London: MacMillan and Co.

Berlin, I. (1969). *Four Essays on Liberty.* Oxford, UK: Oxford University Press.

Beyer, P. (1994). *Religion and Globalization.* London: Sage.

Bishops of England and Wales (1997). *The Common Good in Education.* London, Catholic Education Service.

Blackmore, Sir R. (1700). *A Paraphrase on the Book of Job as Likewise on the Songs of Moses, Deborah, David, on Four Select Psalms, Some Chapters of Isaiah and the Third Chapter of Habakkuk.* London: Churchill.

Blake, N., P. Smeyers, R. Smith, and P. Standish (1998). *Thinking Again: Education After Postmodernism.* London: Bergin and Garvey.

Blake, W. (1997). *The Complete Poetry and Prose.* (D.Erdman, ed., H. Bloom, commentary). New York, Bantam Doubleday Dell Publishing.

Boston, R. (1974). *An Anatomy of Laughter.* London: Collins.

Bourdieu, P. (1992). *The Logic of Practice.* (R. Nice, trans.). Stanford, CA: Stanford University Press.

Boys, M. (2002). Educating Christians in Order that Strangers become Neighbours. *Journal of Religious Education* 50 (2): 10–15.

Brontë. E. (1965). *Wuthering Heights.* Harmondsworth, UK: Penguin.

Bruce, S. (1998). Mission: Impossible. *The Glasgow Herald.* Jan. 28.

———— (2002). *God is Dead: Secularisation in the West.* Oxford, UK: Blackwell.

Bryk, A., V.E. Lee, and P.B. Holland (1995). (new edition) *Catholic Schools and the Common Good.* Cambridge, MA: Harvard University

Buber, M. (1970). *I and Thou.* (W. Kaufmann, trans. and ed.). Edinburgh, Scotland: T and T Clark.

Burke, P. (1992). *History and Social Theory*. Cambridge, UK: Cambridge University Press.

Butler, E., M. Pirie, and P. Young (1985). *The Omega File*. London: Adam Smith Institute.

Callan, E. (1985). McLaughlin on Parental Rights. *Journal of Philosophy of Education* 19 (1)

——— (1997). *Creating Citizens: Political Education and Liberal Democracy*. Oxford, UK: Clarendon.

——— (2000). "Discrimination and Religious Schooling" in W. Kymlicka and W. Norman (eds.). Citizenship and Diversity. Oxford, UK: Oxford University Press.

Campbell, J. (1949 and 1993). *The Hero with a Thousand Faces*. London: Fontana.

——— (1969). *The Masks of God: Primitive Mythology*. London: Souvenir Press.

Carey, J. (1981). *John Donne, Life, Mind and Art*. London: Faber and Faber.

Carr, D. (1999). "Catholic Faith and Religious Truth" in J. Conroy (ed.), *Catholic Education Inside/Out Outside/In*. Dublin, Ire.: Lindisfarne.

——— (2003a). *Making Sense of Education: An Introduction to the Philosophy and Theory of Education and Teaching*. London: Routledge.

——— (2003b). Taking Narrative Seriously: Exploring the Educational Status of Myth and Fiction. Unpublished paper delivered at Philosophy of Education Conference, Miami, FL.

Carr, W. and A. Hartnett (1996). *Education and the Struggle for Democracy*. Buckingham, UK : Open University Press.

Castoriadis, C. (1997). *World in Fragments: Writings on Politics, Society, Psychoanalysis and the Imagination*. Stanford, CA: Stanford University Press.

Central Advisory Council for Education, England (1959). *Vol 1: Report*. London: HMSO.

Chapman, A.J. and H.C. Foot (1996). *Humour and Laughter*. New Brunswick, NJ: Transaction.

Congregation for Catholic Education (1988). *The Religious Dimension of Education in a Catholic School*. Dublin, Ireland: Veritas.

Conroy, J. (1999a). "The Long Johns and Catholic Education" in J. Conroy (ed.), *Catholic Education: Inside/Out Outside/In*. Leamington Spa, UK: Lindisfarne.

——— (1999b). Poetry and Human Growth. *Journal of Moral Education* 28 (4): 491–510.

——— (2000). Citizenship Education and Its Implications for Moral Education: A Scottish Perspective. *Revista Brasileira de Educaçao Médica, Ed.Associaçao Brasileira de Ensino Médico* 24 (3): 16–23.

——— (2001). A Very Scottish Affair: Catholic Education and the State. *Oxford Review of Education*. 27 (4): 543-558.

——— (2003). "What Rough Beast...? On Reading Arendt after the Twin Towers" in M. Peters, C. Lankshear, and M. Olssen (eds.). *Critical Theory and the Human Condition: Past, Present and Future*. New York: Peter Lang.

Conroy, J., M. Boland, and R. Davis (1999). *Values Interventions and the Development of Moral Reasoning in Primary 7*. Glasgow, UK: St. Andrew's College/Gordon Cook Foundation.

Conroy, J. and R. Davis. (1999). "Authenticity, Teachers and the Future of Moral Education" in M. Leicester, C. Modgil, and S. Modgil (eds.). *Values Education in a Pluralist Society*. London: The Falmer Press.

——— (2002). Transgression, Transformation and Enlightenment: The Trickster as Poet and Teacher. *Educational Philosophy and Theory* 34 (2): 255-272

Conroy, J. and D. de Ruyter (2002a). At the Threshold: On Education and Liminality. Paper presented at Philosophy of Education Society of Great Britain, Oxford, UK.

————— (2002b). Preventing Conflict through Contradiction and Contrarian Elements: The Moral Impact of Liminal Education. Unpublished Paper presented at Association for Moral Education, Chicago, IL.

Cooper, L. (1922). *An Aristotelian Theory of Comedy: With an Adaptation of the Poetics and a Translation of the "Tractatus Coislinianus."* New York: Harcourt Brace.

Cox, C.B. and R. Boyson (eds.) (1975). *Black Paper 4, The Fight for Education.* Hull, UK: Critical Quarterly Society.

Cox, C.B. and A.E. Dyson (eds.) (1969). *Black Paper 1,The Fight for Education, A Black Paper.* Hull, UK: Critical Quarterly Society.

Cox, H. (1969). *The Feast of Fools: A Theological Essay on Festivity and Fantasy.* Cambridge, MA: Harvard University Press.

Crick, B. (1990). *Political Thoughts and Polemics.* Edinburgh, Scotland: Edinburgh University Press.

Curren, R. (2000). *Aristotle on the Necessity of Public Education.* Lanham, MD: Rowman & Littlefield.

Dahl, R. (1998). *Matilda.* London, Puffin.

Damasio, A.R. (1994; 1996). *Descartes' Error: Emotion, Reason and the Human Brain.* New York: Grousset/Putnam; London: Papermac.

Davidson, H.R.E. (1964). *Gods and Myths of Northern Europe.* Harmondsworth, UK: Penguin.

Dawkins, R. (2001). No Faith in the Absurd. *Times Educational Supplement* (London). Feb. 23, 17.

Day, J. (1999). "The Primacy of Relationship: A Meditation on Education, Faith and the Dialogical Self" in J. Conroy (ed.) *Catholic Education: Inside/Out Outside/In.* Leamington Spa, UK: Lindisfarne.

Dean, C. (2001a). Backlash against Church School Drive. *Times Educational Supplement* (London). Feb. 23, 3.

————— (2001b). Godless Society Puts Hope in Faiths. *Times Educational Supplement* (London). Feb. 23, 6.

Department for Education and Skills. (2001). Education and Skills: Delivering Results; A Strategy to 2006. London, UK. Government website (cited September 14, 2002). *http://www.dfes.gov.uk/delivering-results/docs/DfES_strategy_Document.doc.* (Visited December 12, 2002).

De Jong, J. and G. Snik (2002). Why Should States Fund Denominational Schools? *Journal of Philosophy of Education* 36 (4): 573–587.

De Rosa, P. (1988). *The Vicars of Christ: The Dark Side of the Papacy.* London: Corgi.

De Sousa, R. (1987) "The Ethics of Laughter and Humour" in J. Morreal (ed.). *The Philosophy of Laughter and Humour.* Albany, New York: State University of New York Press.

Descartes, R. (1911/12). *The Philosophical Works of Descartes.* (E.S. Haldane and G.R.T. Ross, trans. and eds.). London: Cambridge University Press.

Dinneen, P.S. (1927). *FoclOir Gaidhilge agus Bearla.* Dublin, Ireland: Irish Society Texts.

Donnan, H. and T.M. Wilson (1999). *Borders: Frontiers of Identity, Nation and State*. Oxford, UK: Berg.

Donne, J. (1971). *Complete English Poems*. (A.J. Smith, trans. and notes). London: Penguin.

Douglas, M. (1967). "The Meaning of Myth with Special Reference to *La Geste d'Asdiwal*" in E. Leach (ed.). *The Structured Study of Myth and Totemism*. London: Tavistock.

———— (1968). The Social Control of Cognition: Some Factors in Joke Perception. *Man* 3: 361–376.

Dunne, J. (1992). *Back to the Rough Ground: Practical Judgement and the Lure of Technique*. South Bend, IN: Notre Dame Press.

Eagleton, T. (1996). *The Illusions of Postmodernism*. Oxford, UK: Blackwell.

Eco, U. (1983 and 1984). *The Name of the Rose*. London: Pan Books.

Egan, K. (2002). *Getting It Wrong from the Beginning: Our Progressivist Inheritance from Herbert Spencer, John Dewey and Jean Piaget*. New Haven, CT, and London: Yale University Press.

Egéa-Kuehne, D. (1996). Neutrality in Education and Derrida's Call for "Double Duty." *Philosophy of Education Society Yearbook*. *http://www.Ed.uiuc.edu/eps/pes-yearbook/96_docs/egea-kuehne.html*. (Visited September 23, 2002).

Eliot, A. (1990). *The Universal Myths: Heroes, Gods, Tricksters and Others*. New York: Meridian Books.

Erasmus of Rotterdam (1971). *Praise of Folly and Letter to Martin Dorp*. (B. Radice, introduction and notes; A.H.T. Levi, trans.). London: Penguin.

Farnon, J. (1997). "Motifs of Gaelic Lore and Literature" in *An Béal Bocht*, in A. Clune and T. Hurson (eds.). *Conjuring Complexities: Essays on Flann O'Brien*. Belfast, Ireland: Queen's University Institute of Irish Studies.

Ferguson, N. (2001). *The Cash Nexus: Money and Power in the Modern World 1700–2000*. Harmondsworth, UK: Allen Lane/The Penguin Press.

Ferry, L. (1990). *Homo Aestheticus: The Invention of Taste in the Democratic Age*. (R. de Loaiza, trans.). Chicago, and London: University of Chicago Press.

Finn, G.T.P. (2000). A Culture of Prejudice: Promoting Pluralism In Education for a Change. (T. Devine, ed.). *Scotland's Shame?: Bigotry and Sectarinaism in Modern Scotland*. Edinburgh, Scotland: Mainstream.

Finn, M. (1992). *Writing the Incommensurable: Kierkegaard, Rossetti and Hopkins*. University Park, PA.: Penn State University Press.

Flannery, A. (ed.). (1975). *Vatican Council II: The Concilliar and Post-Concilliar Documents*. Dublin: Costello Publishing.

Flynn, M. and M. Mok (2002). *Catholic Schools 2000: A Longitudinal Study of Year 12 Students in Catholic Schools, 1972–1982,1990–1998*. Sydney, Australia: Catholic Education Commission.

Forrester, F. (2000). Schools Beyond Saving. *The Scotsman* (Edinburgh), May 31.

Foucault, M. (1979). *The History of Sexuality, Vol 1: An Introduction*. London: Allen Lane.

Francis, L. (2001). *The Values Debate—A Voice from the Pupils*. London: Woburn Press.

Francis, L., J. Astley, and M. Robbins (2001). *The Fourth R for the Third Millennium: Education in Religion and Values for the Global Future*. Leamington Spa, UK: Lindisfarne.

Freud, S. (1916). *Wit and Its Relation to the Unconscious*. (A.A. Brill, trans.). London: Kegan Paul.

Fridlund, A. (1998). *Beyond a Joke*. London: British Broadcasting Corporation. (Cited November 5, 1998). *http://www.bbc.co.uk/horizon/script.shtml*. (Visited November 16, 1998).

Fried, I. (1998). Beyond A Joke. London: British Broadcasting Corporation. (Cited November 5, 1998). *http://www.bbc.co.uk/horizon/script.shtml*. (Visited November 16, 1998).

Friedman, M. (1962). *Capitalism and Freedom*. Chicago: Chicago University Press.

Fromm, E. (1942). *The Fear of Freedom*. London: Routledge and Kegan Paul.

Frye, N. (1963). *Fables of Identity: Studies in Poetic Mythology*. New York: Harcourt Brace and World Inc.

Gadamer, H.-G. (1975). *Truth and Method.* London: Sheed and Ward.

Gamble, A. (1996). Hayek: *The Iron Cage of Liberty*. Oxford, UK: Polity Press.

Gewirtz, S. (2000). Bringing the Politics Back In: A Critical Analysis of Quality Discourses in Education. *British Journal of Educational Studies* 48 (4): 352–370.

Gilligan, C. (1982). *In a Different Voice*. Cambridge, MA: Harvard University Press.

Giroux, H. (1992). *Border Crossings: Cultural Workers and the Politics of Education*. New York: Routledge.

――― (1996). "Slacking Off: Border Youth and Postmodern Education" in H.A. Giroux, C. Lankshear, P.Mc Laren, and M. Peters (eds.) *Counternarratives: Cultural Studies and Critical Pedagogies in Postmodern Spaces*. New York: Routledge.

Giroux, H.A., C. Lankshear, P.Mc Laren, and M. Peters (eds.) *Counternarratives: Cultural Studies and Critical Pedagogies in Postmodern Spaces*. New York: Routledge.

Glasgow Herald Feature (1998). Challenge to the Separate Schools System. "Upfront on Saturday." *Glasgow Herald*, April 5, 15.

Glasgow, R.D.V. (1995). *Madness, Masks and Laughter: An Essay on Comedy*. London: Associated University Presses.

Golding, W. (1954). *Lord of the Flies*. London: Faber and Faber.

Gooderham, D. (1983). Dialogue and Emancipation: New Horizons in the Development of Religious Education. *British Journal of Religious Education* Spring 5 (2): 59–66.

Gould, E. (1981). *Mythical Intentions in Modern Literature*. Princeton, NJ: Princeton University Press.

Grace, G. (2002). *Catholic Schools: Missions, Markets and Morality*. London: Routledge/Falmer.

Gutiérrez, G. (1999). *The Density of the Present: Selected Writings.* Maryknoll, NY: Orbis Books.

Habermas, J. (2001). *The Postnational Constellation*. (M. Pensky, trans. and ed.). Oxford, UK: Polity Press.

Haldane, J. (1999). "The Need of Spirituality in Catholic Education" in J. Conroy (ed.). *Catholic Education: Inside/Out Outside/In*. Dublin, Ireland: Lindisfarne.

Hand, M. (2002). Religious Upbringing Reconsidered. *Journal of Philosophy of Education* 36 (4): 545–557.

Hargreaves, D. (1997). " Education" in G. Mulgan (ed.). *Life after Politics*. London: Fontana.

Harrison, A. (1989). *The Irish Trickster*. Sheffield, UK: Sheffield Academic Press.

Harrison, B. (1994). *The Literate Imagination: Renewing the Secondary English Curriculum*. London: Taylor & Francis.

Hay, D. (1968). *Europe: The Emergence of an Idea*. Edinburgh, Scotland: Polygon.

Hayek, F. von (1983). *Knowledge, Evolution and Society.* London: Adam Smith Institute.

Heaney, S. (1966). *Death of a Naturalist.* London: Faber and Faber.

——— (1979). *Field Work.* London: Faber and Faber.

——— (1983). *Sweeney Astray.* London: Faber and Faber.

——— (1993). *Seeing Things.* New York: Farrar, Straus and Giroux/Noonday Press.

——— (1995). *The Redress of Poetry: Oxford Lectures.* London: Faber and Faber.

——— (1996). *The Spirit Level.* London: Faber and Faber.

——— (1999). *Beowulf: A New Translation.* London: Faber and Faber.

——— (2002). *Finders Keepers: Selected Prose 1971–2001.* London: Faber and Faber.

Henderson, J.L. (1964). "Ancient Myths and Modern Man" in C.G. Jung (ed.). *Man and His Symbols.* London: Aldus Books.

Hirst, P.H. (1974). *Moral Education in a Secular Society.* London: University of London Press (for the) National Children's Home.

Hobbes, T. (1651). *Leviathan or the Matter, Forme and Power of a Commonwealth Ecclesiasticall and Civil.* London: Printed for Andrew Crooke.

Hopkins, G.M. (1972). *Selected Poems of G.M .Hopkins.* (J. Reeves, ed. and intro). London: Heinemann.

Hull, R. (1985). *The Language Gap.* London: Methuen.

Hutcheson, F. (1750). *Reflections Upon Laughter and Remarks Upon the Fable of the Bees.* (Carefully corrected) Glasgow: Printed by R. Urie for Daniel Baxter.

Hyde, L. (1999). *Trickster Makes This World: Mischief, Myth, and Art.* New York: North Point Press.

Hynes, W.J. (1993). "Inconclusive Conclusions: Tricksters: Metaplayers and Reveller" in W.J. Hynes, W.G. Doty, and C. Murray-Ross (eds.). *Mythical Trickster Figures: Contours, Contexts, and Criticisms.* Tuscaloosa and London: University of Alabama Press.

Hynes, W.J., W.G Doty, and C. Murray-Ross (eds.). (1993). *Mythical Trickster Figures: Contours, Contexts, and Criticisms.* Tuscaloosa and London: University of Alabama Press.

Isaak, J.-A. (1996). *Feminism and Contemporary Art.* London: Routledge.

Jarman, A.O.H. (1991). "The Merlin Legend and the Welsh Tradition of Prophecy" in R. Bromwich, A.O.H. Jarman, and B. F. Roberts (eds.). *The Arthur of the Welsh.* Cardiff, Wales: University of Wales Press.

Jaspers, K. (1962). *Plato and Augustine [from The Great Philosophers, Volume 1].* (H. Arendt ed.; R. Mannheim, trans.). San Diego, CA: Harvest Books/Harcourt, Brace and Company.

Jasper, D. (1999). "How Can We Read the Bible" in L. Gearon (ed.). *English Literature, Theology and the Curriculum.* London and New York: Cassell.

Jefferson, T. (1943). *The Complete Jefferson. Notes on the State of Virginia.* (S.K. Padover, ed.). New York: Duell, Sloan and Pearce.

Jenkins, R. (1994). *Subversive Laughter: The Liberating Power of Comedy.* New York: Free Press.

Jonson, B. (1962 and 1971). *Volpone.* (D. Cook, ed., intro. and notes). London: Methuen.

Joubert, L. (1560 and 1980). *Treatise on Laughter.* (G.D. de Rocher, trans. and annotations). Tuscaloosa, AL: University of Alabama Press.

Judge, H. (2001). Faith-Based Schools and State funding: A Political Argument. *Oxford Review of Education* 27 (4): 463–474.

Jung, C.G. (1954). *C.G. Jung: The Collected Works Vol. 17*. (H. Read, M. Fordham, and G. Adler, eds.). London: Routledge and Kegan Paul.

———— (1961). *Modern Man in Search of a Soul*. London: Routledge and Kegan Paul.

———— (1972). *Four Archetypes: Mother Rebirth Spirit Trickster*. (R.F.C. Hull, trans.). London: Routledge and Kegan Paul.

Kant, I. (1952). *The Critique of Judgement*. (J.C. Meredith, trans.). (Great Books of the Western World, 42: Kant). Chicago: Encyclopaedia Britannica.

———— (1998). *Groundwork of the Metaphysics of Morals*. (M.J. Gregor, trans. and ed.). Cambridge, UK: Cambridge University Press.

Keats, J. (1988) *The Complete Poems* 3rd edition (J. Barnard, ed.). Harmondsworth, UK: Penguin Books.

Keenan, B. (1993). *An Evil Cradling*. London: Vintage.

Ketcham, R.L. (ed.) (1965). *The Political Thought of Benjamin Franklin*. Indianapolis, IN: Bobbs-Merrill.

Kierkegaard, S. (1945). *Concluding Unscientific Postscript*. (D.F. Swenson, trans.). Oxford, UK: Oxford University Press.

Klein, N. (2001). *No Logo*. London: Flamingo.

Komonchak, J. (1968). "Subsidiarity in the Church: State of the Question" in J. Komonchak (ed.). *The Nature and Future of Episcopal Conferences*. Washington, DC: Catholic University Press.

Korten, D.C. (2001). *When Corporations Rule the World*, 2nd edition. San Francisco, CA: Berrett-Koehler Publishers and Kumarian Press.

Kuschel, K.-J. (2000). "The Destructive and Liberating Power of Laughter: Anthropological and Theological Aspects" in E.V. Waldel (ed.). *Concilium: The Bright Side of Life*. London: SCM Press.

Kymlicka, F. (1989). *Liberalism, Community and Culture*. Oxford, UK: Clarendon.

———— (1995). *Multicultural Citizenship*. Oxford, UK: Clarendon.

Lankshear, C., M. Peter, and M. Knobel (1996). "Critical Pedagogy and Cyberspace" in H.A. Giroux, C. Lankshear, P. McLaren and M. Peters (eds.). *Counternarratives: Cultural Studies and Critical Pedagogies in Postmodern Spaces*. New York: Routledge.

Lawrence, I. (1992). *Power and Politics at the Department of Education and Science*. London: Cassell.

Leeming, D. and Page, J. (1996). God: Myths of Male Divine. New York: Oxford University Press

Lenz, L. (1841). *Berlin und die Berliner, Vol 3*. Berlin 5: Droschken-Auctionsscenen

Lewis, C.S. (1961). *An Experiment in Criticism*. Cambridge, UK: Cambridge University Press.

Lyas, C. (1999). "Getting Someone to See" in L. Gearon (ed.). *English Literature, Theology and the Curriculum*. London and New York: Cassell.

Macedo, D.P. (1993). Literacy for Stupidification: The Pedagogy of Big Lies. *Harvard Educational Review* 63 (2): 183–206.

Marshall, J.D. (1996). *Michel Foucault: Personal Autonomy and Education*. Dordrecht, Netherlands: Kluwer Academic Publishers.

Martin, R.A. and H.M. Lefcourt. (1983). Sense of Humor as a Moderator of the Relation between Stressors and Moods. *Journal of Personality and Social Psychology* 45: 1313–1324.

Martin, R.K. (2001). Having Faith in Our Faith in God: Toward a Critical Realist Epistemology for Christian Education. *Religious Education* 96 (2): 245–261.

Maslow, A. (1968). *The Psychology of Being,* 2nd edition, Princeton, NJ: Van Nostrand.

Masschelein, J. (1998). World and Life or Education and the Question of Meaning (of Life). *Interchange* 33 (1): 1-20.

——— (2000). Can Education Still Be Critical? *Journal of Philosophy of Education* 34 (4): 603–616.

——— (2001). The Discourse of the Learning Society and the Loss of Childhood. *Journal of Philosophy* of Education 35 (1): 1–20.

McClelland, V.A. (ed.) (1992). *The Catholic School and the European Context, Aspects of Education, No. 46.* Hull, UK: University of Hull.

McGough, R. (1999). *The Way Things Are.* Harmondsworth, UK: Penguin.

McLaren, P. (1986). *Schooling as a Ritual Performance: Towards a Political Economy of Educational Symbols and Gestures.* London: Routledge and Kegan Paul.

——— (1995). *Critical Pedagogy and Predatory Culture.* New York: Routledge.

McLaughlin, T. (1984). Parental Rights and the Religious Upbringing of Children. *Journal of Philosophy of Education* 18 (1): 75–83.

——— (1999). "Distinctiveness and the Catholic School: Balanced Judgement and the Temptations of Commonality" in J.Conroy (ed.) *Catholic Education: Inside/Out Outside/In.* Leamington Spa, UK: Lindisfarne.

Mehlman, J. (1993). *Walter Benjamin for Children: An Essay on His Radio Years.* Chicago: University of Chicago Press.

Merson. M. (2000). Teachers and the Myth of Modernism. *British Journal of Educational Studies* 48 (2): 155–169.

Millbank, J. (1998). The Politics of Time: Community, Gift and Liturgy. *Telos* 113 (Fall): 41–67.

Miller, A. (1968). *The Crucible: A Play in Four Acts.* Harmondsworth, UK: Penguin.

Monro, D.H. (1963). *Argument of Laughter.* South Bend, IN: University of Notre Dame Press.

Morreal, J. (1987). "A New Theory of Laughter" in J. Morreal (ed.). *The Philosophy of Laughter and Humour.* Albany: State University of New York Press.

MORI GTC (2003). Teachers on Teaching: A Survey of the Teaching Profession, Topline Results (Cited January 7, 2003) *http://www.mori.com/polls/2002/gtc-topline.shtml* (Visited January 30, 2003).

Morris, A. (1998). By Their Fruits You Shall Know Them: Distinctive Features of Catholic Education. *Research Papers in Education* 13 (1): 87–112.

Morton Smith, J. (1995). *The Republic of Letters: The Correspondence Between Thomas Jefferson and James Maddison, 1776–1826.* New York: W.W. Norton and Co.

Muir, F. (1987). *What A Mess and the Hairy Monster.* London: A.C. Black.

Muldoon, P. (1998). *Hay.* London: Faber and Faber.

——— (2000). *To Ireland I.* Oxford, UK: Oxford University Press.

Munro, D. (1997). Enterprise Culture To Be Central to Schools. *The Times Educational Supplement* (Scotland). Nov. 14, 1997: 1.

Murphy, J. (1971). *Church, State and Schools in Britain, 1800–1970*. London: Routledge and Kegan Paul.

Na Gopaleen, M. (Flann O'Brien). (1968). *The Best of Myles*. (K. O'Nolan, ed.). London: Picador.

———— (1941). *An Beal Bocht*. Dublin, Ireland: An Press Náisiúnta.

Nezu, A.M., C.M. Nezu, and S.E. Blissett (1988). Sense of Humor as a Moderator of the Relation between Stressful Events and Psychological Distress. *Journal of Personality and Social Psychology* 54: 520–525.

Nietzsche, F. (1966). *Beyond Good and Evil*. (W. Kaufmann, trans. and commentary). New York: Random House.

Noddings, N. (1992). *The Challenge to Care in Schools*. New York: Teachers College Press.

Norman, E. (1979). *Christianity and World Order*. Oxford, UK: Oxford University Press.

Novak, M. (1982). *The Spirit of Democratic Capitalism*. New York: Simon and Schuster.

———— (1993). *The Catholic Ethic and the Spirit of Capitalism*. New York: Free Press.

O'Brien F. (1973) *The Poor Mouth*. (P. Rower, trans.). London: Picador.

O'Hainle, C. (1997). "Fionn and Suibhne in At Swim-Two-Birds" in A.Clune and T. Hurson (eds.). *Conjuring Complexities: Essays on Flann O'Brien*. Belfast, N.Ireland: Queen's University Institute of Irish Studies.

O'Hare, P. (1999). Catholic Ambiguity or Sectarian Certainty? *Religious Education* 94 (1): 111–116.

O'Riain, P. (1972). A Study of the Irish Legend of the Wild Man. *Eigse*, xiv: 179–206.

Otto, R. (1959). *The Idea of the Holy*. (J.W. Harvey, trans.). Harmondsworth, UK: Penguin.

Oxford University Press (1986). *The New Oxford Book of Australian Verse*. (Chosen by L. Murray). Oxford, UK: Oxford University Press.

Pelton, R. (1980). *The Trickster in West Africa*. Berkeley and Los Angeles: University of California Press.

Peters, M. and C. Lankshear (1996). "Postmodern Counternarratives" in H.A. Giroux, C. Lankshear, P.Mc Laren, and M. Peters (eds.) *Counternarratives: Cultural Studies and Critical Pedagogies in Postmodern Spaces*. New York: Routledge.

Peters, R.S. (ed.). (1973). *The Philosophy of Education*. Oxford, UK: Oxford University Press.

Pilger, J. (2002). *Reporting The World*. London: Barbican Art Galleries.

Pittock, G.H.M. (1999). *Celtic Identity and the British Image*. Manchester, UK: Manchester University Press.

Plath, S. (1967) *The Colossus*. London: Faber and Faber.

———— (1971). *Crossing the Water*. London: Faber and Faber.

Plato (1982). *Philebus*. (R. Waterfield, trans.). Harmonsworth, UK: Penguin.

Plessner, H. (1970). *Laughing and Crying: A Study of the Limits of Humam Behavior*. (J.S. Churchill and M. Grene, trans.). Evanston, IL: Northwestern University Press.

Poliakoff, S. (1999). *Shooting the Past*. London: Methuen.

Pollard, S. (2001). *A Class Act: World Lessons for U.K. Education*. London: Adam Smith Institute.

Pope John Paul ll. (1994). Apostolic Letter to the Bishops of the Catholic Church on Reserving Priestly Ordination to Men Alone. Vatican website.

http://www.vatican.va/holy_father/john_paul_ii/apost_letters/documents. (Visited July 1, 2002).

Pratt, M.L. (1992). *Imperial Eyes: Travel Writing and Transculturation*. London: Routledge.

Provine, R. (1998). Horizon: Beyond a Joke. BBC website. (Cited November 5, 1998). *http://www.bbc.co.uk/horizon/script.shtml*. (Visited November 16, 1998).

———— (1996). Laughter *American Scientist* 84: 38-45.

Qualifications and Curriculum Authority on behalf of the Citizenship Advisory Group (1998). Education for Citizenship and the Teaching of Democracy in Schools: Final Report of the Advisory Group on Citizenship. London: Qualifications and Curriculum Authority.

Quality Assurance Agency for Higher Education (2000). The Standard for Initial Teacher Education in Scotland. Quality Assurance Agency website (Cited June 2000). *http://www.qaa.ac.uk/crntwork/benchmark/itescot/context.htm*. (Visited February 8, 2003).

Quinn, J.R. (1996). The Claims of Papacy and the Costly Call to Unity. http://www.usao.edu/-facshaferi/QUINN.HTML. (Visited June 5, 2002).

Redfern, H.B. (1986). *Questions in Aesthetic Education*. London: Allen and Unwin.

Ricoeur, P. (1976). *Interpretation Theory: Discourse and the Surplus of Meaning*. Fort Worth: Texas Christian University Press.

———— (1977). *The Rule of Metaphor*. (R. Czerny, ed.). Toronto: University of Toronto Press.

Riu, X. (1999). *Dionysism and Comedy*. Lanham, MD: Rowman & Littlefield.

Rorty, R. (1989). *Contingency, Irony and Solidarity*. Cambridge, UK: Cambridge University Press.

———— (1999). *Philosophy and Social Hope*. Harmondsworth, UK: Penguin Books.

Rosenzweig. F. (1985). *The Star of Redemption*. (W. Hallo, trans.). Notre Dame, IN: University of Notre Dame Press.

Rossetti, C. (1984). *Christina Rossetti: Selected Poems*. (C.H. Sisson, ed.). Manchester, UK: Carcanet.

Rousseau, J.-J. (1968). *The Social Contract*. (M. Cranston, trans. and intro.). Harmondsworth, UK: Penguin.

Russo, J. (1997). "A Jungian Analysis of Homer's Odysseus" in P. Young-Eisendrath and T. Dawson (eds.). *The Cambridge Companion to Jung*. Cambridge, UK: Cambridge University Press.

Sacred Congregation for Catholic Education: (1988). *The Religious Dimension of Education in the Catholic School*. London: C.T.S.

Santner, E. (2001). *On the Psychotheology of Everyday Life: Reflections on Freud and Rosenzweig*. Chicago: Chicago University Press.

Sawicki, M. (1988). *The Gospel in History; A Teaching Church; The Origins of Christian Education*. New York: Paulist Press.

Schama, S. (1990). *Citizens: A Chronicle of the French Revolution*. London: Vintage.

Schapiro, T. (1999). What Is a Child? *Ethics* 19 (4): 715–738.

Schiller, F. (1967). *On the Aesthetic Education of Man: In a Series of Letters English and German Facing*. (E.W. Wilkinson and L.A. Willoughby, eds., trans., intro, and commentary). Oxford, UK: Clarendon Press.

Scottish Consultative Council on the Curriculum. (1999). The School Curriculum and the Culture of Scotland: A Paper for Discussion and Development. Dundee, Scotland: SCCC.

Scottish Executive and Learning and Teaching Scotland (2001). *The Balance and Structure of the Curriculum: 5–14 National Guidelines.* Edinburgh, Scotland: The Stationery Office.

Scruton, R. (1974). *Art and Imagination: A Study in the Philosophy of Mind.* London: Routledge and Kegan Paul.

———— (1983). *The Aesthetic Understanding: Essays in the Philosophy of Art and Culture.* Manchester, UK: Carcanet.

———— (2001). *The Meaning of Conservatism.* Basingstoke, UK: Palgrave.

Shaw, G.B. (1964). *Heartbreak House.* Harmondsworth, UK: Penguin.

Shelley, P.B. (1967). *Poetical Works.* (T. Hutchinson, ed.). London: Oxford University Press.

Short, G. (2002). Faith-Based Schools: A Threat to Social Cohesion? *Journal of Philosophy of Education* 36 (4): 559–572.

Skinner, Q. (2000). Why Does Laughter Matter to Philosophy? The Passmore Lecture. Australian National University Online. *http://socpal.anu.edu.au/pdf-files/passmorelect2000.pdf.* (Visited May 8, 2002).

Smith, M. (2002). The School Leadership Initiative: An Ethically Flawed Project. *Journal of Philosophy of Education* 36 (1): 21–39.

Sobrino, J. (1978). *Christology at the Crossroads.* London: SCM.

———— (2001). *Christ the Liberator: A View from the Victims.* Maryknoll, NY: Orbis.

Sobrino, J. and F. Wilfred (eds.) (2001). *Globalization and its Victims.* London: SCM Press.

Speaker's Commission on Citizenship (1990). *Encouraging Citizenship: Report of the Commission on Citizenship.* London: HMSO.

Spinner, J. (1994). *The Boundaries of Citizenship.* Baltimore, MD: Johns Hopkins University Press.

Spinner-Halev, J. (2000). *Surviving Diversity.* Baltimore, Md.: The John Hopkins University Press.

Starrs, C. (1998). "Call to End Segregation Criticized." *Glasgow Herald*, Feb. 9: 4.

Stephenson, P. (2001). *Billy.* London: Harper Collins.

Sullivan, B.T. (1993). Economic Ends and Educational Means at the White House: A Case of Citizenship and Causistry. *Educational Theory* 43 (2): 161–179.

Tate, N. (1996). Two Worlds, One Purpose. *Times Educational Supplement* (Scotland), November 29, 11 .

Taylor, C. (1995). *Philosophical Arguments.* Cambridge, MA: Harvard University Press.

Thomas, G.P. and C.J. McRobbie (1999). The Potential of Metaphor for Investigating and Reforming Teachers' and Students' Classroom Practices. *Educational Practice and Theory* 21 (2): 87–102.

Townsend, M.L. (1992). *Forbidden Laughter: Popular Humour and the Limits of Repression in Nineteenth-Century Prussia.* Ann Arbor: University of Michigan Press.

Truzzi, M. (1974). *Verstehen: Subjective Understanding in the Social Sciences.* Reading, MA: Addison-Wesley.

Turner, V. (1967). *The Forest of Symbols: Aspects of Ndembu Ritual.* Ithaca, NY: Cornell University Press.

———— (1969 and 1995). *The Ritual Process: Structure and Anti-structure.* New York: Aldine deGruyter.

————— (1974). *Drama, Fields and Metaphors: Symbolic Action in Human Society.* Ithaca, NY: Cornell University Press.

UK Government (2001). Government Outlines Further Anti-terrorist Measures Online. *http://www.pm.gov.uk/output/page 3617.asp.* (Visited July 4 2002).

UNESCO (1996). *A Model of Educational Development.* Paris: UNESCO.

Van Gennep, A. (1960). *The Rites of Passage.* (M.B. Vizedom and G.L. Caffee, trans.). Chicago: University of Chicago Press; London: Collins.

Warnock, M. (1980). *Imagination.* London: Faber and Faber.

Way, E.C. (1994). *Knowledge, Representation and Metaphor.* Oxford, UK: Intellect.

Welsford, E. (1935). *The Fool: His Social and Literary History.* London: Faber and Faber.

Wheatcroft, P. (2001). Do We Really Want Our children to Receive a Sectarian Education? *The Times* (London), February 13: 20.

Winch, C. (2002). The Economic Aims of Education. *Journal of Philosophy of Education* 36 (1): 101–118.

Wogaman, J.P. (2000). *Christian Perspectives on Politics.* Louisville, KY: Westminster John Knox Press.

Woodiwiss, A. (1997). Behind Governmentality: Sociological Theory, Pacific Capitalism and Industrial Citizenship. *Citizenship Studies* 1: 1.

Žižek, S. (1991). *Looking Awry: An Introduction to Jacques Lacan through Popular Culture.* Cambridge, MA: Massachusetts Institute of Technology Press.

Index

aboriginal 74, 123, 138, 143, 145f
abuse 2, 97, 105, 119, 135, 140,
    175
    sexual 31, 173f
advertising 11, 25, 141, 190
Aeschylus 120f
Aesthetics 138, 142, 153, 158, 172,
    190
alterity 60, 83, 89f, 98–100
ambiguity 5, 7, 9, 27f, 49, 55, 59,
    72, 79f, 88f, 92, 111, 113f, 116,
    123, 126–130, 134, 138f, 149,
    152–158, 164, 177f
Amish 139f, 176
Anthropology 53, 98, 186
anti-semitic 182
archein 93
Arendt, H. 6, 19, 21ff, 32ff, 36, 45,
    49–52, 71ff, 87f, 90f, 98, 140,
    148, 154, 189–192
Aristophanes 96–105
Aristotle 22, 38, 78, 83f, 106, 146,
    184f
arithmetic 6, 9f, 118, 132, 134f, 162
arts 11, 64, 106, 130f, 138, 141f,
    147, 159–162, 173
Audi, R. 139, 164, 175
Augustine, St. 189–193
Averintsev, S. 98–101

Bakhtin, M. 101, 121
Baudrillard, J. 141, 190
Bauman, Z. 26
Beattie, J. 95f
Belah, R. 172, 188f
benchmarks 4, 25, 40, 103, 116ff
Benjamin, W. 106
Beowulf 148

Berger, P. 94, 104
Blackmore, J.D. 96
bios 21–23
Black Papers, the 46
Blake, W. 43f, 49f
borders 5, 37, 49, 53–55, 68f, 72
Bordieu, P. 189
Boston, R. 100, 128
Brontë, E. 151
Bruce, S. 28, 67, 172, 175, 182ff
Buddha, the 10, 55
Buddhism 93, 169, 178, 189
Buber, M. 56, 63, 88
bureaucracy 36f

Callan, E. 167, 170, 182–186
Callaghan, J. 116
Campbell, J. 120, 130
capital 18
capitalism 34, 46, 138, 147, 171,
    178, 193
caritas 193f
carnival 106, 119, 121,
Carr, D. 31, 114f
Castoriadis, C. 6, 118, 135, 147, 160
Catholic
    church 28–34, 39, 169
    education 13, 31, Ch. 6
Catholicism 59, 60, 72, 128, 145,
    153, 172
celtic 112, 121–130
Chesterton, C.K. 105
childhood 40, 44f, 48ff, 52, 54, 59,
    64, 72f, 83, 95, 104, 112ff, 131,
    164
church 28–32, 39, 96, 124, 128,
    153, 169–187

citizen 5, 19, 26, 28, 35, 37ff, 44,
   48, 57, 70, 82, 85, 102, 114,
   140, 172, 183f
citizenship 44, 47f, 102, 147, 184
closure 25, 23, 25, 29, 34, 38–40,
   43, 61, 102, 118, 129, 139f, 151,
   160, 180f
   discursive 3–7, 16, 25, 35, 43,
      52, 57f, 60, 62, 64–74, 112,
      115f, 118, 122, 128, 133f,
      138f, 140ff, 1147, 149, 153,
      161, 173f, 192
   linguistic 39
   market 130
   philosophy of 168
   political 2, 92
   senses (of the) 139
comedy 79, 86, 94, 97f, 106, 121,
   130
communitarians 24
communitarianism 64
communitas 55–57, 61, 63f, 66,169
competences 25, 103, 116, 118, 135
conservative 20, 23, 47, 49, 70, 73,
   172, 185
   neo- 49, 74
consumption 1, 17, 22f, 26, 59,
   130,180, 187–193
corporation, the 17, 38, 51f, 112,
   116, 121, 133, 149, 187, 190
   global 142, 147, 152, 155, 168
   transnational 2, 17
Coyote 119
creativity 4, 91, 118, 156
Crick, B. 47, 74
critical reflection 6, 38, 188
cupiditas 189, 190, 193ff
Curren, R. 167, 183–186

Dahl, R. 94
daimon 6, 38
Dante 149

Davis, R.A. 65, 135, 149
death 1, 31, 54, 59, 82ff, 156, 158
democracy see liberal
dissenus 19, 92, 98, 102, 104f
Donne, J. 145f
Douglas, M. 125, 134

Eco, U 82
economy the 3–7, 16–19, 24–32,
   37, 84, 117,
   188
economics 3, 25, 44, 46, 51, 113,
   186, 196
   liberal 65
   education
   political 45f
   rationalism 116
education
   and advertising 190
   and aesthetics (see also poetry)
      142
   and anxiety 121, 190
   and christianity 13, 29, 31f,
      182f, Ch. 6
   and citizenship 44, 48, 102, 147
   and death 59
   and economy 6, 9, 32, 49, 51,
      87, 117, 135, 192
   and experience 45
   and the "Great Education
      Debate" 116
   higher 8, 135
   and justice 66
   and laughter 8, Ch. 3
   and the person 10, 13, 66, 69,
      82, 133
   political 43, 45–48, 73, 81, 89,
      98
   and pressure groups 26
   purpose 1, 3, 7, 25, 31, 58, 88,
      139

as a social good 3, 19, 31, 34, 36f, 47, 57, 133
and the teacher 4, 103, 105, 160, Ch. 4
and religion Ch. 6
emotion 68, 88, 143, 149ff, 180,
and the brain 86, 92
and corruption 83, 93
and choice, 33
and depth 71
empowerment 9, 70, 93f, 102, 122f, 164
encounter 22, 24, 55ff, 60, 62f, 64, 69, 88, 132, 143ff, 146, 163,
Enlightenment, the 10, 99, 154
en-massing 11, 26f, 88, 98ff
erastianism 175f
eruption 67f, 79ff, 89, 169, 178
ethics 162, 195f
eudaimonia 183

Fear 1, 3, 5, 9, 35, 84ff, 92–97, 95, 104f, 119, 189f
Ferry, L 147
fool, the 167, 176f
Francis, St. 169
Fromm, E. 5, 93
Frye, N. 145f, 159, 160
Fukayama, F 40
Fianna 128
flourishing
communal 18, 38, 73, 117, 140, 179, 194
human *see* human flourishing
political 85

gati 93, 108
Genesis 4, 22
Gewirtz, S. 51, 116
Giroux, H. 48, 53, 69f, 74, 190
globalisation 3, 7, 11, 16–24, 27f, 30, 38f, 65, 99, 147,152,193

God 78, 96, 111, 119,121, 153, 191, 193
gods 97, 126, 156
Greenpeace 169f

Haldane, J. 31, 59
Habermas, J. 17f, 38f, 72
habitus 103ff, 161, 189
Hargreaves, D. 20f
Heaney, S. 53, 65, 71, 123ff, 148, 151, 157f, 162, 164f
Heidegger, M. 147
Hegel 2, 18
Hermes 119ff, 130
Hobbes, T. 78, 82, 84f, 91
Hopkins, G.M. 67, 152f
human
being 9, 12,18, 29, 38, 45f, 50, 64, 68ff, 79f, 82ff, 88f, 93, 98,112, 121, 132, 149, 152, 159, 161, 175, 193
flourishing 1, 16, 19ff, 24, 27ff, 35, 82, 84, 95, 102, 117, 129f, 150, 153–158, 174, 177, 179ff, 184ff, 194–198
humour 84f, 86, 94, 97,130
Hynes 119,130

ideologies 24, 54, 128, 175
I—It/I—Thou 56
Iktome 119
imagination 11, 35, 44, 50, 52, 59, 65, 73, 105, 113, 118, 124, 130
innocence 43f, 50, 52, 114, 157
individualism 160
interstitial 8,11, 20, 40, 49f, 65, 58, 60, 103f, 132, 138, 146, 164, 169, 187
Irish 66, 71, 83f, 86, 111f, 122, 124–130, 157
Irony 59, 96, 98, 105, 126, 141f, 151

Jasper, D. 142, 160
Jaspers, K. 192
Jenkins, R. 77, 92, 101
Jonson, B. 111, 176f
Jung, C.G. 11, 119f, 120, 122, 153f,
    157
justice 25f, 35, 69, 167, 172, 175,
    183–187, 190, 192f
    education for 66
    social 46, 70
    redistributive 47, 178f

Kierkegaard, S. 18
Komonchak, J. 30

Lailoken 124
language 4, 16, 25, 34, 39f, 45, 65,
    68, 72, 97f, 117, 123, 131, 138–
    157, 161, 176, 195
    of ambiguity 123
    of care 34
    and development 138
    of the economy 25, 39
    of education 25
    of the oppressed 125
    of poetry 125, 150
    of religion 176
    logical 11
late industrial society 40
Lascaux 119
les hommes des letters 32
Lessing 165
Lewis, C.S. 138
liberal
    curriculum 68
    democracy 1ff, 7f, 12f, Ch1,
        43, 45, 48, 51ff, 57, 60, 67,
        70–77, 95–99, 102, 105,
        115f, 126, 130, 132, 138,
        140ff, 156, 163, 167ff, 170–
        183
    education 68ff

individualism 49, 160
philosophers 28f, 139f, 162,
    170
state 12, 32, 37ff, 168, 171,
    175f, 195
limen 72, 106, 121, 130
literature 11, 71,73, 121f, 130f,
    134, 142, 146, 154, 159
Loki 119f
Luddite 65
Lyas, C. 161f

Machiavelli 83
management 25, 33f, 65, 117, 150
    behaviour 21,115
    total quality 116
Marx, G. 99
Marx, K. 22, 38, 99
Masschelein, J. 21, 23
Maui 119
Merson, M. 51, 116f
McGough, R. 148
McLaren, P. 48, 52, 58, 69f, 190
Merlin 122, 124
Merson, M. 51, 116f
metaphor 4, 6ff, 11f, 22, 25, 38f, 44
    52f, 57f, 60, 66, 68f, 72, 85,
    111f, 117, 129–139, 149–153,
    159, 164, 168
    economic 4, 7
    liminal, 12f, 53, 68, 113, 117,
        118–122, 132f, 168
Millbank,J. 2
Milky Way, the 143
morality 9, 117, 124, 173
Muir, F. 94
myth 7, 11,93, 112, 118f, 123f,
    126–135, 143ff, 148,152
    proto- 124
mythological 118ff, 123
mythopoeic 11, 19, 163

National Socialism 3, 90
NaGopaleen (see O'Brien, F.)
natality 6, 22, 24, 59, 182, 191
National Curriculum, the 141
neo-liberals 25, 33, 46, 65, 194

O'Brien, F. (see NaGopaleen)
Ó Criomhthain, T. 127f
Otto, R. 143

Paine, T. 38
parody 99, 105, 121, 126ff
Parousia 31
Paulin, T. 162
pedagogy 60ff, 65, 68, 74, 115
  critical 48
  borderland 60, 68–73
performativity 25, 51, 74
Pilger, J. 62f, 69
Pittock, G.H.M. 128
Pius XII 30, 41
Plath, S. 156f
play 7f, 10, 44, 73, 86, 105, 126
Plessner, H. 79ff, 84, 86, 88f, 99, 101
poet, the 12, 53, 124f, 129, 131f, 142, 146f, 149, 153f, 158, 162, 164
Pol Pot 63
Poliakov 100
polity, the 5, 10, 13, 17f, 24, 28f, 33, 44f, 55, 58, 67, 71, 97f, 105, 114, 121, 129, 139, 159, 171, 174, 177f, 181–186, 188, 194
  liberal-democratic 12, 16, 20, 39, 43, 77, 92, 140, 156, 176, 179, 194
postmodern 38, 65, 72, 96, 106, 132, 148, 153, 179f
poverty 1, 34, 49, 140f, 169
power 2, 4, 6, 8ff, 17f, 25f, 30, 34, 36, 38f, 48f, 53, 55, 59, 61, 67,
  70, 73, 80, 82, 87, 90, 93f, 95ff, 102f, 105, 116, 120, 124, 129, 130, 138, 146, 148, 157, 173, 179, 189, 193
  anti-/disruptive 4, 39, 129
  of language 4, 152f
  liminal 149
  re-creative 121
  symbolic 11
Pratt, M.L 54
prattein 993, 107
Prometheus 119ff, 130
public
  discussions 1, 6, 183
  good 19, 167, 187f
  institutions 36, 168
  schooling 167, 184, 193
  sphere/spaces 9, 13, 27, 36, 40, 151, 185f
  transport 27

Quadragesimo Anno 30
Quakers 169
Qualifications and Curriculum
  Authority 47

Ratzinger 29, 34
Raven 119
religion 2, 5, 7f, 10, 12, 18, 30, 31, 35, 54, 60, 74, 128, 134, 138, 145, 152, 162ff, 171–181, 186, 189
religious education 74, 131, 163f
revolution
  American 32, 35
  French 32, 34f, 148
  Irish 126
  Russian 101
Rousseau, J.-J. 5, 28, 35, 172f
Rosenzweig, 6
Richards, I.A. 150
Ricouer, P. 150

rites de passage 59

Santner, E. 6, 32, 109
Schama, S. 35
Schiller, F. 144, 160
Scottish
    Consultative Council on
      the Curriculum 138
    Executive 51, 196
    Literature 130
    philosopher 85, 95
    schools 21
Scruton, R. 47, 144, 158
seanchaidhe (storyteller)
Self, the 5, 11,24–27, 32, 38f, 43,
    46, 57, 59, 61, 65, 68, 79ff, 88f,
    92f, 95, 98, 101, 133, 139, 143,
    147, 164, 186, 191f
self, the 5f, 22, 24, 27, 36, 38f, 56,
    68, 80, 88f
    92, 133, 139, 143
    acting 87, 101
    amoral 120
    and alterity 98
    and the body 59, 79f, 81, 89,
      99, 186
    education for the 6
    enmassing of the 11, 57
    erasure of the 5, 26, 82
    hidden 81
    individuated/unique 5, 22, 32,
      34, 37, 56, 82, 101
    inner 103
    modern 148
    surplus 5ff, 27f, 31, 38ff, 43,
      56f, 65
shaman 10, 119, 24, 129
Shakers 169
Shelley, P.B. 120f
Sobrino, J. 34
social contract 28, 108
Spinner-Halev, J. 67, 139, 170, 196

state, the 1, 12f, 17ff, 30, 32–37,
    39, 46, 52f, 55, 66, 82, 95ff, 99,
    121, 167, 170, 175, 180–185,
    193f
    administration 77
    just 13
    liberal 26, 32, 37ff, 108, 171,
      176, 195
    liberal-democratic 2, 36, 38,
      117, 170, 175, 180, 194
    nation 18, 38
    papal 29
stranger, the 36, 57, 88, 90
structured spaces 62, 64
structures 57, 62, 72, 169
    administrative 30
    anti- 61
    curriculum 51
    democratic 171
    of domination 69
    linguistic 157
    normal 37, 54
    psychic 119
    social 20, 31, 49, 53, 55
subsidiarity 30, 36f, 41
Sweeney 123f

Taylor, C. 27, 103f, 186
technology 10, 21, 100, 159
teleology 23, 89, 195
theocracy 126, 175
threshold 7, 30, 32, 36, 53, 66f, 80f,
    86, 101, 121, 133, 140, 144,
    148f, 151, 164, 168, 186
trickster 7–11, 50, 69, 96, 100, Ch
    4, 137, 143f, 163f, 174, 178
truth 10, 23, 30, 97, 100, 121, 139,
    149, 151, 154, 156, 164, 174,
    176f, 179f, 184
Tsimshian 134
Turner, V. 53–58, 61–67, 169, 171